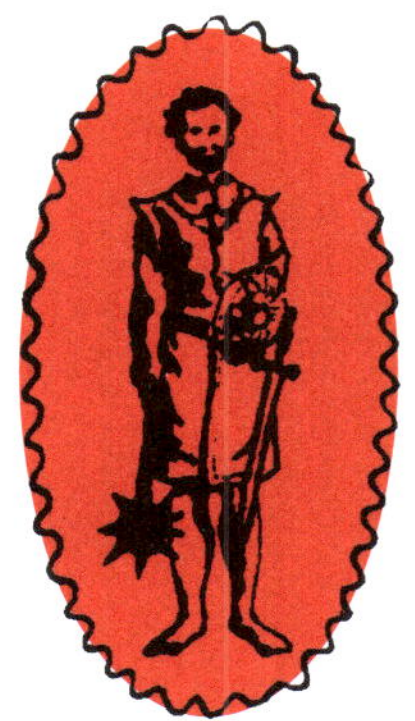

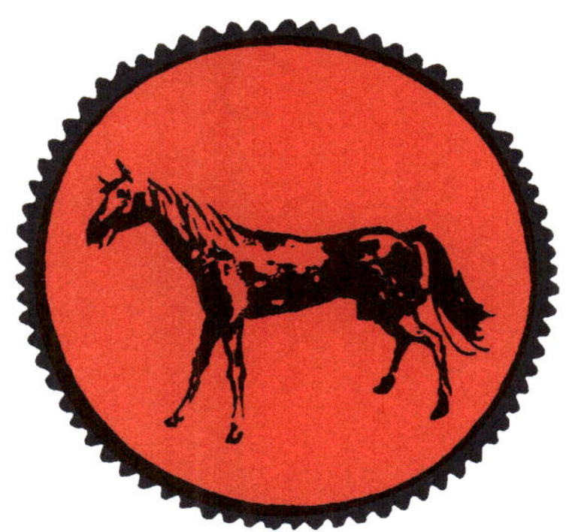

WHAT TO DO IF YOU SEE A NAKED ANIMAL

1. Provide temporary covering for the animal using an overcoat, shawl or blanket.
2. If no immediate covering is available, lead animal gently to nearest shed or area hidden from public view.
3. Report the location, complete description of animal and any identifying marks by telephone to your nearest SINA headquarters.

REMEMBER: "Decency today means Morality tomorrow."

Society for Indecency to Naked Animals
507 Fifth Avenue
New York 17, New York

INSIDE SINA
The Society for Indecency to Naked Animals

The Abel Treasury No. 7

First edition published by J&L Books

Editor: Andrew Lampert
Production & Design: Jason Fulford

ISBN 978-0-9993655-9-5

Printed in Denmark by Narayana Press

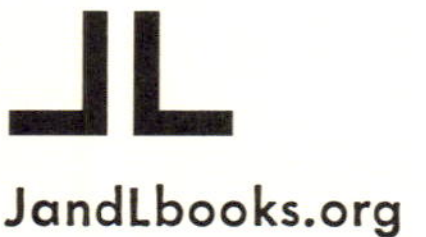

JandLbooks.org

INSIDE SINA

At last... the absolutely true story of The Society for Indecency to Naked Animals as relayed by its creator Alan Abel.

The idea for the clothe-the-animal movement struck me while driving through Texas in the autumn of 1955. I was on the way to the Texas Women's University in Denton to deliver a talk about my theatrical experiences. My job at that point involved traveling hundreds of miles at a time to give technical, historical and amusing music demonstrations at high schools, junior colleges, rotary clubs and wherever I could land a booking. I had been working as a professional percussionist since my tour of duty in the Army Air Force band during World War II. Only a couple of weeks earlier I had produced *Safari*, an off-Broadway revue featuring comedian Milt Kamen that closed after four performances. How embarrassing.

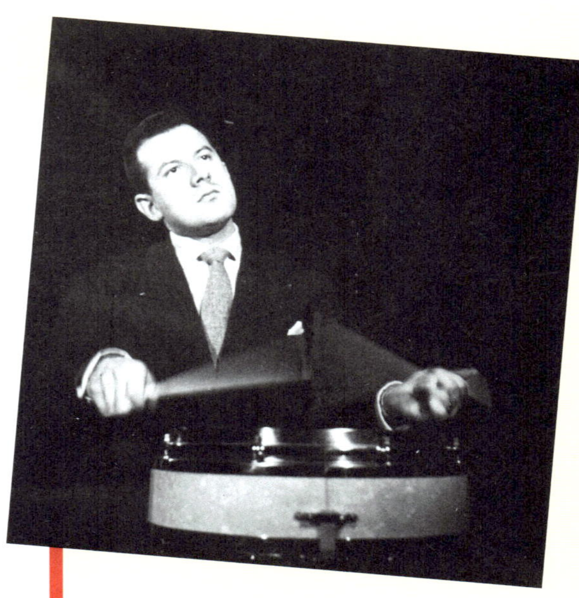

Sitting behind the wheel, still thinking about the months of work and thousands of dollars that had gone down the drain, I wondered how I could possibly encourage eager young students. Shouldn't I level with them that show business is a cold, calculating struggle? This dreary thought ran through my mind as I rounded a bend and suddenly halted. Just ahead was a herd of cattle languidly crossing the highway, oblivious to traffic, with only a solitary sheep dog in charge. My car was the first in a long stream of vehicles, and another line was building from the opposite direction. One of the cows joined her boyfriend, a ferocious-looking bull, on the far side. There they quietly embraced and began carrying on a most torrid love affair.

A woman driver alone in the lead car facing me was obviously mortified. She put her head down on the steering wheel and covered both ears with her hands. I could see two men in the car behind hysterically laughing, first at her and then at the animals. A middle-aged couple in my rear-view mirror looked the other way, as rigid as English Pointers, pretending not to notice.

Meanwhile, the rest of the cows couldn't have cared less. Nor the dog. He was busy with his job and seemed to be the understanding type.

At last it was over. The culprits in congress separated and the road was clear for passage. The embarrassed lady's car leaped forward with an engine roar and screeching tires. As she sped by me, her taut facial expression suggested the strain she had endured during those few minutes. But why did she cover her ears? As each car passed, I caught glimpses of passengers reacting with hilarity, disgust and indifference. The kaleidoscopic effect was quite amusing.

Gotham's ALAN ABEL, Erudite "Professor", Will Divulge "The History of the Drum"!

THE TIMES-PICAYUNE

Alan Abel demonstrated a droll, dry wit in a dissertation on the history of drums that we found hilarious. It's intelligent humor and the crowd roared with delight.

THE BILLBOARD

Sally Sweetland and Andy Roberts helped to keep up the good standard with their song numbers, and Alan Abel quite stopped the show with his comic drum act.

ALAN ABEL—deft, droll and double-talking . . .

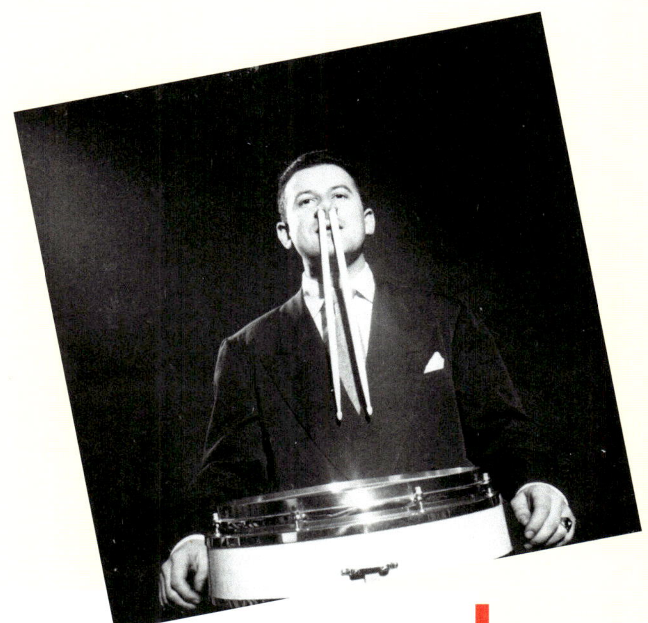

Driving on, I was unable to forget the incongruity of that scene, the way that nature's interruption of modern man's mechanical order had managed to paint a composite portrait of humanity's confused sexual attitudes. Animals, after all, are nature's creatures and will do what comes naturally. To an animal, the world is a bedroom. They have no sense of sin. More arresting to me was the human reaction, because it demonstrated the tangle of conflicts between our society's mores and taboos versus its actions. I began to think of a satirical story line that poked fun at people's foibles and would involve the civilizing of naked and lewd animals.

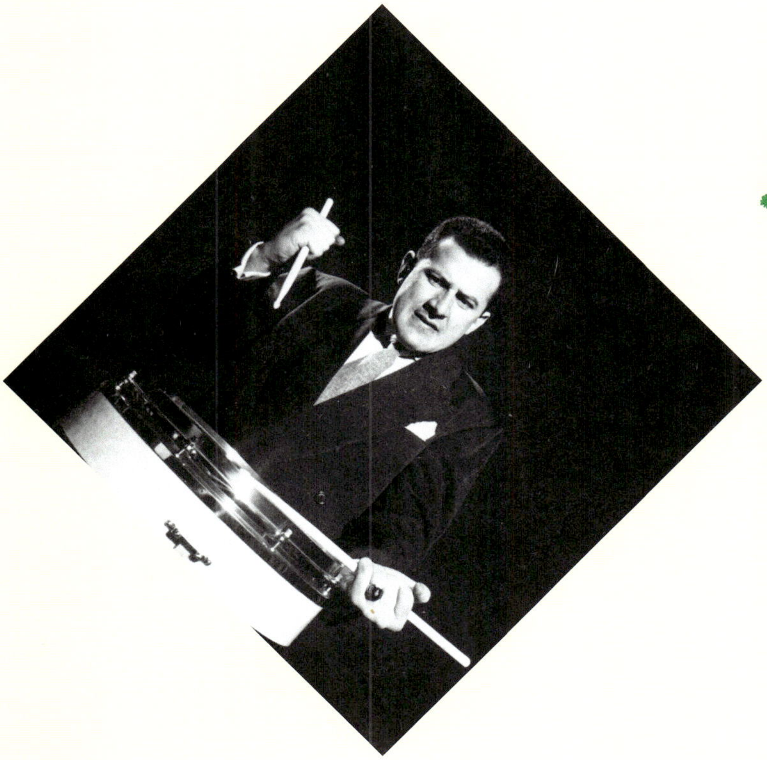

THE NEW YORKER

THE TALK OF THE TOWN

Mr. Abel is also, we learned in the course of a visit we paid to his apartment, on West End Avenue, one day performer in night clubs like One Fifth Avenue and Café Society, where he does a humorous monologue on the history of drumming over the past two thousand years;

Ideas

Sr. Citizens Home for Swingers (Voice Ad)

Merchandising Idea
"YUK" visual on all Poison bottles (decals available) to warn pre-school children

BELL PRODUCTIONS
507 FIFTH AVENUE
NEW YORK 17, N. Y.
OXFORD 7-5893

Ad Net on stick to grab waiters — a la dog catcher device.

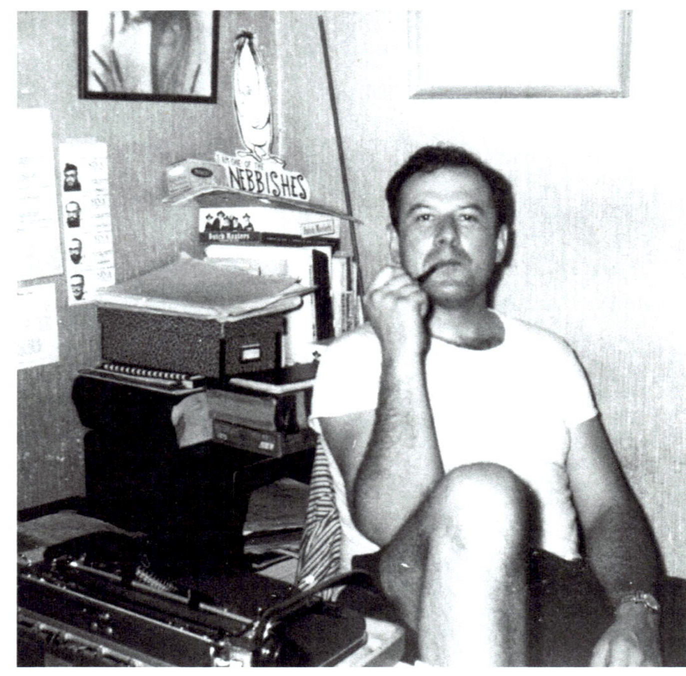

Transplanting of black, white + yellow limbs to erase racial bias

Every writer knows the exhilaration generated by an idea that's going to work. An idea that starts easily and leaps forward practically on its own, staying far enough ahead of your pencil or typewriter to keep you in hot pursuit. With three hours to spare before my lecture, I felt inspired to write about a man named G. Clifford Prout, who had inherited $400,000 with the condition it be spent on his father's last wish that all animals be clothed to cover their nakedness. Composed as a contemporary report, the substance of this original draft remained the same throughout the run of The Society for Indecency to Naked Animals.

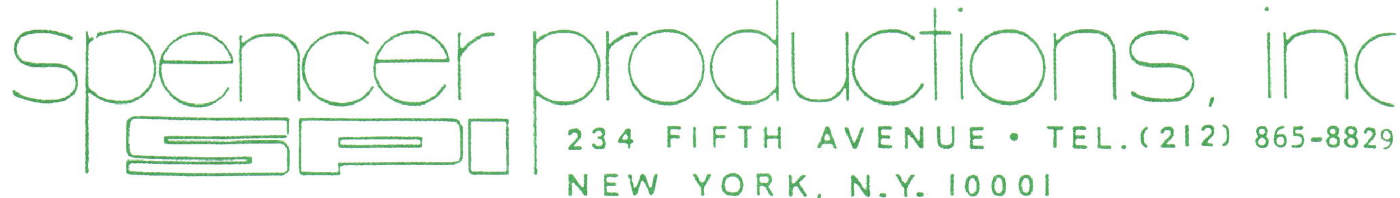

News Release

FOR IMMEDIATE RELEASE

Last week in St. Louis I met G. Clifford Prout Jr., Leader of an unusual organization called the Society for Indecency to Naked Animals, or SINA for short. It is Mr. Prout's belief that all domestic animals should wear clothing for the sake of decency. He points out that we human beings, who are biologically animals, share our food, our love, and our homes with our pets. Then we should also share our decency with them.

The SINA philosophy for clothing all animals was initially prescribed by Mr. Prout Sr., who passed away last year leaving a will estimated at $400,000 to his son. There was a provision in that will that the inheritance was to be spent solely for promoting decency and morality through SINA. Otherwise all the money would go to the Missouri State Department of Highways for the widening of roads and the improvement of toll houses.

Since his father's passing, Clifford Jr. has been diligently spending vast sums of this money for his dedicated cause, travelling all over the world, lecturing, and forming new SINA chapters.

According to Prout, children habitually dress their dogs and cats because of a socially learned stimulus to look decent. Little Johnny sees his parents clothed. He looks at himself and he is clothed, but Rover is stark naked! Unable to ignore the sight of Rover's immodesty, the child puts doll clothes on him. But how do his parents react? They rip off the clothes, calling Johnny a sissy. He cries and trouble begins as a double standard is permanently fixed in his little but impressionable mind.

Mr. Prout added that when children are denied the healthy habit of dressing their pets, they rebel against their parents, school, and community, in that order.

spencer productions, inc
SPI
234 FIFTH AVENUE • TEL.(212) 865-8829
NEW YORK, N.Y. 10001

(2)

"Try and explain to a three-year-old girl why her cat must remain in the nude,' he said. 'You can't. She becomes frustrated over the prevailing hypocrisy and joins a gang engaged in street fighting, muggings, and robberies. School dropouts, unwed mothers, and other forms of anti-social behaviour called juvenile delinquency are these youngsters' expressions of their contempt for the adult world they will inherit. So, the sooner we clothe these naked animals the better our chances are that we'll bring up young people to be decent citizens.

There are now over 25,000 honorary members of SINA who have taken the pledge to clothe all animals, including those of their neighbours and any strays prowling back-yards. These determined moralists carry emergency animal clothing in their cars, can spot a naked animal at fifty feet, and then clothe him in twelve seconds flat! (Mr. Prout himself holds the present SINA time record for catching and dressing a dog in nine and a half seconds.)

Those people who wish to organize SINA chapters in their own communities must take an oral and written emotional stability test to determine their general fitness, attitude, and leadership potential. Mr. Prout said he devised the test himself and it helps weed out the crackpots, thrill seekers, and other undesirables who would attempt to infiltrate SINA, possibly undermining the cause.

'Decency Today Means Morality Tomorrow' is the motto composed by Mr. Prout that is prominently displayed in every member's home, framed on walls, carved above fireplaces, embroidered on pillow cases, or chiselled into front pavements.

Mr. Prout drove me back to my motel after a meeting and urged me to write the truth about SINA; that he wasn't spending his father's fortune unwisely, contrary to some vicious and slanderous articles against him. I listened as he spoke with a quiet air of confidence and determination usually reserved for men of importance. I was impressed. The Society for Indecency to Naked Animals could someday rule the world.

My next move was to send copies of the article to various magazines with a note suggesting they spread the news about Prout's organization. I was careful to alternate between using my name and a handy alias, Bruce Spencer. He was a press agent who almost exclusively worked to promote the efforts of Alan Abel. We both received nothing but rejections.

EDITORIAL OFFICES

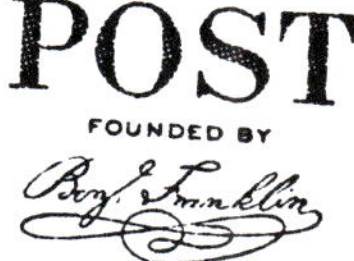

ROBERT SHERROD
EDITOR

666 FIFTH AVENUE
NEW YORK CITY 19

November 9, 1955

Dear Mr. Abel:

We regret that we cannot encourage you to submit the article outlined in your letter. Unfortunately, this subject does not seem to be a possibility for the POST.

The competition for space in the POST is very keen, since dozens of manuscripts are submitted for every one we can publish. Therefore, the number of encouragements must be limited. Furthermore, the idea is deplorable.

Thank you for writing to us.

Sincerely,

Elizabeth Evans

Elizabeth Evans
Editorial Assistant

Mr. Alan Abel
Vice President
SINA
507 Fifth Avenue
New York, New York
EE:mr

THE CURTIS PUBLISHING COMPANY

I found a fellow in Peekskill, N.Y., who had a hand press. He printed bundles of SINA flyers that I bought by the pound.

I left them wherever I traveled — on motel desks, store counters, restroom sinks. I also mailed them to newspapers and radio shows. When I saw an aerial on a building in a town I was passing through, I went inside and explained the cause. More often than not I was welcomed on the air right away.

CLOTHE ALL ANIMALS

Join SINA
Society for Indecency to Naked Animals

TO

Protect our children from the sight of naked horses. cows, dogs and cats.

CLOTHE ALL ANIMALS

Article IV from SINA'S Constitution reads:
"Be it resolved that the members of SINA shall devote their time and energy to clothe all naked animals that appear in public, namely horses, cows, dogs and cats, including any animal that stands higher than 4 inches or is longer than 6 inches."

JOIN A LOCAL CHAPTER OF SINA TODAY!

New York, St. Louis, Dallas, Los Angeles.

CLOTHE ALL ANIMALS!

"Decency Today Means Morality Tomorrow."

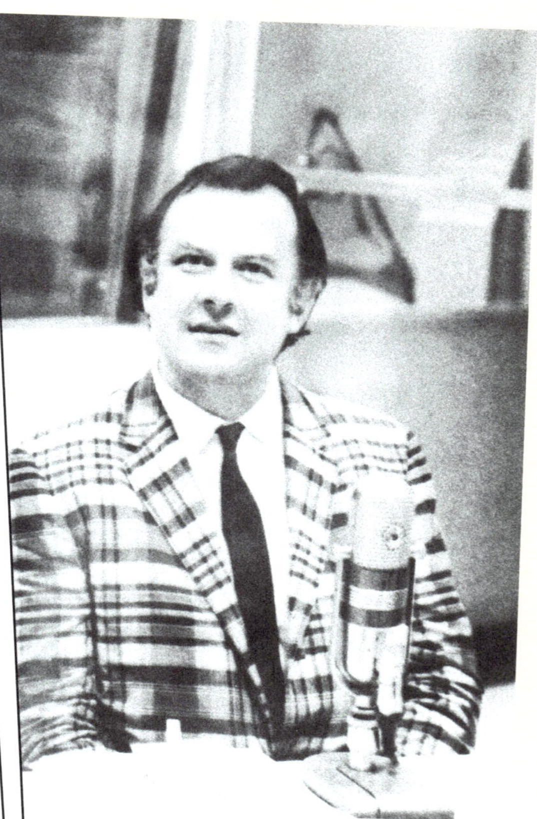

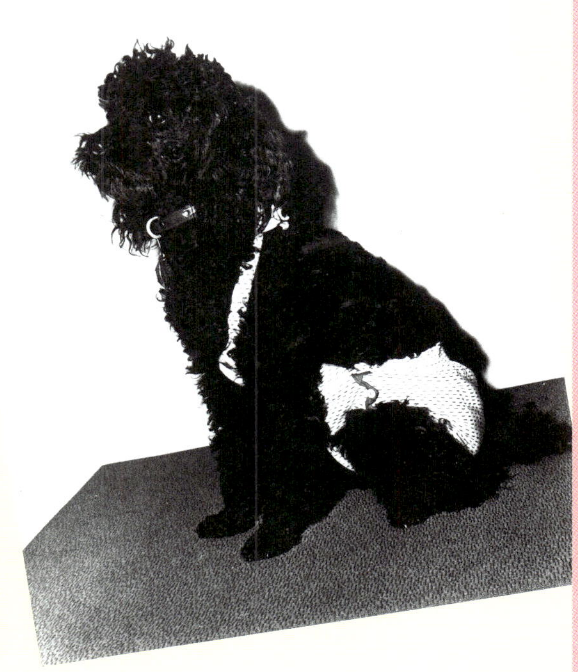

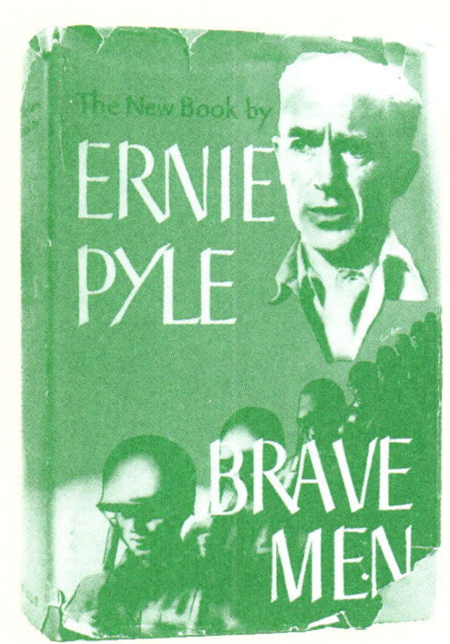

How To SPREAD Your Leaflets

by Bruce Spencer

1. Sit down casually and pretend to read a book.*
2. Yawn, rub your nose or scratch, gradually sliding a hand to an inside breast coat pocket (men) or a purse (women) for a single SINA leaflet.
3. CONTINUE READING AT ALL TIMES.
4. Carefully slip the leaflet under your left leg.
5. Rise with dignity and walk slowly away, head held high, with a slight smile on your face. You have done your job well and are ready for a SINA drop elsewhere.

NOTE:
Limit your SINA droppings to public benches and seats in hotels,bus stations,train terminals and wash rooms ... wherever people are bound to gather.

Good luck and remember that only one single leaflet is necessary for maximum effect. It will be eagerly read and passed from person to person. On the other hand, a pile of leaflets will be swept away by the custodian. And there is always the danger of your being cited for littering.**

I have found during my extensive travels from Coast to Coast that the leaflet is SINA's most potent missile!

---

*I usually carry a copy of "Brave Men" by Ernie Pyle everywhere I go.

**If you are ever cited for loitering or littering in the performance of SINA duty, and are a member in good standing, contact SINA National Headquarters in New York as soon as possible. We have some powerful and influential members in politics who may be able to help you out of your difficulties.

Back home in New York City, I met Paul Burke, owner of the Majestic Buick agency at 55th and Broadway. He complained that his show window didn't attract customers. I had previously staged the world's longest marriage proposal in the window of a Village boutique, and a 67-hour, 11-minute, 47-second-long snare drum solo in the window of Henry Adler Music Co.; ideas were not a problem. I suggested a never-ending debate inside the Buick showroom on the subject of "The Role of the Dog in Society." Burke went for it.

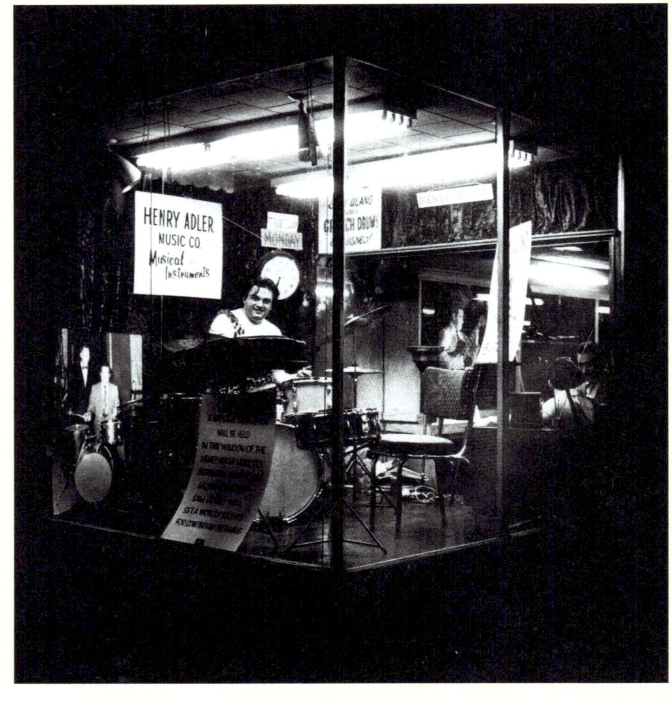

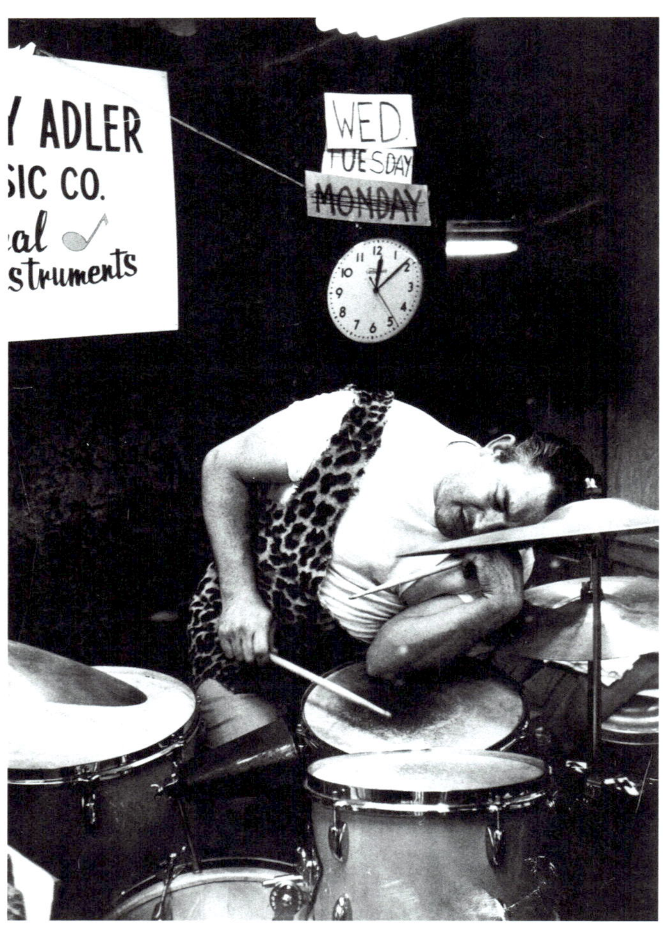

I narrowed down the hundreds of actors and actresses who responded to my trade paper ads to those who had a flair for comedy and could speak extemporaneously. As it turns out, a man named Buck Henry was the last to audition, and he was by far the best. Especially effective was a bit where he held two chemistry tubes aloft, one containing white crystals, the other with a clear liquid. With deadpan deliberation, Buck poured the liquid into the tube of crystals, then swished the mixture back and forth until it erupted in frothing foam. The audience outside the window gasped, leaning in with rapt attention as he downed the concoction (which was actually Bromo Seltzer).

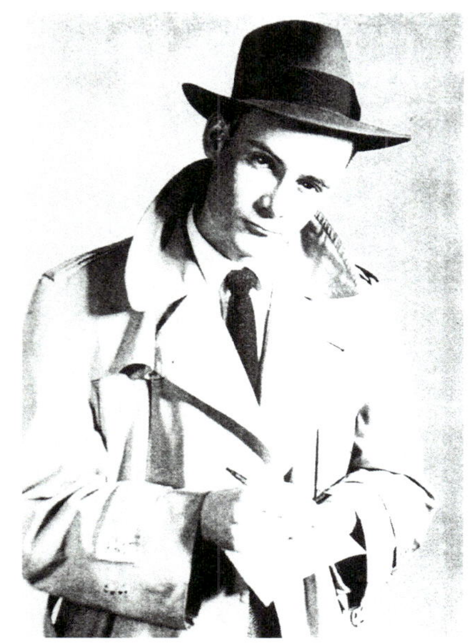

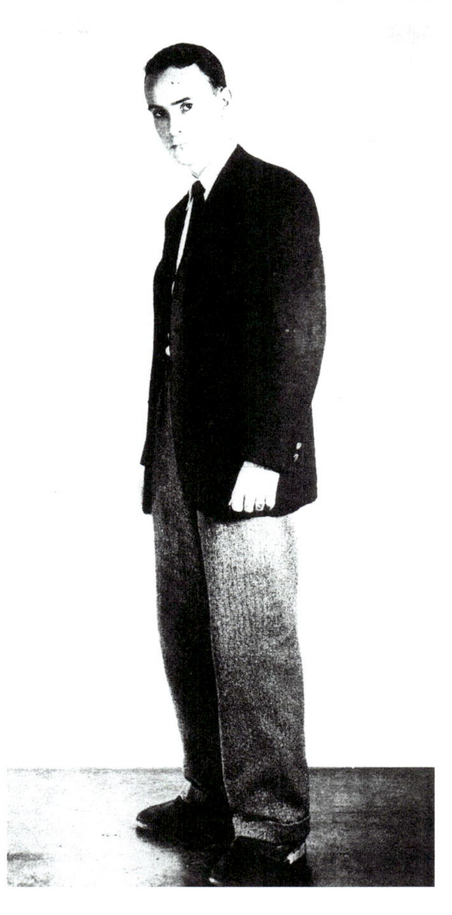

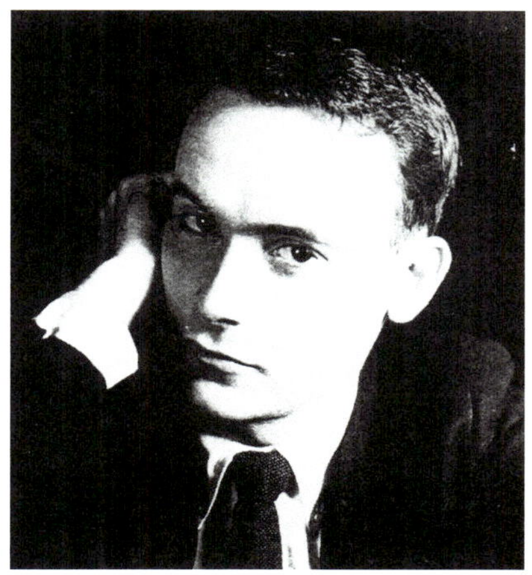

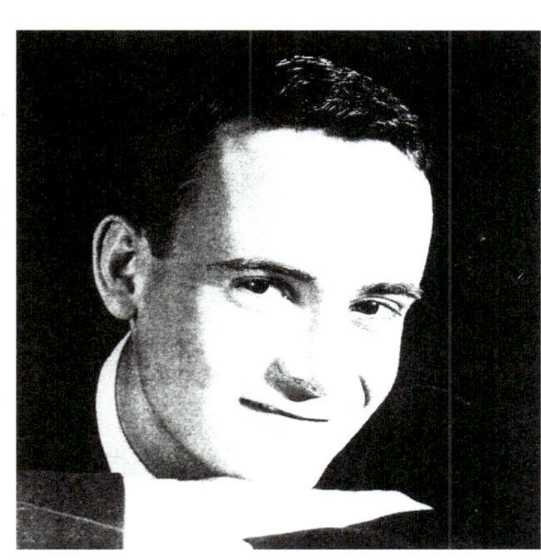

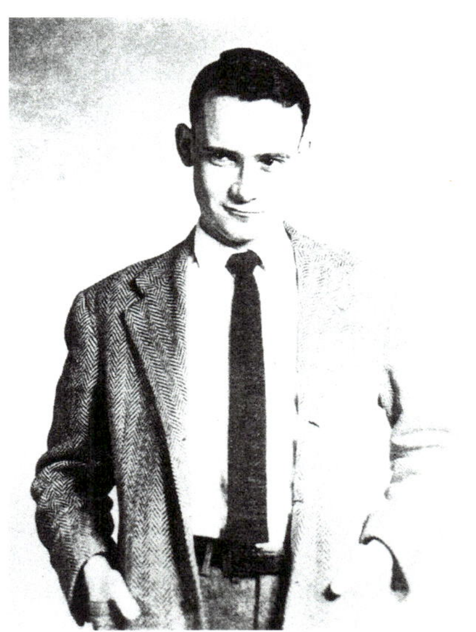

Buck Henry (Zuckerman)
141 W. 10 St.
TE 2-9388 (Service)
WA 9-0056 (home)

Broadway: "Bernardine"
"Life With Father"
Subway Circuit: " " "
Stock: Dennis, Fairhaven, Norfolk, Keene etc.
T.V.: Philco, GE, Studio One, Montgomery, etc.
Night Club Comic-MC
Comm. Films: Gerald Prod., New England Films
Industrial Shows: GE, Int'l Finance

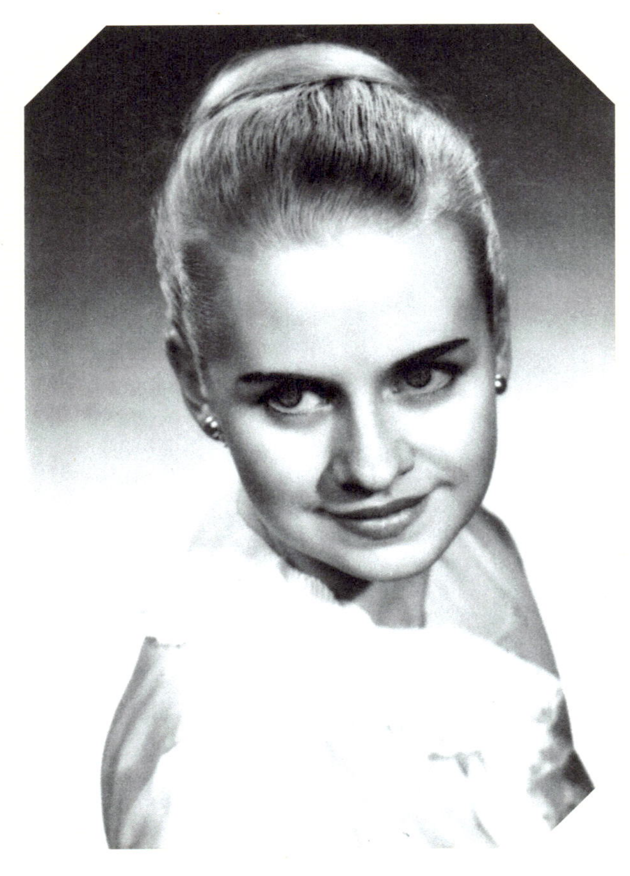

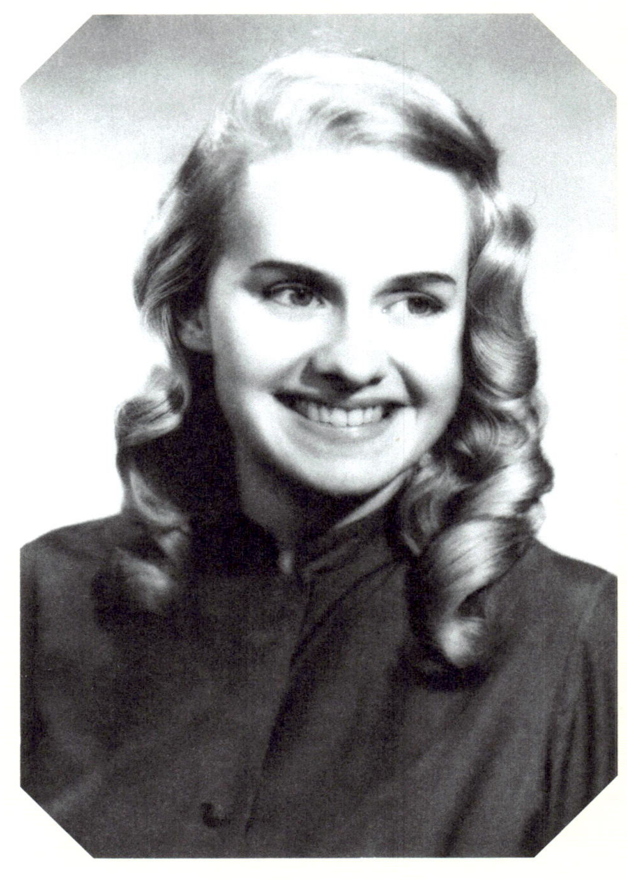

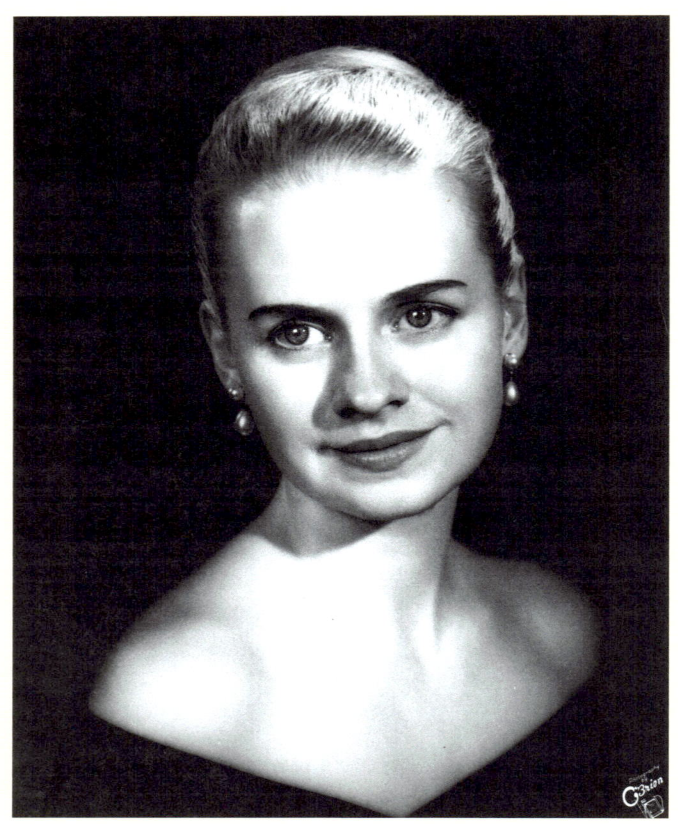

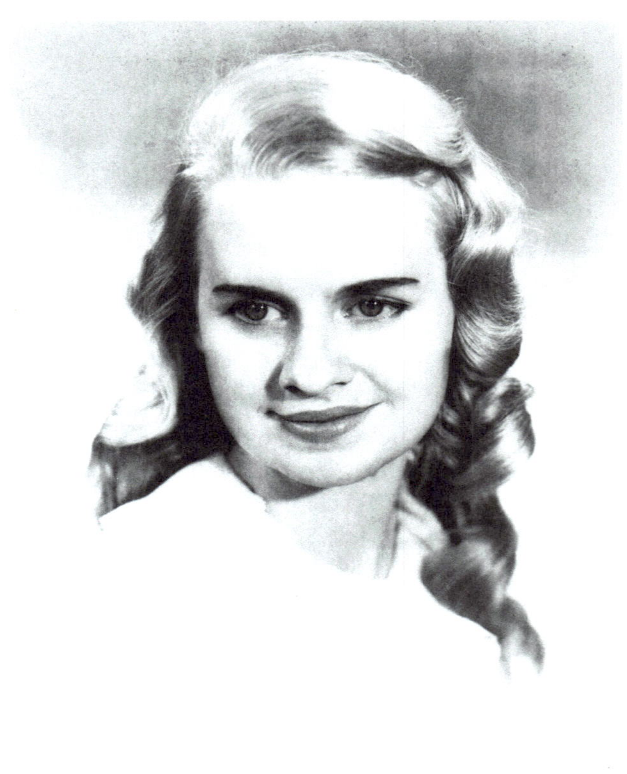

It wasn't long before I went back out on the lecture circuit to deliver my humorous percussion recitals. I arranged to have a New York answering service periodically forward my mail to the post office in the next town where I was scheduled to appear. One day, I received a bunch of resumes from actors responding to an ad for my company Bell Productions in the trade paper *Show Business.* I hadn't actually run an ad. Stuck with unsold space, the paper simply reprinted one of my previous notices. Among the headshots was a beguiling young blonde actress from Cincinnati. I am also originally from Ohio. I figured I should have her in for an interview when I return to the city.

Jeanne Allgeier came to meet me at my office at 507 Fifth Avenue, which was actually a rented broom closet filled by a desk and two chairs. She talked about her summer stock experiences in Cincinnati and Myrtle Beach, and mentioned an upcoming performance in T.S. Eliot's *Sweeney Agonistes.* Would I care to come see the show? The phone rang; it was Sylvia at the front desk, who quietly alerted me that a process server was waiting for me at the entrance.

So, I kept talking to Miss Allgeier, and after an hour the interview became a conversation. She had a sense of humor and seemed to dig mine. We chatted until another phone call told me the coast was clear. And then we talked some more.

I went to see her in the Eliot play and later drove to Andover, New Jersey, to watch her perform as Pearl in *Tobacco Road.* I was impressed. Her long blonde hair dangling over her shabby dress: I was falling in love. Another tour intervened, but I wrote to Jeanne every day and looked forward to her letters sent by general delivery. Our courtship transpired by mail.

Meanwhile, I continued to leave SINA leaflets wherever I traveled. One morning while trying to rouse myself, I switched on the television to find *Today* show host Dave Garroway talking in his laid-back style. Nearly falling asleep again, I wished for something happening on the tube to wake me up. It struck me that he should be talking about SINA. So I wrote to him in April 1959, saying, "I travel a lot and everywhere I go so goes your program. The thought came to me, Mr. Garroway, that you might wish to discuss my movement to clothe all naked animals for the sake of decency, which is called SINA, the Society for Indecency to Naked Animals...."

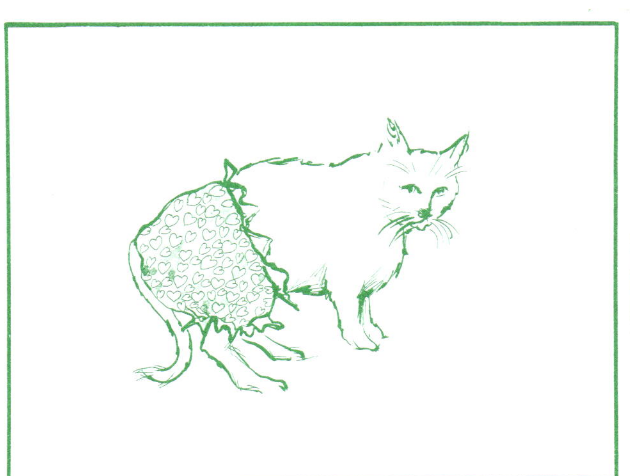

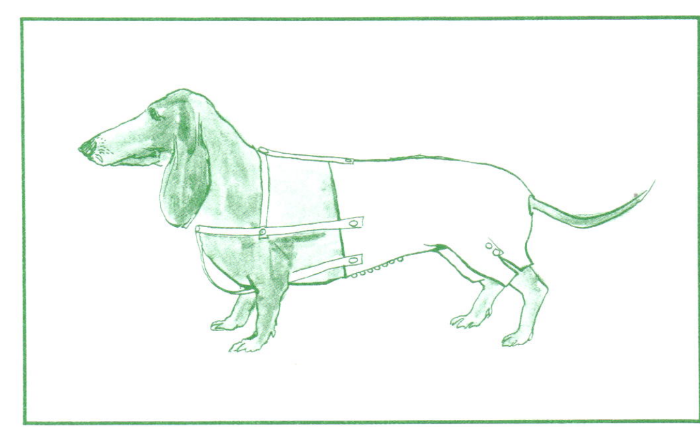

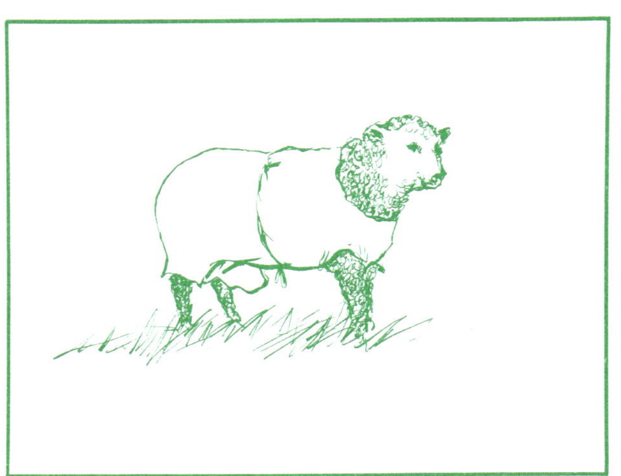

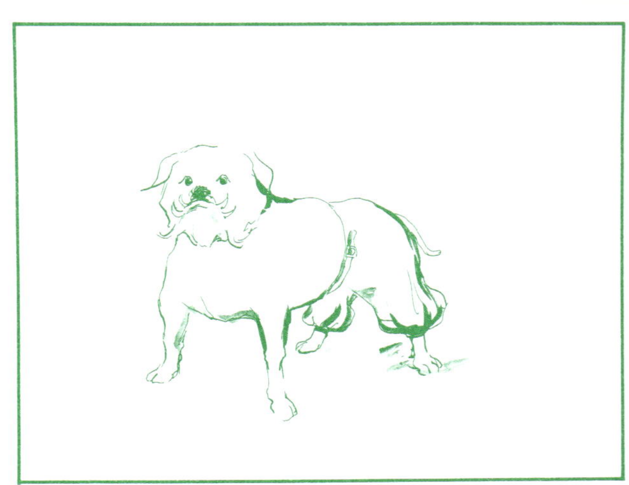

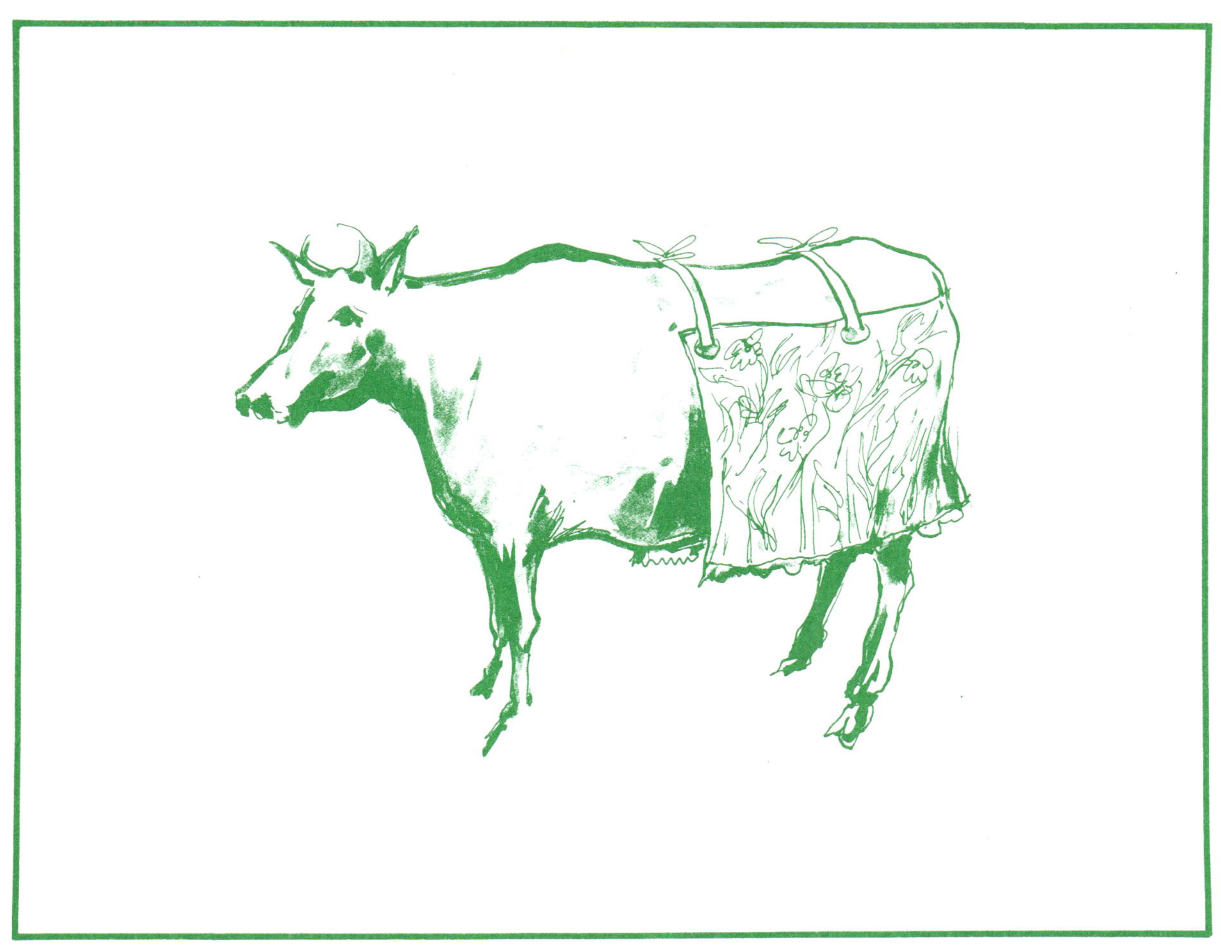

I waited. Sure enough, a message from *Today* came into my answering service. Returning the call, I spoke with a producer who asked very direct questions. Who was I? Why did I join this organization? I explained I was a used tire salesman. I claimed that I had devoted my life to this cause after attending a SINA meeting in St. Louis and was now the organization's vice president. Where was this Mr. Prout? He was, of course, in Kansas City, soliciting new members. "But he'll be in New York City in a couple weeks," I added, figuring my lecture tour was coming to a close. I would pose as Prout myself. I promised to send him literature. Hanging up, I hurriedly rang my artist friend, George Wayne, to create sketches of dogs and cats in proper garments. Farm animals, too.

As tempted as I was to get nationwide exposure, I realized that school administrators would take a dim view toward someone from SINA lecturing their students. Disinclined to jeopardize my primary source of income, I needed someone else to be zealot moralist G. Clifford Prout. This nimble-minded person could espouse the cause I had introduced in radio and phone interviews. He needed to be a good improviser who could look truly concerned about animal nudity. Buck Henry came to mind.

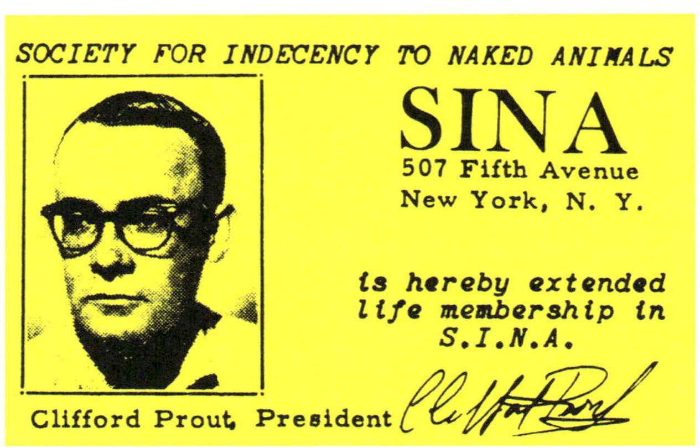

Thankfully, Buck was free and willing to be the face of the SINA movement. On May 27, 1959, he appeared as Prout on *Today*, exclaiming to Garroway that, "There are naked animals everywhere! They are on the streets and sidewalks — a public disgrace to our children — and along the highways, causing accidents as motorists take their eyes off the road to watch nude cows and bulls. These animals are not grazing — they are hanging their heads in shame! So don't let your moral standards sink lower and lower due to naked animals. It's a shocking situation and I am spending every single minute of every single day and every last dollar of my father's money to correct this evil... Remember our motto is:

"Decency Today Means Morality Tomorrow"

The Lima Citizen

Lima Owned Lima Edited Lima Dedicated

LIMA, OHIO, THURSDAY, MAY 28, 1959 Phone CA 5-8050

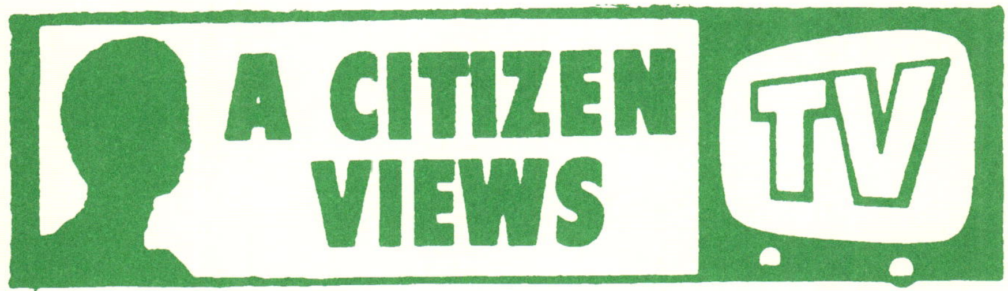

By HOPE STRONG
Citizen TV Critic

Watching the first 15 minutes (7 to 7:15 a. m.) of Dave Garroway's "Today" show Wednesday was an experience viewers cannot soon forget.

Dave interviewed a man whose name escapes us but is the head of the Society for Indecency (or Decency, we missed that, too) to Naked Animals. This purveyor of morals among the animal kingdom is trying to stir Americans into clothing domesticated animals—such as cows, dogs, cats and horses.

His society, he claims, has between 20 and 30,000 members throughout the country and actually has an office in New York City. The man claims seeing naked animals is bad for our children and apparently their parents. His argument goes something like humans are clothed, why not animals that live with humans.

Further, the man showed a sketch for proposed "comfort stations" for animals that could be erected on city street corners.

Garroway handled the interview with finesse and equilibrium that would have toppled lesser mortals. He concluded by informing viewers that perhaps this interview had no place on TV but "we thought you ought to know."

Charles Van Doren's comment was ours: "This man is the world's biggest practical joker." Frank Blair added it was the silliest thing he had ever heard of. And some of the animals on the show in their proposed garb was silly.

(Is it not fantastic what you learn these days on television.)

Physics. Dr. Harvey E. White will lecture on "Chain Reactions."

—— 7:00 ——

(2) (5) (12) **TODAY—Dave Garroway.** "Today" reports on the formation of a new society concerned with "The Indecency of naked animals." New styles in beach wear will be modeled in the studio. Luz Morales, a new singer from the Philippine Islands, will entertain. Fay De Witt, singer and comedienne, will be "Girl-of-the-Week."

(10) **HOME AND INDUSTRY**

—— 7:30 ——

(2) (5) (12) **TODAY—Dave Garroway (Cont'd)**

(10) **VACATIONLANDS—Travel**

—— 8:00 ——

(2) (5) (12) **TODAY—Dave Garroway (Cont'd)**

(4) (10) **NEWS—Richard C. Hottelet**

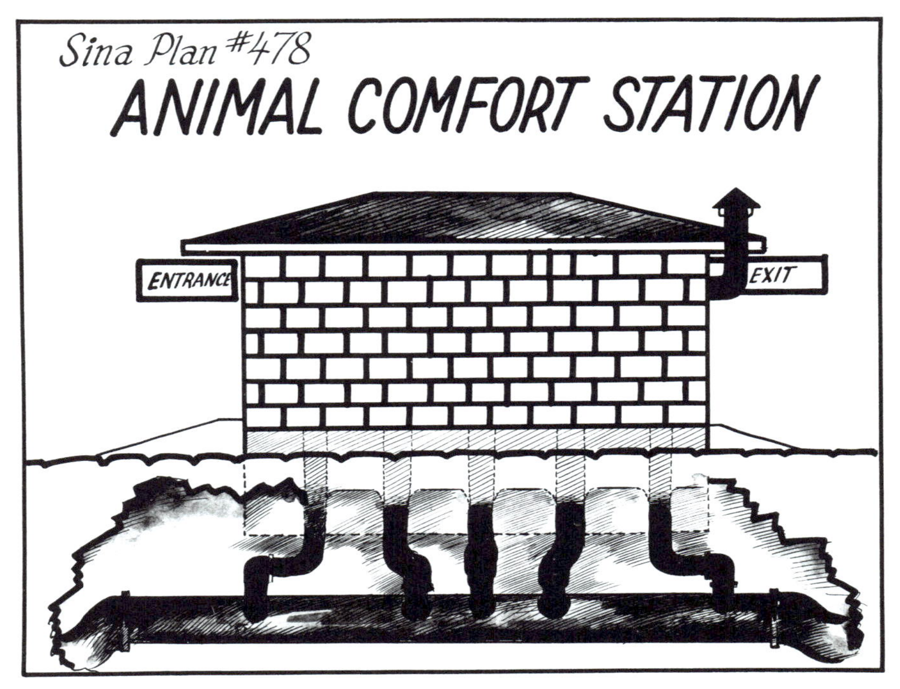
Sina Plan #478
ANIMAL COMFORT STATION
ENTRANCE
EXIT

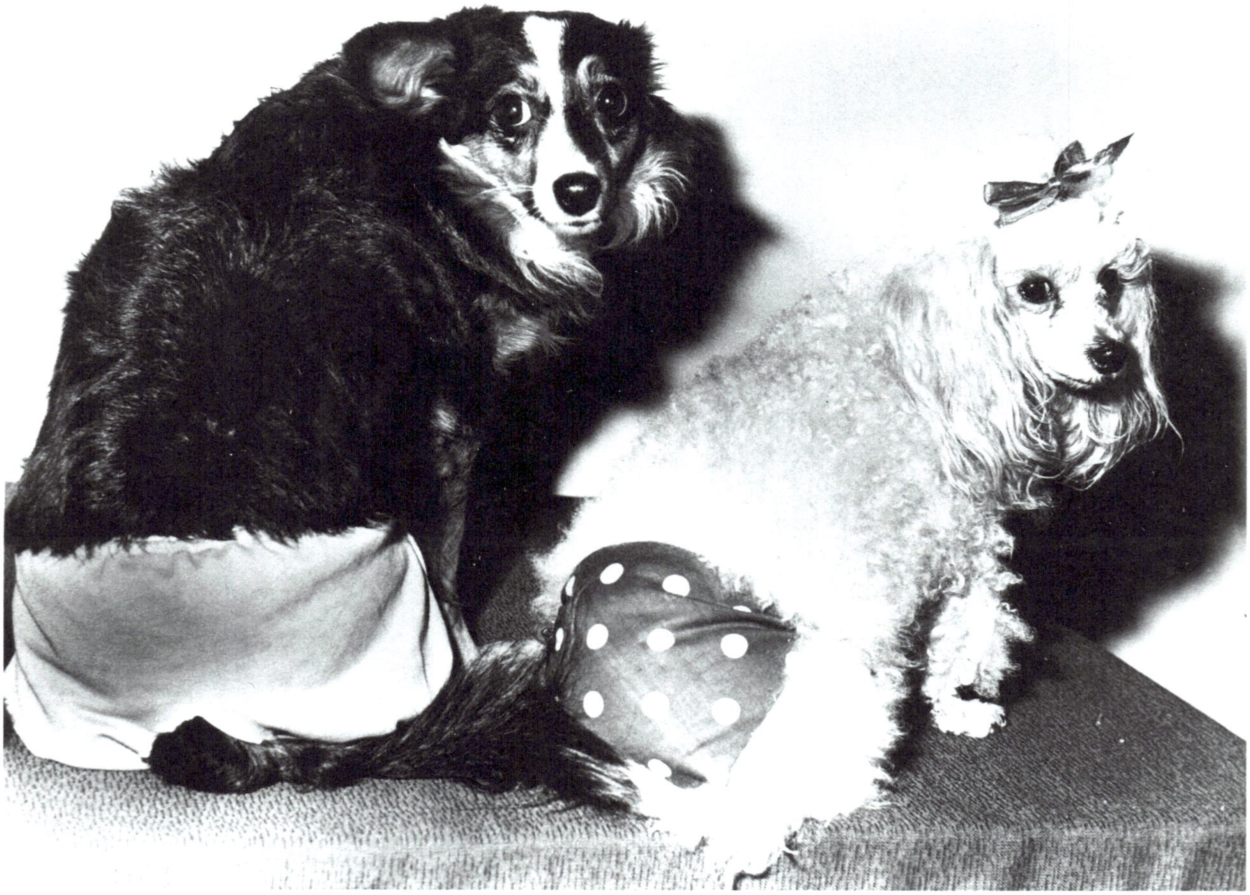

June 23, 1959

keep

Dear sir:

I think you have flipped in plane english. I have heard of nuttie thing in my life time, but this has gone to far. You'd never see my dog in a dress if you'd pay me. In my thinking you should see a very good doctor. You should have some one tighten you screws, there must be a few of them loose or some of them missing.

Bags of mail appeared at 507 Fifth Avenue: letters expressing amazement that such an organization existed, most written in anger, others thanking SINA for dealing with a long unresolved problem. There was occasional suspicion that it was a joke, but people tended to believe Prout. As long as Buck kept a straight face and said he was serious about his moral crusade, who could challenge the man's sincerity?

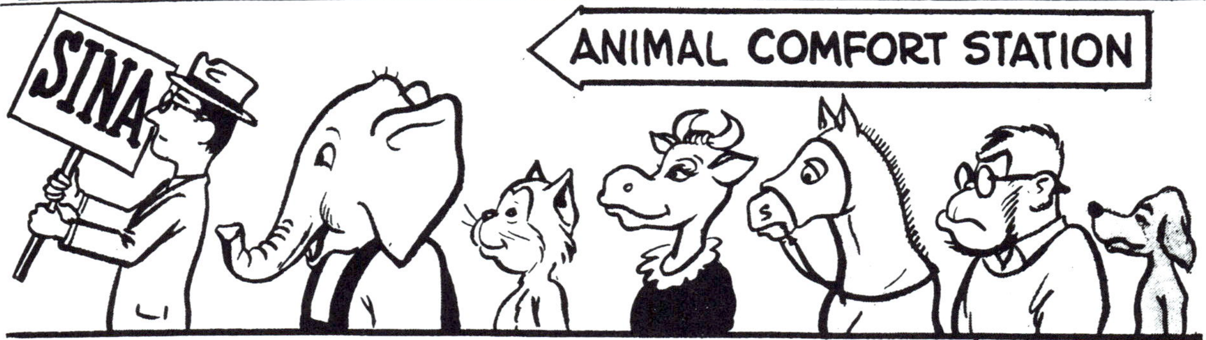

A New Style in Clotheshorses?

Modest, He'd Put Shorts on Nags

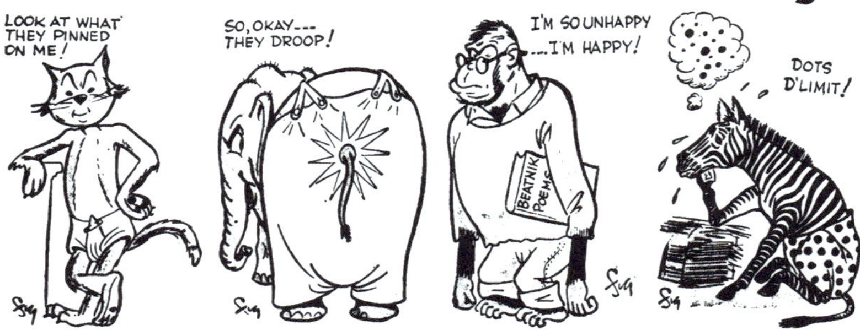

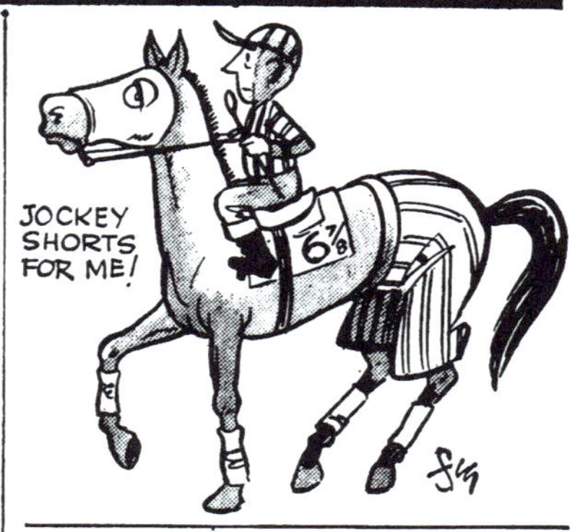

By PHIL SANTORA

THE specter of gorillas clad in bikinis, racehorses in Bermudas, black panthers in jockey shorts and elephants in overalls looms—like a nest of pink snakes with plaid eyes and orange elbows—on the not too distant horizon.

If G. Clifford Prout has his way, all animals will be decently clothed in the near future. Cows, which have been brazenly exhibiting their udders, will be covered by a Mother Hubbard sort of garment similar to the ones unhappy Solomon Islanders were forced to wear by zealous missionaries.

The racehorse of the next generation, Prout hopes, will prance to the post wearing an outsized pair of Bermuda shorts in the colors of his stable.

"Thousands attend horseraces," he said solemnly, "and see horses come out naked as the day they were born. This is not good for impressionable people and certainly it is a bad influence on children.

"I think the horses would be perfectly content—and it wouldn't affect their running ability—if they wore shorts bearing the colors of their owners. It would even add color to the race."

YOU SHOULD SEE ME IN MY UDDER DRESSES!

PROUT, who has spent most of his life (he's 29) studying everything about anything, is a slim, good-looking chap bearing a strong resemblance to Wally Cox. Some months ago, he organized SINA, which stands for Society for Indecency to Naked Animals and it's anyone's guess as to whether he's a leg-puller or really serious about his crusade to put clothes on animals.

School children, he said, are subjected to the sight of dogs scouting trees and hydrants or in the throes of unabashed necking. The morals of cats are equally uncertain and disturbing.

Diapers for cats, shorts for dogs and horses and eventually a working agreement with zoo authorities—these are the aims of Prout's organization.

There was the obvious question. Dogs, cats and horses are notoriously clumsy with zippers and . . .

"THAT IS a problem," said G. Clifford (the G. doesn't stand for anything), "but we're working on it. We hope to design a sort of breakaway pair of shorts—like the jerseys they wear in football games. We haven't all the answers yet."

G. Clifford Prout

Prout claims that putting clothes on cattle, horses and other fauna will also cut down on auto accidents. He claims that motorists gaze at animals in the meadows and run into trees.

He didn't say how many motorists would drive headlong into bridge abutments after staring at cows in Mother Hubbards and horses in gaudy shorts.

The idea, claims Prout, came to him in St. Louis and has spread like cholera to several other cities.

"It's perfectly natural," Prout said. "If we follow a course in society, we should follow it to the logical end where it concerns animals. The Stone Age man went unclad and little by little began wearing the hides of animals and then — eventually — modern clothes. There is no reason why animals can't be trained the same way."

Prout says he's a philosophy major who has attended several universities—including Stanford, Dartmouth and Tubigen, which is in Germany not far from the dwelling place of the Black Forest cuckoos.

He's unmarried and looks like a well-scrubbed beatnik. His office is a small room at 507 Fifth Ave. He's been on several TV shows and thus far no one has discovered whether he has his tongue wedged in his cheek.

He claims that SINA isn't seeking money, that only recently a letter arrived with a dollar enclosed and he sent it back. Money for the project comes from "private sources."

Prout has also advocated the widespread use of comfort stations for animals. It is not beyond reason, he contends, to install these at intervals so that dogs, cats, horses and other animals can be trained to use these unusual facilities.

In this connection, a study group is examining basic designs for animal clothing.

After leaving Prout, which we did with mixed feelings, we paid a visit to the Bronx Zoo to do a series of interviews with friends of ours.

THE penguins were skipped, since they already are nattily attired in evening clothes, besides which even a penguin can't tell the sex of another penguin—a situation which has resulted in much face-slapping among these birds.

Wilhelm the Wolf chuckled at the thought of putting shorts on the inhabitants of the zoo. "Chalk me up with some sheep's clothing," he quipped.

Leona the Lioness was much more interested—even wistful. "Frankly," she said, "I like the idea—with reservations. I've always wanted a Dior gown and a few gingham dresses for just pacing around the cage. There's a hitch, of course. Putting pants on horses is illogical."

How so, Leona?

"Well," she said thoughtfully, "we're fed horsemeat here and I can just see myself combing pieces of shorts from my teeth."

A LADY elephant said she didn't think her husband would look good in shorts. She added: "I don't think there's a question of morality involved at all. Kids come here to see us snatch peanuts and apples with our trunks, not because we're chorus girl types."

Tillie the Tigress ran her paws over her slim hips and snorted. "Putting clothes on a tiger," she said, "would be like draping the Venus de Milo or forcing Gypsy Rose Lee to wear coveralls. The first tailor who comes into this cage with a tape measure is going to lose an arm."

"Somehow," said Andy the Orangutan, "I can't see myself in a pair of denim pants, dirty sneakers and sports shirt. I'd look like a beatnik."

WE explained to the leopards that Prout claims some 34,764 members scattered like buckshot from coast to coast and up in Canada, but they just coughed politely and looked at each other.

The laughing hyena just kept on laughing—perhaps a bit more hysterically. The zebra mumbled something about getting out of convict's stripes, but was worried about polka dots.

The grizzly bear rumbled: "He better not come around here. I eat these college guys for breakfast."

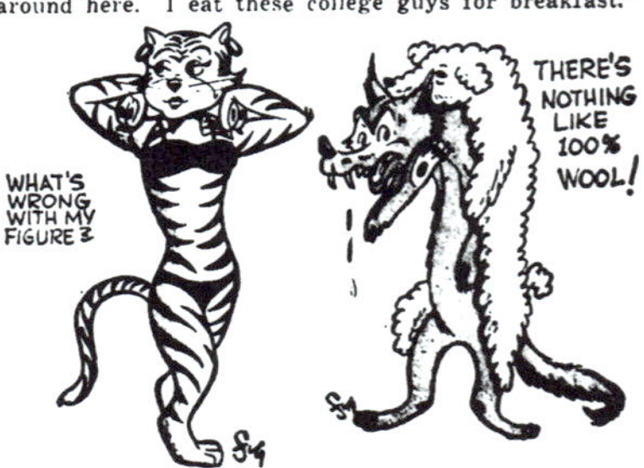

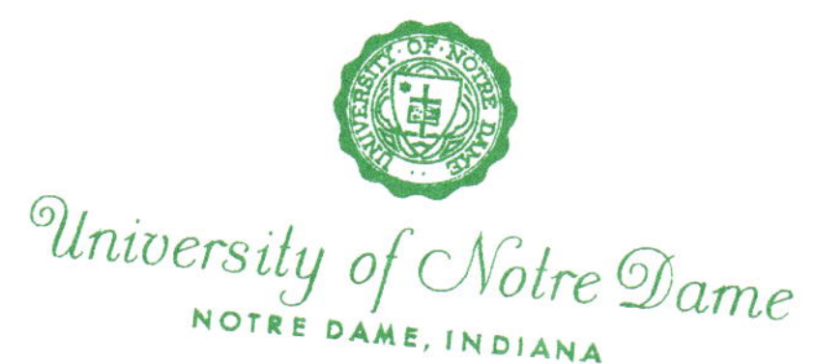

University of Notre Dame
NOTRE DAME, INDIANA

Jack Pigman
144 Farley

Mr. Bruce Spemser
S.I.N.A.
507 5th ave.

Dear Sir:

After listening to your arguements I have only one comment: BULLSHIT!!!.
Never in my life have I heard such an illogical and morally unjustified arguement.

Sir, I would like to know how you justify your arguement, therefore I am requesting that you send me any information on your movement. Once again let me state that I see no sense in your arguement therefore this letter should not be included in your"70% favorable response".

Yours truly,

Jack R. Pigman, Jr.

Jack R. Pigman,JR

Pulitzer Prize-winning writer Phil Santora from *The Daily News* wrote a feature on SINA, as did *The New York Herald Tribune*. *The London Evening News* sent Jack Gold to get the story. Even though there were suggestions that it might be a "leg-puller," more stories cropped up, some written with a smile or a smirk, each generating yet more interest. Prout appeared on *The Jack Paar Show*, and there were calls from Art Linkletter and Johnny Carson. A couple weeks later, on June 14, Garroway interviewed Prout again on *Monitor*, NBC's weekend network radio show. After a lengthy exchange, Garroway asked Prout in a rather deliberate fashion if he happened to know an actor by the name of Buck Henry. Prout responded that he knew Buck Henry rather well. Uh-oh, I thought, the jig is up. It was fun while it lasted.

Well, as it happened, a week later *Today* brought Prout on as a guest again. He delivered the same message, stating, "To take a child to the zoo is like taking him to a nudist colony!" He even sang the SINA Marching Song with only his head showing from behind a cardboard medieval knight. While it was completely preposterous, Buck's identity was not challenged. This is how the SINA legend grew, one television appearance leading to another, each newspaper article begetting a follow-up. The news clipping service I ordered got expensive. I tried to reply to as much written correspondence as I could; the avalanche of mail consumed my days when I wasn't on the road.

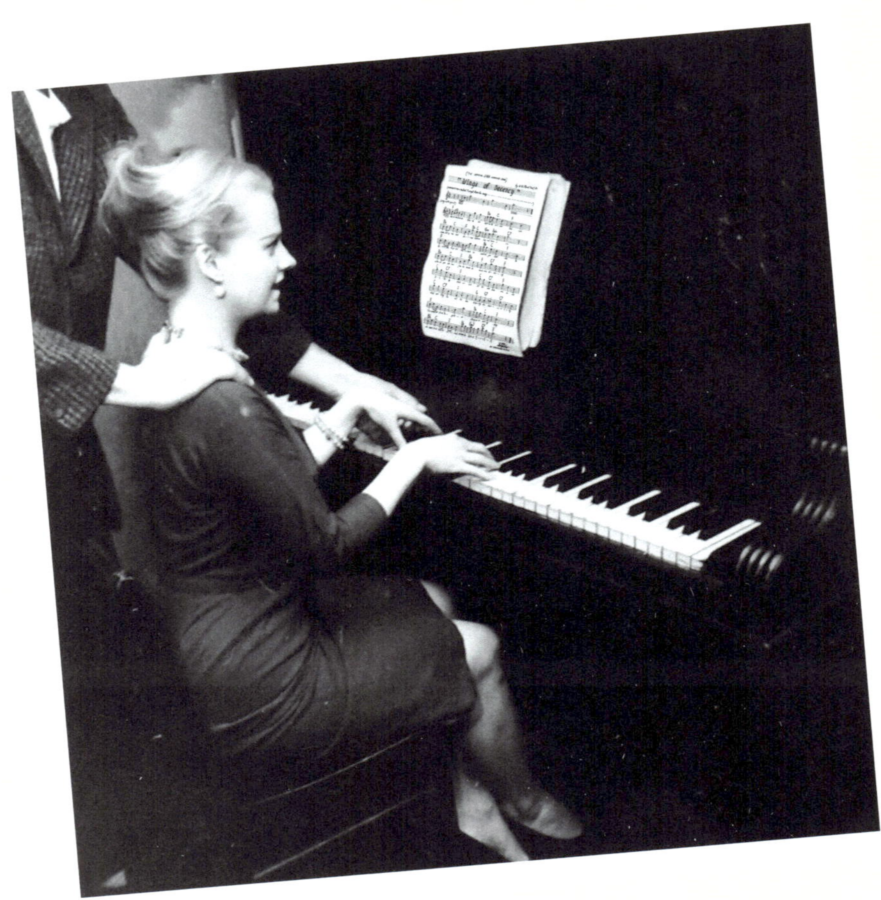

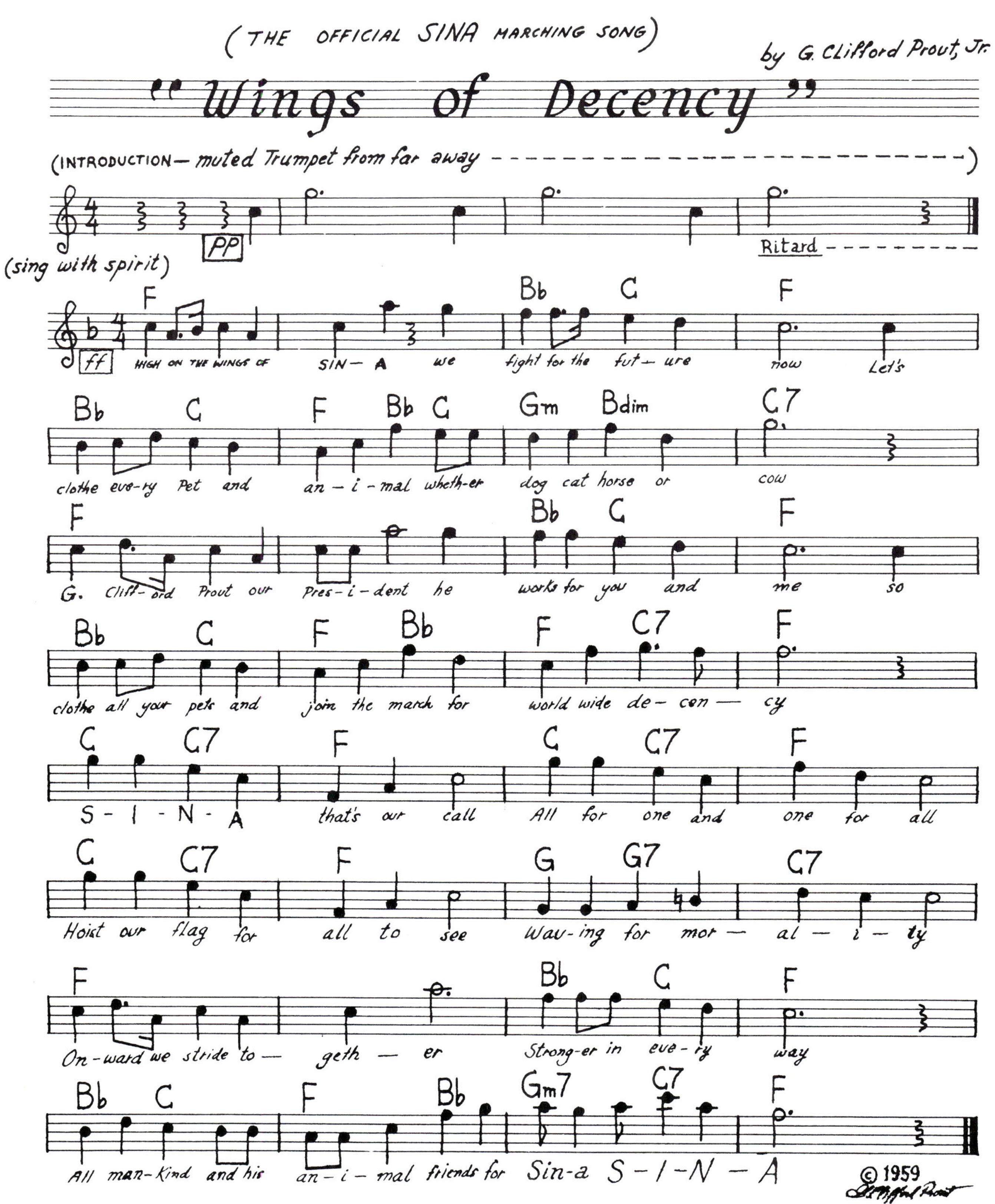

PROPERTY OF SINA

Dear Buck:

I've thought of another grabber for any interviews you do: admit that we do receive a lot of mean and nasty letters but we understand them; i.e. we have had our staff psychiatrist analyze these letters and he has revealed, along with our handwriting expert, that these people are using SINA as a scapegoat for their own personal frustrations! That will really open the gates and flood response with the greatest tidal wave yet! So hang on to it and l t's see what happens.

Write soon and stay cool. Anything can happen at anytime!
Later, AA

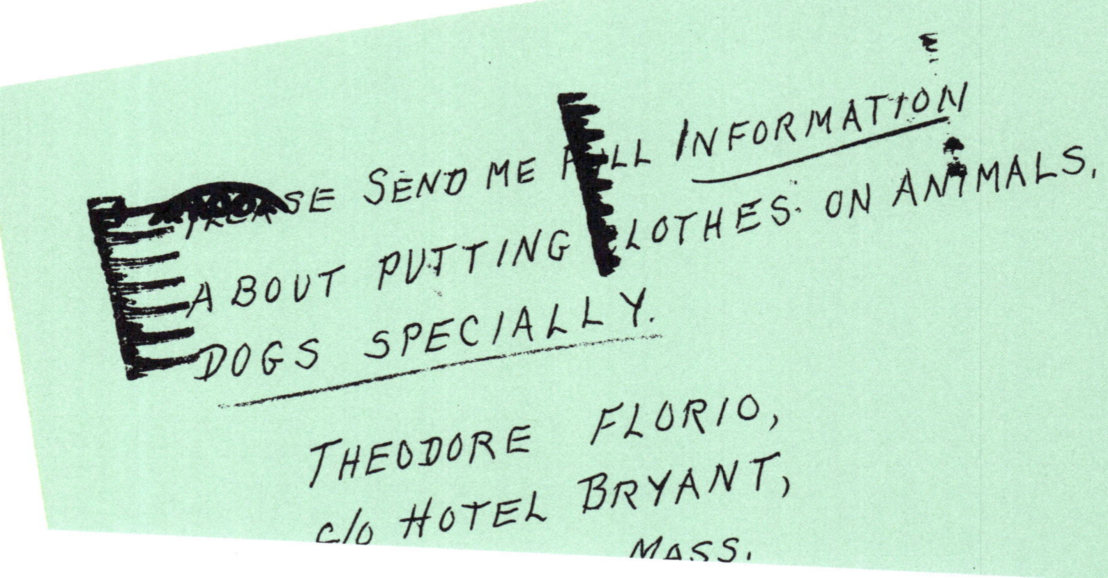
PLEASE SEND ME FULL INFORMATION ABOUT PUTTING CLOTHES ON ANIMALS. DOGS SPECIALLY.

THEODORE FLORIO,
c/o HOTEL BRYANT,
MASS.

Gentlemen: Would you please inform the North Sacramento City Council of what methods should be used to further the aims of your society.

Please send information to:
Mayor Olga Roth,
City Hall,
North Sacramento, California.

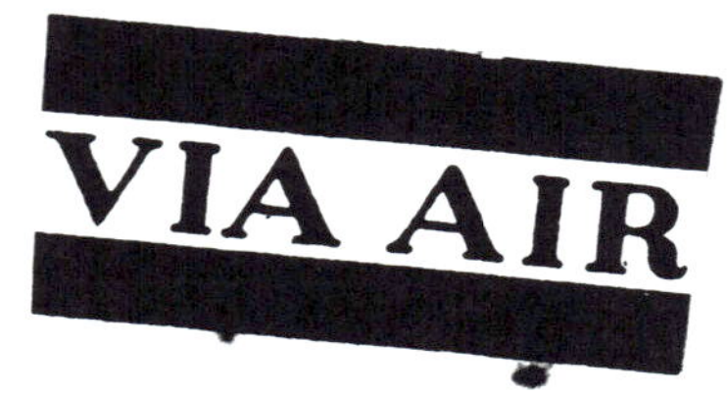

Dear Sir,
I am so very interested in joining your organization for promoting decency. Please send me patterns for my cow, Ermertrude and my cat, Blackie.

Sincerely,
Miss Elaine Murphy
33 Appleton St.
Manchester
New Hampshire

June 24, 1959

Dear sirs:

I would appreciate your kindness in sending me some information or literature concerning your organization.

Please let me know also whether members … ay
dues and how much it … ear.

Idiots what Insane
Asylum did you fools
escape from
Sane J. Mooser

PANTS ON A HORSE??

Dear John

I f this man wasn't jokeing about this crazy idea, then I say "Able's not Stable". The above would make a good song title perhaps but can you picture a clothing store for cows etc.? I dont know where Mr. Al[...] mind, but, I know where he keeps [...] and I think he should stay i[...] In reference to what he said abo[...] Rose Lee, not being worthy of a l[...] in his little dream world. becau[...] Well I don't know. but seems to [...] has more respect for animals tha[...] And Gypsy Rose Lee is human[...] life. present life or future life[...] Mr. Ables finisness. She has [...] ears. and I f I would have talke[...] I would have left your show on [...] and knees. My opion of Mr. Ab[...]

I watch your show every mo[...] it very much. Judy has a wonder[...] Joe Negri, can not be beat play[...] I play one also, but would give most [...]

over Please

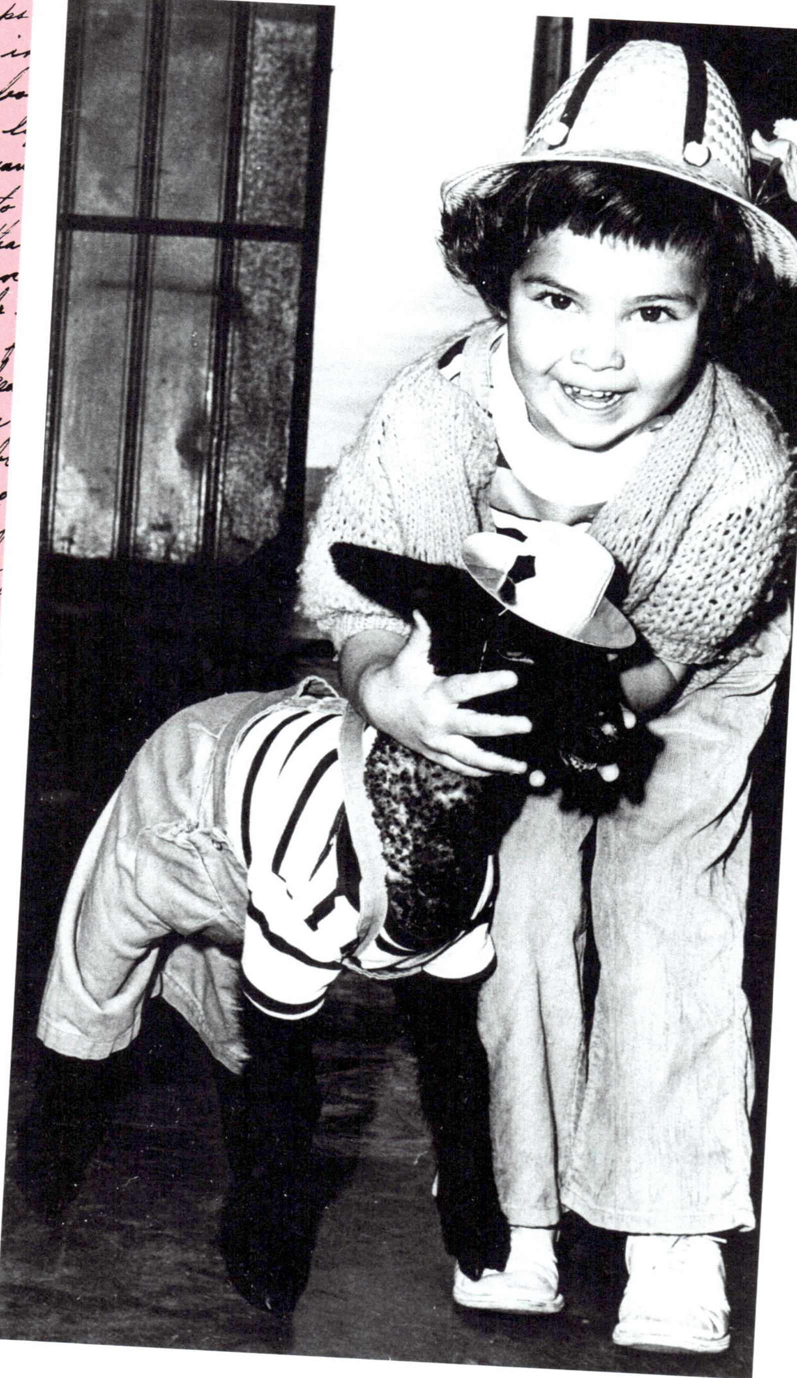

Please check ON Nac and cats & dog & Rabits Keep by Mr. E. W. French and Mrs. L. Horn of 162 Ferry St, Hudson, N.H. 03051. Two seprate family which need Attention or Summons

A. Friend

After reading articles in the newspaper, I am greatly interested in your organization.
Would you please send me some of your free patterns for animal clothes?

Thank you —

LC

Miss Debbie Dokken
535 Montrose Lane
St. Paul

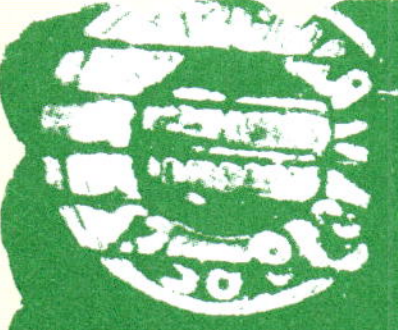

4307-20th Street
San Francisco, 14, Calif.

S I N A
507-5th Avenue
New York, New York

Gentlemen: Will you kindly send me literature on your organization, also patterns for cat's clothing - I have many cats (4 in all) and they weigh between 8 and 12 lbs. each - in other words, they are NOT small. Thank you.

W. S. Doran (Mrs.). LC

1510 Unionport Road
Bronx 62, New York

SINA
507 Fifth Ave.
New York 17, N. Y.

Gentlemen:

Last night on the Jack Paar show, you asked for opinions. As a graduate student in Sociology, having minored in Psychology, here is my opinion:

I assume that the reason you wish to clothe animals is that you don't want children and adolescents to observe the animal's genitals, male or female. It is not enough that we cover people. Now animals too must be taken into the fold. Allow me to ask one question: What is wrong with the genital parts? Why should they be differently treated from any other part of the body? Your answer that they are different in each sex is invalid. Men have bearded faces, while women and children are smooth. This is a sexual characteristic. Why do we not cover these parts also? Or, let us cover our entire bodies to conceal our sex.

It is true that one of the severe problems of juveniles in our society is their unhealthy attitude towards sex and sexuality. This is due to the paradox of a culture which tries to be two different things at the same time:

1- Sexually restrictive and secretive. We condemn and suppress sexuality in children and adolescents. The child is punished or threatened for masturbatory and/or sexually exploratory behavior, when in reality, masturbation and sexual exploration may be an essential part of his psychosexual development. The child is not allowed to witness parental coitus. We speak freely about and uncover all parts of the body except the genitals and the female breasts.

2- Sexually stimulating. You cannot deny that the main interest of advertising, entertainment, etc., is the scantily clad woman and the sexually tinged situation.

Let us get one thing straight. There is nothing wrong with sex. It is an acceptable natural urge just like eating and sleeping. There is nothing wrong or immoral about the sexual parts. The penis is as much a part of the body and just as honorable as the index finger. If a child wants to know about sex, he should be told, just as he is about food, drink, trees, grass, or God. If he exhibits sexuality or an interest in sex, he should be encouraged, and his parents should be delighted, just as they are when he exhibits an interest in food and eats well. If he asks about the function of sex organs, he should be shown and told, just as he is about teeth, hair, fingers, etc.

Since the child is left in the dark about parental coitus, and kept from seeing human genitals (often he is even discouraged from seeing and exploring his own genitals), observation of animals is practically the only outlet left. Children on farms have much healthier attitudes because of this.

Unfortunately, we have not yet progressed to a stage of sexual freedom where children can intimately see, observe, experience and understand sex. When we do, many unhealthy attitudes will be erased, and many of our juvenile problems will be solved. But until we do, observation of animals remains a healthy area. The less we let children and adolescents see of genitals and sexuality, the more they will be driven to pornography and dirty movies which show genitals and the sex act in a secretive and often perverted and unhealthy situation.

By attempting to clothe animals, you are setting mental health and our society back at least one hundred years. I know you mean well, but you are wrong.

Please do not increase our problems by your foolish actions. Psychiatrists, Psychologists, Social Workers and others are working to make us a healthier, more productive people. The greatest experts in the fields are against you. Intelligent minds like yours should be directed towards forward-thinking, helpful campaigns for mental health. Your reactionary and poorly thought out campaign can only serve to produce more neurotic and unhappy individuals, and increase the rates of delinquency and crime.

Your reply will be appreciated, and is eagerly awaited.

Very truly yours,

Richard H. Stark

Richard H. Stark

I did most certainly make time for Jeanne. She enjoyed helping me with the mailings, stuffing envelopes in the wee hours after her acting classes and between performances in children's theater. I asked her to marry me; she said, "Yes." We visited her family's home and they warmly welcomed me. We also went to meet my family in New Philadelphia, Ohio, where they now lived.

Jeanne still remembers my mother's words to me in the next room: "She's a nice girl, but I hope you're not thinking of marrying her!" Wanting to avoid a lot of conflict, we drove back to New York, where we got hitched at City Hall. Jeanne's mother was upset and my mother took to her bed... but both recovered.

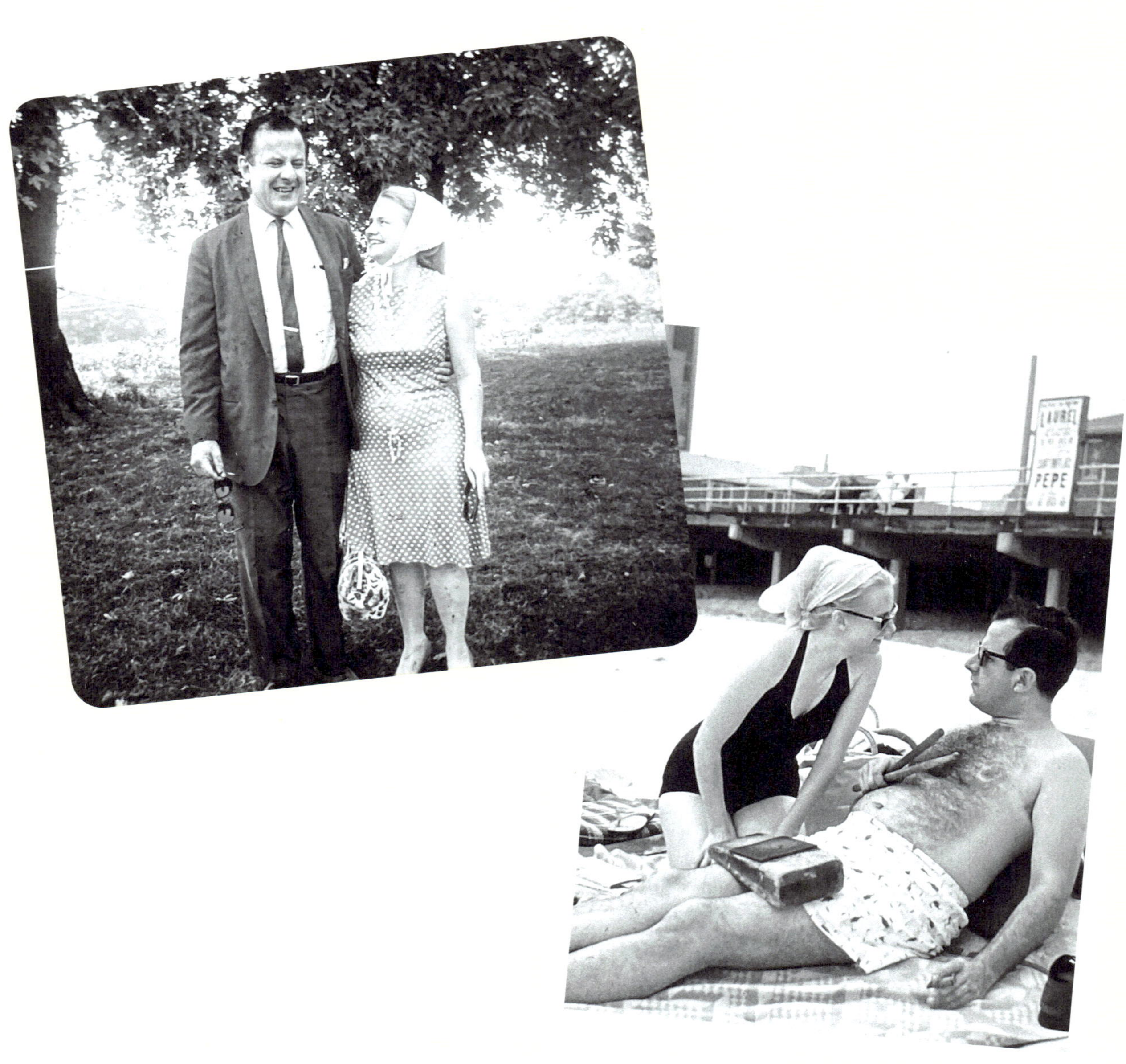

Los Angeles Times

★ SUNDAY, JUNE 17, 1962 Section C—7

PAUL COATES

They Want to Clothe Animals

I was always under the impression that it was the hot California sun beating down on us that made us all so delightfully nutty.

But the past week it's been completely overcast.

This leaves me at a loss to explain the existence of a young man named Alan Abel.

Abel, a graduate of Ohio State University, is vice president of a New York society known as SINA. Spelled out, that's the Society for Indecency to Naked Animals, a title which still has me confused.

Abel took time from his schedule of public appearances and lectures to meet with me last week and outline the purposes of his society.

"First of all," he assured me, "we are nonprofit and self-sufficient. We're dedicated solely to the cause of decency among animals that are higher than 4 in. or longer than 6 in."

★

By "decency," he clarified, he meant putting clothes on them. "There are presently some 825,000 domestic animals in public view without clothing in Los Angeles County alone. We are organizing SINA chapters here and all across the nation to combat this inconsistency."

"Inconsistency?" I questioned.

"That humans are attired and animals are not," he said.

SINA, with offices on New York City's Fifth Ave., is headed by G. Clifford Prout, who claims that the "foundation" was bankrolled to the tune of $200,000 through a trust fund set up by his late father.

Vice president Abel travels some 50,000 miles annually spreading the word.

"The reception I receive, generally speaking, is excellent," he told me. "Because of our work, many people have re-evaluated their thinking regarding naked animals. Just in the last few days, I helped launch three new SINA chapters in the San Diego area.

"We try to be realistic in our campaign," he added. "For example, I'm

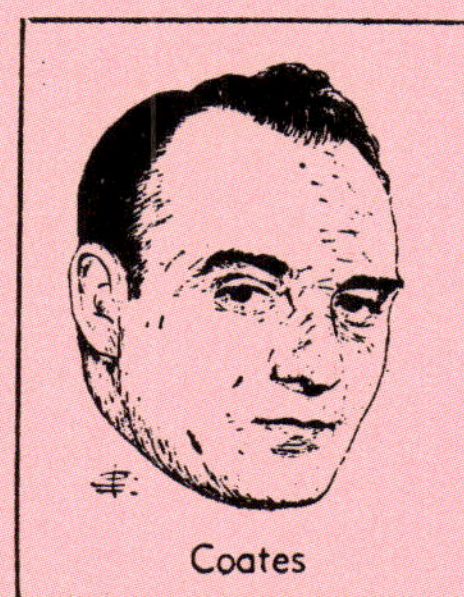

Coates

not going to attempt to put pants on cattle roaming the range in some obscure area of Montana. However, farm animals—cows, mules, sheep, and the like — animals you can see along roads and highways, certainly should be dressed.

"I'd hate to estimate how many auto accidents are caused by drivers whose attention was distracted by a naked cow or horse grazing in a meadow by the side of the road."

Also among SINA's immediate targets, Abel revealed, are race horses, dogs and cats, and zoo animals.

"When parents take their children to a zoo, they might just as well take them to a burlesque theater," he said. "That reminds me of a terribly immoral scene which was put into the display window of an airline office on Fifth Ave. It was an Arizona resort scene. And right in the middle they had a large papier mache horse — not a stitch of clothes on the animal! You can imagine how impressionable children would react to that."

Abel was visibly upset at the thought.

"So," he went on, pulling himself together, "we began writing letters to the Fifth Ave. Assn., demanding that it take some action against the airline. All we asked was that the animal's hind quarters be clothed in boxer shorts."

The association did contact the airline, and the airline—according to Abel —bowed, at least partially, to the forces of decency. It removed the horse from the display window.

"We don't expect to win our fight overnight," Abel admitted. "It takes time to educate public opinion. And until we do, we'll have to put up with the hecklers. You know, in every crowd, there's always one crackpot."

★

I nodded in enthusiastic agreement. "Tell me one more thing," I asked. "How do the animals you've succeeded in dressing react to their new station in life?"

"Oh, they're all for it," Abel assured me hastily.

"Well," he qualified, "they might fight it a little at first—like a Tennessee farmboy in his first pair of shoes. But they always come around to our way of thinking and end up much more well-adjusted than they were to start with."

"There's a delicate question I must raise," I said to Mr. Abel.

"And what is that, sir?"

"If you clothe animals, will they be able to tell the difference?"

"The difference?"

"Will the boy animals know for sure which ones are the girl animals?"

"You're a human animal," Abel old me disdainfully, "and you wear clothes. Can you tell the difference?"

And, of course, I had to admit that I can. The girl human animals are the ones in the Capri pants.

I spent considerable time writing and disseminating press releases filled with Prout's head-scratching declarations about SINA's meetings and triage efforts. We also began mailing out monthly newsletters chock full of more erroneous information. SINA continued barreling along until Buck moved to California to join the staff of talk-show host Steve Allen as a writer-performer. We agreed to keep SINA alive, and he promised to appear as Prout when he could. In January 1962, Jeanne and I also ended up journeying out West because I had signed onto what would be my last five-month school tour there. This gave me the opportunity to meet with columnist Paul Coates in Los Angeles, which drew more media interest.

CORRECTION

A number of well known people on radio and television have been mispronouncing SINA as "Sēēna", "Cīna", "Sāna" and even "Shina!" The correct and only pronunciation is S Ĭ N A as in winna or dinna. Please keep that in mind. Thank you.

Society for Indecency to Naked Animals

507 Fifth Avenue
New York 17, N.Y.

MARCH 1962 NEWSLETTER-ALAN ABEL, EDITOR

Please address all mail to the editor in care of our New York office.

Some 46 members of the Southampton SINA Chapter #12 (Long Island) held an outing on Shelter Island where they spent a week-end playing checkers and studying the local wild life. Miss Valerie du Pont was a guest lecturer at the gathering and she discussed her work in clothing animals, with an eye towards creative fashion designs. This was of special interest to the women present and Miss du Pont said she would make special trips in the future to the Masters School in Dobbs Ferry and Sarah Lawrence College in Bronxville, New York where many students would be awaiting her fashion tips along with the decent aspects of clothing all animals. Miss du Pont herself was charmingly dressed in a casual frock of white chiffon appliqued with Alecon lace and with short sleeves.

* * * * * * * * * *

Your editor plans to spend the next four months in California since we have received many hundreds of inquiries from that state. The groundwork will be laid to establish key SINA chapters in San Diego, Palm Springs, Los Angeles, Fresno, and San Francisco. A public relations firm will be retained in Sacramento to push through legislature that will make it mandatory in the state of California for all animals higher than 4 inches or longer than 6 inches to be decently clothed so that their vital areas are covered.

* * * * * * * * * *

G. Clifford Prout, President of SINA, entertained several members of the press with a buffet luncheon at his Greenwich Village garden apartment Sunday March 4th. In response to the many comments on the delicious meat loaf served, Mr. Prout has received permission from SINA member Rose Anne Roth to disclose the actual recipe as follows:

SINA MEAT LOAF

2 pounds lean ground chuck
2 eggs
one-half cup bread crumbs or cracker meal
one-half teaspoon baking powder
one-eighth teaspoon salt
one-eighth teaspoon pepper
one-half teaspoon parsley flakes
a few grains of celery, onion, and garlic salt.
MIX THOROUGHLY THEN ADD ONE HALF CUP COLD WATER,SLOWLY. MIX UNTIL PLIABLE IN HANDS AND NOT TOO STIFF OR MUSHY.
Shape into two large loaves; pour a little ketchup on top of each loaf then add water to about half of the pan. Add salt and pepper to suit taste. Bake at 350 degrees until nicely brown on one side; then turn and brown the other side. Complete baking time should be around two hours. Good luck.

Society for Indecency to Naked Animals
507 Fifth Avenue
New York 17, N.Y.

JUNE 1962 NEWSLETTER-ALAN ABEL, EDITOR

Please address all mail to the editor in care of our New York office.

SINA members will be interested in knowing that your editor appeared in an interview program on television last month in Los Angeles that brought an unprecedented amount of response from the public. Paul Coates, veteran newsman, conducted the interview and did his best to bring out the best points in the SINA movement. We received several letters in New York as a result of the telecast and Mr. Coates's office had several hundred responses by mail plus numerous phone calls and telegrams. They plan to repeat the program in the near future due to this heavy demand. The program is also transcribed on tape for a repeat performance in San Francisco.

* * * * * * * *

President Prout has disclosed the text of a letter mailed over his signature to the Radio Corporation of America and we print the contents in full for the benefit of our membership:

Brig. General David Sarnoff, Chairman of the Board
RADIO CORPORATION OF AMERICA
30 Rockefeller Plaza
New York, New York

Dear General Sarnoff:

I would like to call your attention to the fact that the dog "Nipper", as used by RCA VICTOR RECORDS, which I believe is under your jurisdiction, is portrayed completely naked.

This of course is in violation of our SINA code of ethics and is certainly not in keeping with any high standards of decency which we feel your company tries to maintain. Many members of SINA, the Society for Indecency to Naked Animals, have been concerned over this portrayal of "Nipper" and feel as I do that a strong note of protest is in order.

The many thousands of members of SINA throughout the world have pledged their time and energies to see that all naked animals be clothed, whether alive or as an imitation such as your "Nipper." I'm sure you will agree that the demoralizing effect remains the same whether a naked animal is real or made of clay!

We sincerely hope that you will take decisive action in either clothing "Nipper" or changing this trademark. And please keep in mind the tremendous purchasing power behind the SINA membership that is ready and willing to back up its demands.

Thanking you for your co-operation, I remain

Respectfully,
G. Clifford Prout, President

My next employment was at the advertising agency Guild, Bascom & Bonfigli in San Francisco. It's a good thing Dave Bascom was amused by my SINA sideline. *The San Francisco Chronicle* called. Reporter George Draper wanted a story with Prout and myself. Moreover, he wanted us to dress animals in the San Francisco Zoo. Buck just happened to be available for a week before going back to New York for a new job as a writer on *The Garry Moore Show*.

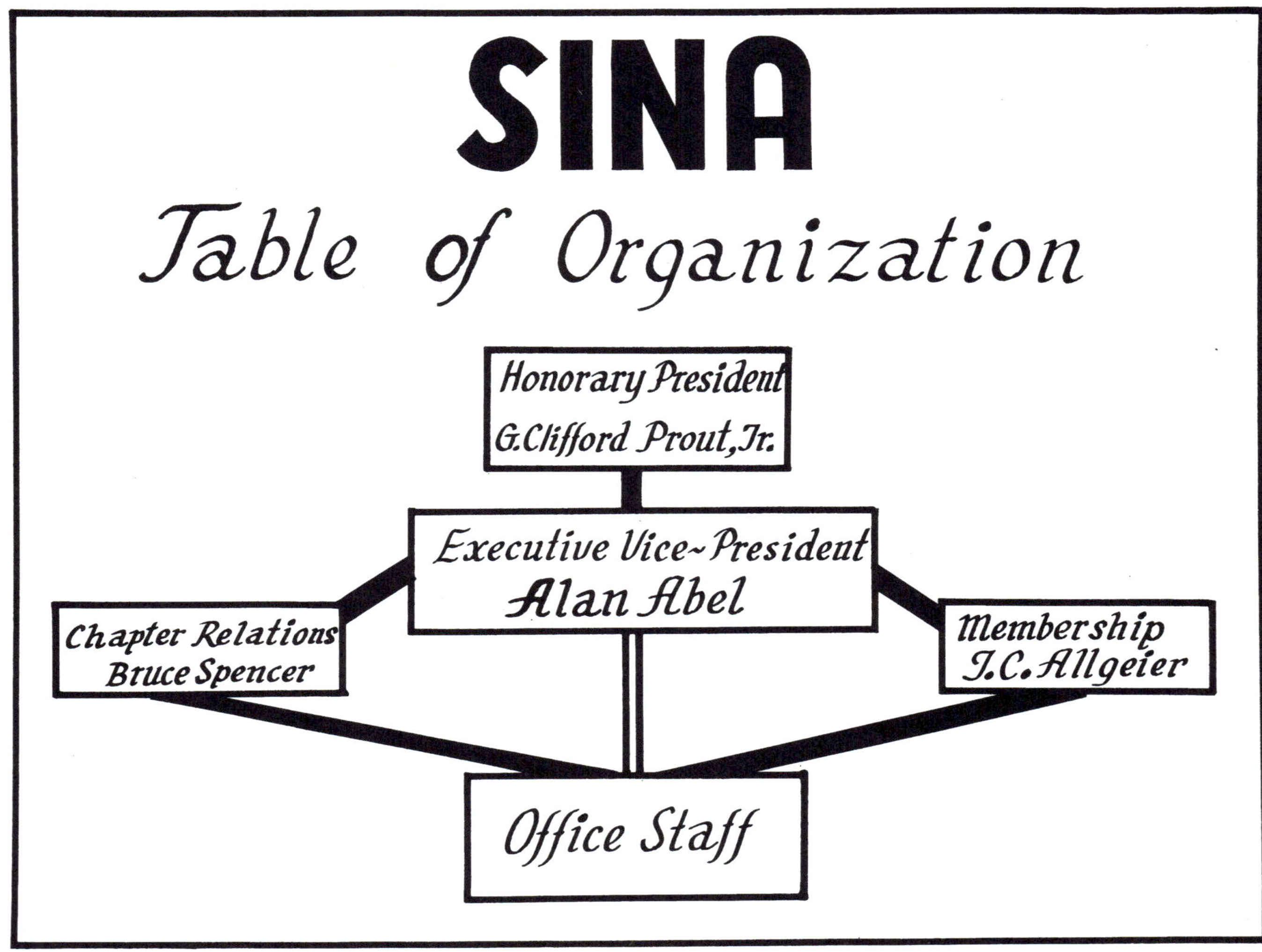

2900 Scott Street
San Francisco 23, Calif.
July 14, 1962

Dear Buck:

Glad to know you are back! The CHRONICLE wanted to take some pics and interviews of you but I begged off saying you were in Monte Carlo, however, there's no reason why you can't have a change of heart!

As I mentioned, all expenses will be paid. Another aspect I didn't mention was that the CHRONICLE also owns KRON-TV and has agreed to pay the costs of holding a half hour live discussion on SINA if their story produces enough mail pull, discussion, etc.

The latter to me represents the real victory and that's what I'm shooting for; I told the reporter handling the SINA story that in order to do a TVer we would have to import our people from L.A. and this would call for rehearsals, transportation, housing expenses, etc. and they have no objection......so I know there will at least be the loot available to pay the bills for doing a half hour live.

But we'll have to wait and see on that score. It would be great if you can get in Wednesday evening so we could go over all details and plan to stay Thurs. and Friday at least. I'll set the interviews and pics for Thursday and then leave Friday for meeting the execs and Bascom at the agency.

I don't know what happened to all the charts and drawings so poor George Wayne is making them all over again and will send them out today from N.Y. so we'll have all the visual stuff on hand.

I've been posing as the V.P. of SINA. This week-end I'm doing all the press releases and other printed stuff so as to be available for the paper.

Bob Guy at KCOP also wants the panel to appear on his station in August but I'm holding off until we resolve things up here.

I've written a number of TV spots for the agency that would be right down your alley so I hope that can be wrapped up.

Will talk to you Monday eve.

Best,

AA

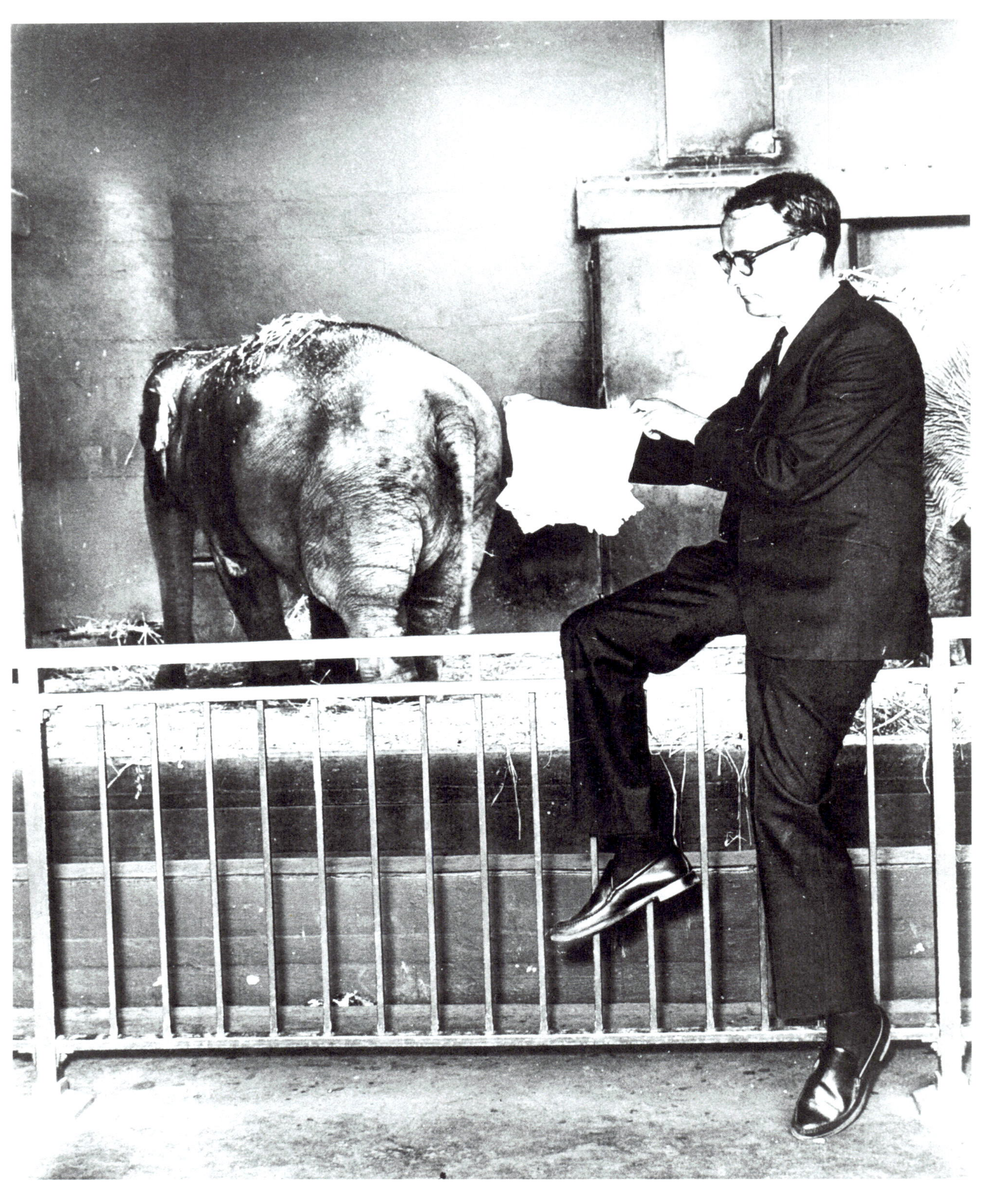

President Prout registers concern over a pair of shorts that look too small for an elephant.

Joined by another friend, Sasch Rubinstein, we attempted to dress a camel, elephant, bear, giraffe and rhinoceros with clothes sewn by Jeanne and Charlene, Sasch's wife. Or at least appear to be dressing them. We held up the skirts and pants and posed a lot. Wild animals aren't keen on being dressed.

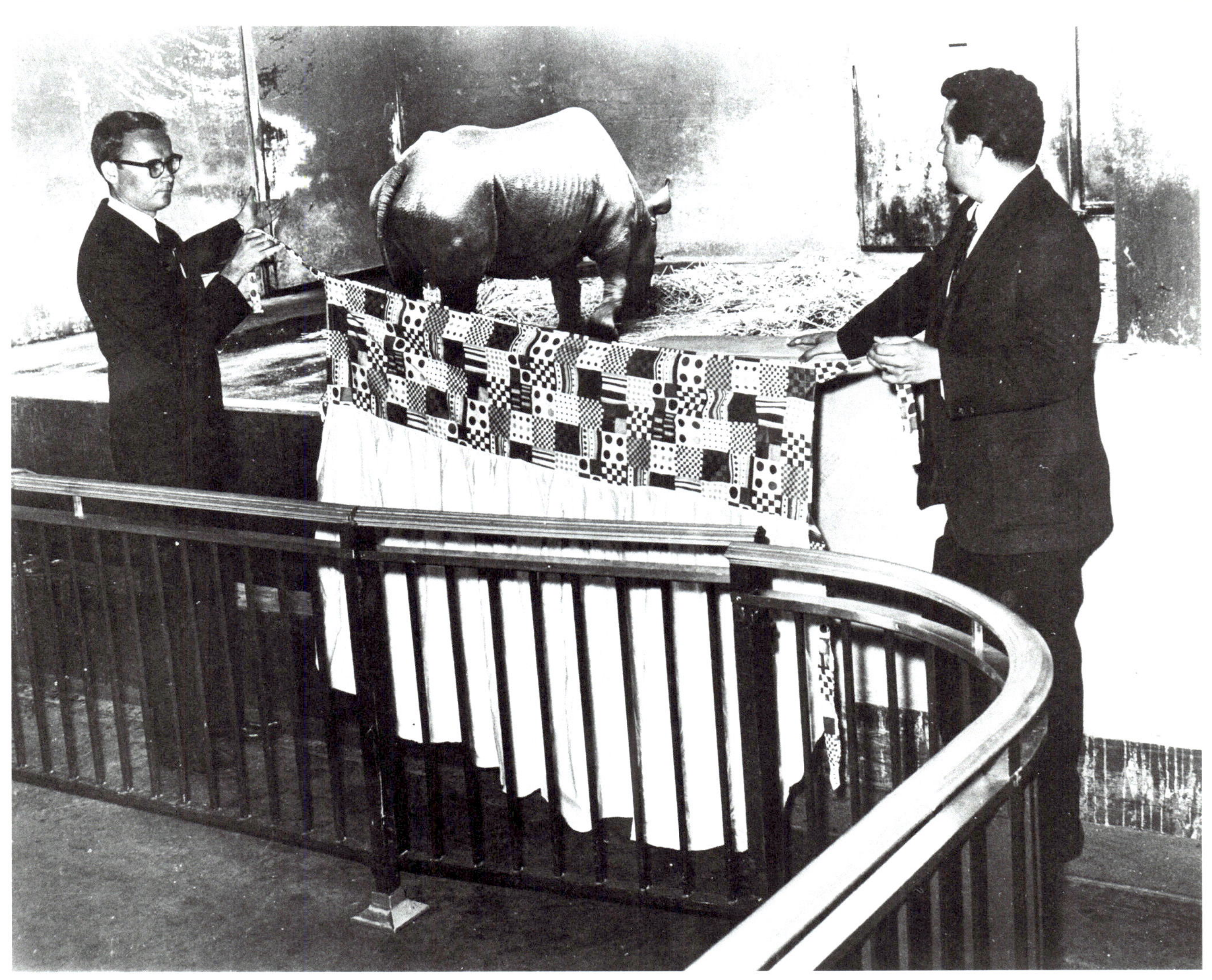

G. Clifford Prout and Sasch Rubinstein approach a rhino silently from the rear, a safe procedure for clothing a wild animal.

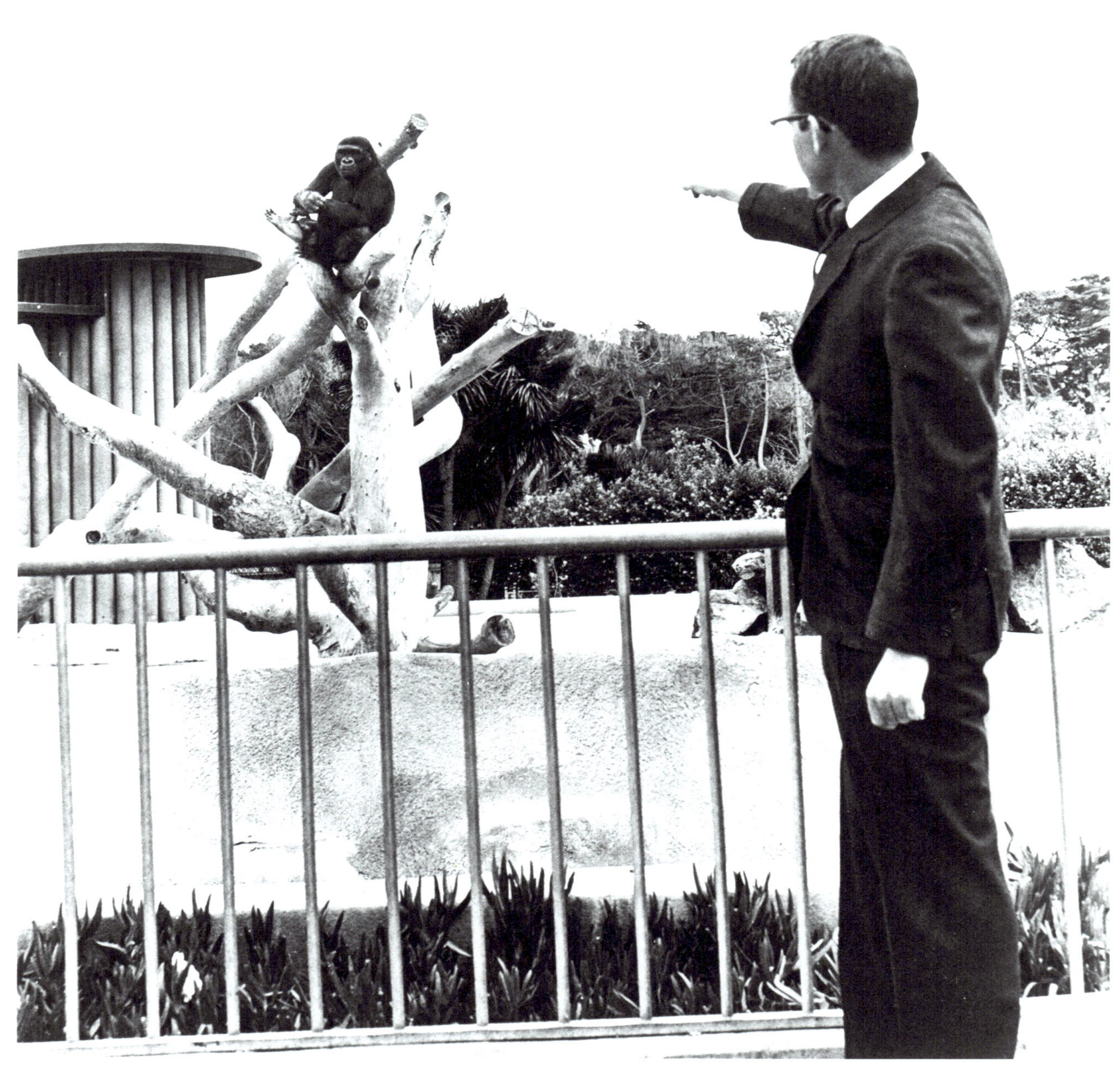

SINA President Prout points with shame at a nude ape perched on a tree in full view of men, women and children.

Much to the delight of the zoo visitors, Buck ran after an elusive fawn. A gorilla eyed us with indignation while the photographers snapped pictures and a bull with horns made very threatening snorts. We passed garments back and forth while trying to dodge the directions of Mr. Draper: "How about that water buffalo? That tiger looks pretty naked." I was relieved when they finally threw us out.

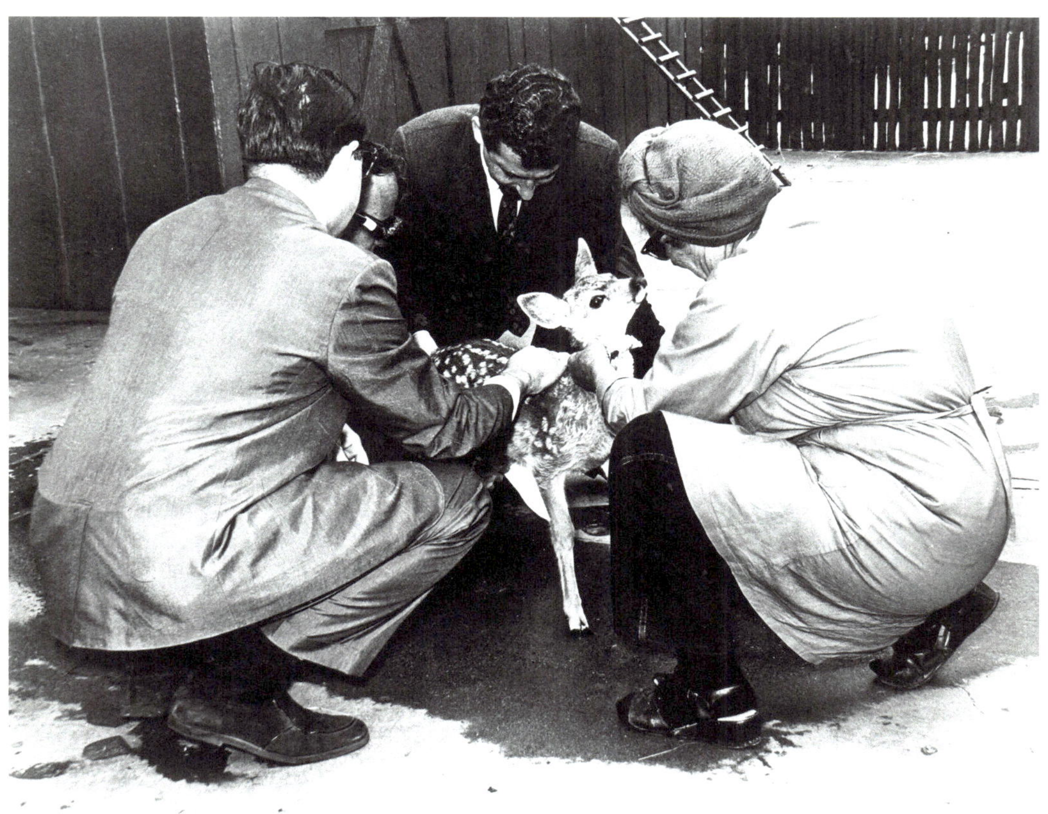

A baby deer is quickly and expertly clothed by SINA officers in 14 seconds!

A few days later, on Monday, August 13, 1962, I picked up the *Chronicle* in total amazement. On the front page in bold headlines "Exclusive: War Against Naked Animals" and a lengthy story about Prout's campaign against immorality. The next day another front-page headline: "Exclusive: San Francisco Center of War on Naked Animals," a continuation of SINA's pronouncement that San Francisco was a moral disaster area. The paper milked the story for two more days! There was such a deluge of calls from radio, TV and newspaper reporters that Jeanne and I could hardly handle all the interviews. Papers around the country picked up the story. A month later *The National Enquirer* ran its own full-page article using the same photos.

EXCLUSIVE

'War' Against Naked Animals

THE WEATHER

Bay Area: Fair with patches of morning fog. High temperatures 70 to 86; lows 50 to 55. Westerly winds 10 to 20 miles an hour. See Page 30.

San Francisco Chronicle

THE VOICE OF THE WEST

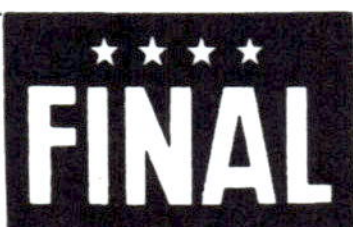

98th YEAR No. 225 | CCCCAAA | MONDAY, AUGUST 13, 1962 | 10 CENTS  GArfield 1-1111

Two Russians in Orbit

Giants Top L.A. Again

See Sports

Crusade Against Naked Animals

By George Draper

A New Yorker fighting to advance the cause of morality by clothing the "vital areas" of naked animals slipped into San Francisco yesterday.

In addition to his determination, he has an estimated $400,000 to back his plan.

Armed with the title of president of the 38,794-member Society for Indecency to Naked Animals, he answers to the name of G. Clifford Prout Jr.

He carries his heavy ammunition on the animal situation in a briefcase bulging with charts and graphs.

A CRUSADER

Prout, an unobtrusive but relentless crusader, wears the costume of an Ivy Leaguer and the flickering smile of a politician.

He modestly describes himself as "a left winger in the humane movement."

Prout and his devoted followers believe animals should conduct themselves much like people — particularly where natural functions are concerned — if decency is to triumph over immorality in this world.

And the question of suitable attire for the "vital areas" of our four-legged friends, he said, is at the heart of this challenging problem.

IT'S 'DECENCY'

"If you stop to think about it for a minute," Prout suggested, "you'll discover it's just a matter of decency."

Prout and his organization, which is known for short as SINA, have designed bikinis for stallions, half slips for cows, boxer shorts for certain small animals and knickers for bulldogs.

The nationwide (and global) tentacles of the SINA organization are controlled by Prout and his three salaried lieutenants from a bustling office in the heart of Manhattan.

There, at 507 Fifth avenue, they oversee the design of functional clothing for the pertinent parts of a variety of quadrupeds. They carry on a vast correspondence

See Page 16, Col. 1

Stores Open Until 9 Tonight

He's Against Nudity

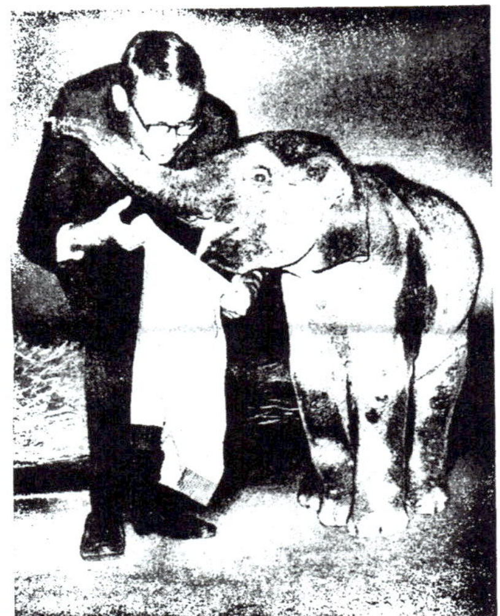

G CLIFFORD PROUT JR. AND LULU
"It's just a matter of decency"

A 90-Day Boat Trip to S. F.--Alone

By Jonathan Root

A 23-year-old Japanese auto parts salesman sailed into San Francisco Bay aboard a 19-foot sloop yesterday after a 90-day voyage alone from Japan.

His name is Kenichi Horie and he arrived without passport because Japanese officials had refused to give him one for what they termed a "suicidal" trip.

Officials of the Japanese Maritime Safety Agency in Osaka, informed that Horie had arrived safely, in good health and high spirits, were astonished.

"What!" exclaimed one. "We'd given him up for dead."

Horie sailed from his home at Osaka on May 12 in de-

See Page 2, Col. 1

KENICHI HORIE
"You want sake?"

Herb Caen Is Back--- **Page 29**

Brown Signs Oroville Dam Pact Today

By Jackson Doyle
Chronicle Correspondent

Sacramento

The biggest single construction contract ever awarded by California, for the tallest earthfill dam in the world, to be financed by the biggest bond issue ever authorized anywhere for any purpose.

That is what Governor Edmund G. Brown will approve in Los Angeles this morning when he signs a $120.9 million contract for construction of the main embankment and related features of

See Page 18, Col. 1

Soviet Spaceships 'In a Formation'

Pilots Can See One Another

A.P., U.P. & Reuters

Moscow

The Soviet Union yesterday fired off a second cosmonaut, putting him into an orbit so near to that of Major Andrian Nikolayev, that the two pilots could see each other and talk by radio.

The two Soviet spaceships were orbiting the earth in "group formation" at an altitude of more than 100 miles, according to Moscow Radio.

And in a continuing demonstration of another space first, their weightless movements in their space cabins were televised from time to time to Russian TV sets.

This morning the two orbiting spacemen awoke from a night's sleep and did calisthenics in their capsules, Moscow Radio reported.

Both cosmonauts were feeling "excellent."

A THIRD ONE?

A rumor floated through Moscow that a third cosmonaut would join them today.

Available sources in Moscow were inclined to doubt it, however, and Premier Khrushchev, in a message to one of the pilots, seemed to

See Page 10, Col. 1

'Fantastic' Leap Toward the Moon

London

The twin Soviet space flight brought a forecast from British scientists yesterday that the "fantastic" achievement might cut by half the time it will take man to reach the moon.

Sir Bernard Lovell, director of the Jodrell Bank radio observatory, said the flight was "the most remarkable development man has ever seen."

Kenneth Gatland, a leading member of the British Interplanetary Society, said if Vostok III and Vostok IV rendezvous in space the Russians will have taken "the vital step toward lunar flight."

Gatland and the society's secretary, Leonard Carter, predicted that the Russians were aiming to land a man on the moon within three or four years.

Gatland said a rendezvous would mean that spaceships could be refueled in orbit around the earth before being fired off toward the moon.

Dr R. L. Smith-Rose of the British Radio Research Station at Slough pointed out that the two spaceships have two opportunities to rendezvous every 24 hours on the basis of their orbital paths.

Lovell did not exclude the possibility of a space meeting but he thought the main mission of the twin probe was to further test communications and navigation in space.

Reuters

'Dead' Girl Phones ---Macabre Mixup

A San Leandro girl told police last night "I'm still alive"—after her father had identified her "dead body" hours earlier.

The Highway Patrol said the father identified a body at Fairmont Hospital. A girl was killed in an auto accident at 8:55 a.m. yesterday in San Leandro.

But his daughter called police and said she had heard of her "death" on a news broadcast.

CONFUSION

The girl's call, at 9:30 p.m., stirred three agencies to investigate—and it was late last night before the confusion began to clear.

A borrowed car contributed mainly to the mixup, officers said. They pieced the story together like this:

A young woman was killed when she was tossed out of her cartwheeling auto on South Davis street in San Leandro. She was dressed in pajamas and a coat and carried no identification.

Highway Patrol officers found the car was registered

See Page 14, Col. 4

THE INDEX

Who Am I? See Clue on Page 32

EXCLUSIVE S. F. Center of War on Naked Animals

THE WEATHER

Bay Area: Fair with fog near the ocean. Highs Tuesday, 68-85 degrees; lows, 52-58. Westerly winds 12-24 miles an hour in the afternoon. **See Page 22.**

San Francisco Chronicle
THE VOICE OF THE WEST

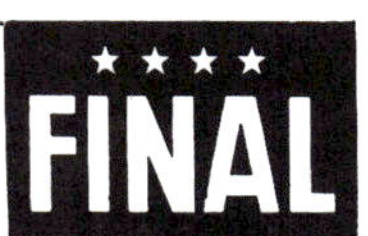

98th YEAR No. 226 | CCCCAAA | TUESDAY, AUGUST 14, 1962 | 10 CENTS | GArfield 1-1111

Address to Nation

Kennedy Says Tax Cut Now 'Not Justified'

United Press

Washington

President Kennedy told the country last night that he will not seek an immediate tax cut.

He said that if the economy should demand it, he'll call Congress back to act on one before year's end.

The President also promised again to request next year, at the latest, a "top to bottom, across-the-board" reduction in personal and corporate income taxes — retroactive to next January 1. He said key members of Congress already had assured him of quick action on this.

While the economy is by no means up to Administration goals, Mr. Kennedy said, it does not require the stimulus of a tax cut now. Even if one were sought, Congress would not approve it, he added.

The President said that the Administration plans to cut taxes because "our present tax system is a drag on economic recovery and economic growth, biting heavily into the purchasing power of every taxpayer and every consumer . . ." Then he added:

"Let me emphasize, however, that I have not been talking about a different kind of tax cut, a quick, temporary tax cut to prevent a new recession . . . In the ab-

See Page 20, Col. 1

A Whipping

Perth, Australia

Birch twigs have been ordered from Britain for the first whipping of a sexual offender in Western Australia in 50 years, prison officials announced here yesterday.

Reuters

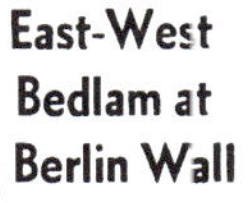

East-West Bedlam at Berlin Wall

Associated Press

Berlin

Crowds of enraged West Berliners made repeated attempts last night to storm the hated Red wall that has divided this Communist-encircled city for one year.

Blocked by hundreds of West Berlin Police from reaching the barricade, the demonstrators attacked vehicles carrying Soviet officers and soldiers.

The crowd, cursing and booing the Communists, hurled beer bottles, paving blocks and stones, smashing the windows of a Russian bus taking soldiers back from duty at the Soviet war memorial in West Berlin.

BRICKS

A brick hurtled through the rear window of a Soviet sedan following the bus. A second sedan was pelted with beer bottles.

This was the first anniversary of the wall and there had been officially expressed

See Page 12, Col. 1

Crusader at Work

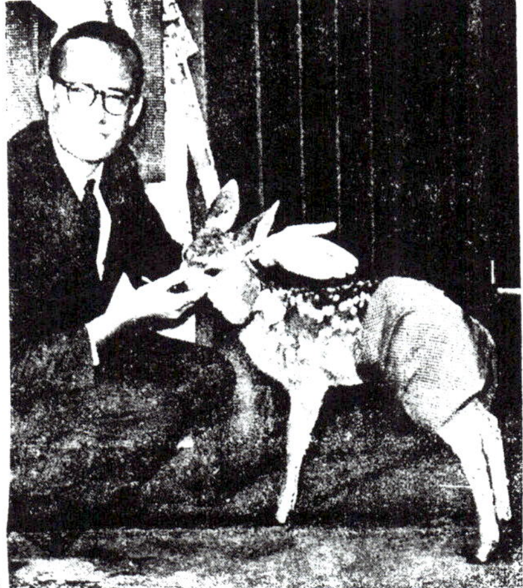

G. CLIFFORD PROUT AND FAWN
Nothing like it in a deer's world

Carpenters Bar Talks in Washington

By Kirk Smith
Labor Correspondent

Local carpenters rejected a proposal yesterday that they take their bargaining troubles to a Washington, D.C., mediation conference.

And C. R. Bartalini, leader of 18,000 carpenters in San Francisco, Marin, San Mateo and Alameda counties, sharply criticized the intervention of Secretary of Labor Arthur Goldberg, who suggested the mediation.

Goldberg said Sunday he wanted the carpenters and contractors, who cannot agree on wages for a new contract, to meet with William Simkin, director of the Federal Mediation Service, in Washington, D. C., on Thursday.

AVAILABLE

Richard Boyle, spokesman for the employers, said "we will be available."

Bartalini said nothing could be accomplished in Washington, D. C., that could not be done in San Francisco.

"If in the opinion of em-

See Page 20, Col. 3

WHO AM I?
See
Today's Clue
Page 24

Blame the Beasts

City Called 'Moral Disaster Area'

By George Draper
(Copyright, 1962, by Chronicle Publishing Co.)

San Francisco was declared a "moral disaster area" yesterday by G. Clifford Prout Jr., the New York crusader who believes bikinis, bloomers, knickers and shorts should cover the "vital areas" of naked animals.

Prout, president of the non-profit Society for Indecency to Naked Animals, delivered his harsh judgment of the city's moral status following a blitzkrieg inspection tour of prime animal centers here.

"There is an incredible amount of laissez faire in terms of tolerance of naked animals in San Francisco. This adds up to blatant immorality," fumed the usually gentle Manhattan moralist.

President Prout, who wears an Ivy League business suit while snooping for facts about animal nudity, said there is a definite correlation between the city's abnormally high rates of alcoholism and suicide and the vastness of its undressed animal population.

'Deterioration'

"The moral deterioration triggered by the sight of so many naked animals," Prout added, "also helps to explain why there is so much juvenile delinquency and adult crime."

The more unsavory aspects of beatnik life, Prout added, are "part and parcel of the naked animal situation."

SINA, the non-profit organization so zealously directed by Prout, is spending an estimated $400,000 over a 10-year period in its crusade against naked beasts.

The crusade headquarters at 507 Fifth avenue, New York, distributes free patterns for SINA-designed dog, cat and goat clothing and mails out a vast amount of SINA propaganda.

SINA lobbyists are currently pulling strings behind the scenes for Federal legislation against domesticated animals displaying their "vital areas" in public.

Membership

Membership in SINA is approaching a claimed 40,000. A life membership costs nothing, Prout main-

See Page 18, Col. 1

A Space Rendezvous?

Two Cosmonauts Maneuver Closer

Moon-Trip Mileage Dwarfed

A.P. & U.P.

Moscow

One of the two Russians orbiting the earth passed the million-mile mark and there were indications today that the cosmonauts might have attempted a fantastic rendezvous in space.

Major Andrian Nikolayev, who was hurled into space Saturday aboard Vostok III, began his fourth day in space. Somewhere in the vicinity, Lieutenant Colonel Pavel Popovich, who was launched into an almost identical orbit Sunday, was beginning his third.

An American, Dr. A. L. Jones of the Standard Oil Co. (Ohio) research center in Cleveland, said he believed the Russian spaceships had come together, "sometime before noon yesterday." He said he also thought that both men were now in one craft.

"One reason we believe they may have had the rendezvous is there are no voice transmissions from Vostok IV," he said. "We will know

See Page 14, Col. 3

Record 78 for S. F., With a Little Smog

The temperature in San Francisco set a record yesterday, but elsewhere in the Bay Area it was just seasonably warm.

The Weather Bureau reported a 10:50 a. m. high of 78 in downtown San Francisco, the hottest August 13 ever. The previous high for the date was 76 in 1929.

There was a touch of smog, too, but somewhat below the eye-smarting level. The Air Pollution Control District recorded a reading of .22 parts of oxidents per million parts

See Page 20, Col. 3

Churches Backed

Supervisors Join School Race Row

Four Supervisors yesterday asked the Board of Education to join with irate parents and community groups in settling the raging Central Junior High School controversy before the fall term begins.

They urged that the school "reflect as nearly as possible the racial makeup of the city and should be maintained as a happily integrated school." The resolution was introduced at a meeting of the Supervisors.

Two other groups took strong stands against a predominantly Negro school in separate actions yesterday:

1—The Inter-City Council of the Presbytery of San Francisco, an arm of the United Presbyterian Church of the United States, criticized school leaders for failure to take immediate action.

2—The Grattan Parents and Friends Committee announced last night they would not send their children to Central Junior High School unless the student body is predominantly white.

In doing so the parents, whose children graduate from Grattan Elementary School to the new Central Junior High School, joined a previously announced boycott by the National Associa-

See Page 16, Col. 4

Central Just Temporary, Spears Says

San Francisco's new Central Junior High School was described yesterday as a "purely temporary expedient" that very well may be out of business in two-and-a-half or three years.

Superintendent of Schools Harold Spears said he felt the controversy over the school and its racial pattern of 40 per cent white and 60 per cent non-white, is "getting people worked up over nothing."

"I wish the public realized Central is not a permanent

See Page 16, Col. 3

100 Battle Fire Atop Russian Hill

More than 100 firemen battled a three-alarm fire atop Russian Hill last night as several hundred apartment dwellers thronged the scene.

The blaze broke out in the third and fourth-floor apartments of 1100 Lombard street at 9:36 p.m. and caused an estimated $25,000 damage before it was controlled an hour later.

Twenty-six pieces of equipment jammed the intersection of Lombard and Hyde streets, halting cable car traffic.

India Prepared For Border Talks

New Dehli

Prime Minister Nehru said yesterday his government is prepared for preliminary talks with Communist China to try to remove tensions.

Associated Press

THE INDEX

The War Against Naked Animals

He Aims to Put Pants On Dogs, Slips on Horses And Even Bikinis on Cows!

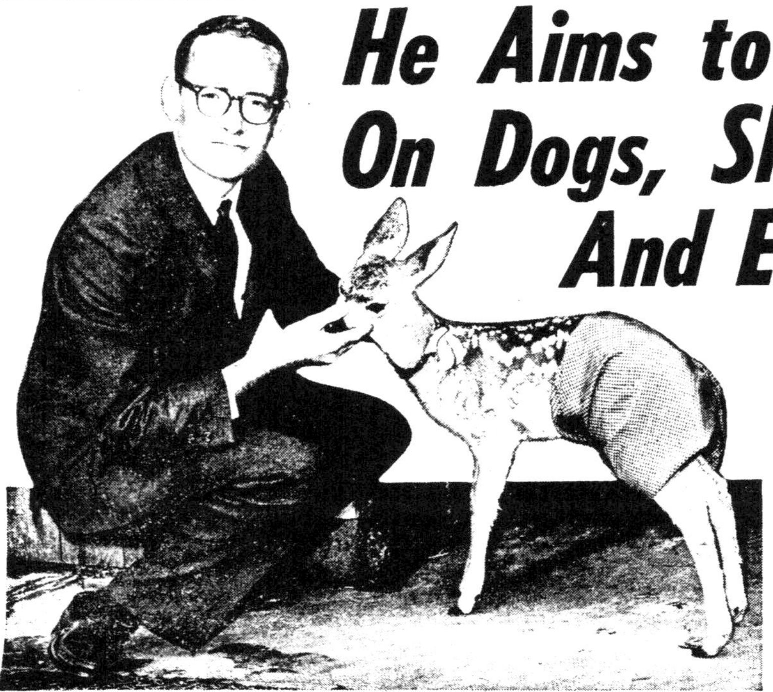

BAMBI COVERS UP: Deer's vital areas have been covered up to the satisfaction of G. Clifford Prout, president and founder of the Society for Indecency to Naked Animals.

Crusader Claims Their Nudity Is Ruining American Morals

By **BERNARD HENRY**

G. Clifford Prout has declared war on naked animals.

As President of the Society for Indecency to Naked Animals — known as SINA — Prout has dedicated 10 years of his life to clothing the "vital areas" of animals.

He wants dogs to wear pants and horses to wear half slips.

He's designed bikinis for cows and even trousers for elephants.

"It's a matter of decency," Prout explained. "Naked animals are ruining the moral standards of America."

Prout began his campaign against unclothed animals in 1956, when he received $400,000 in his father's will.

The money had to be spent within 10 years, according to the terms of the will, and it had to be used for "improving the moral climate of animals."

Prout immediately formed SINA, with headquarters at 507 Fifth Avenue, New York City, and began preaching for animal clothing.

At first Prout found people were turning a deaf ear to his pleas to cover up naked animals.

"Nobody realized what a terrible moral menace naked animals really are," he said.

"People went to zoos and leered at naked gorillas and monkeys without knowing how these animals were undermining their morals."

And whenever Prout approached authorities for aid in his campaign he was rebuffed.

"A mounted patrolman in Central Park gave me a summons for speaking without a permit," he said.

"I retaliated by giving the cop a SINA summons for contributing to the delinquency of his horse."

As more and more people read the monthly SINA newsletter and heard about his work Prout started meeting with more success.

"We now have 40,000 members from coast to coast," he said. "We have a Washington lobby to influence animal legislation.

"We distribute patterns for animal clothing through the mail, and SINA has 14 emergency clothesmobiles spotted around the U.S. ready to rush in to any area where animal morality is low."

Prout believes that all animals have a built-in sense of modesty and that they prefer to wear clothes.

"People who don't clothe their animals are at fault," he said.

Whenever Prout hears about a case of animal nudity, he sends a letter to the offending person.

In 1959 he wrote to Northwest Orient Airlines complaining about a naked horse in the company's show window in New York.

Last June he sent a letter to David Sarnoff, board chairman of RCA, pointing out that the RCA trademark — a dog called Nipper — was immodest.

Besides the mail campaign, Prout personally visits U.S. cities to press his drive for animal modesty.

Last August, in San Francisco, Prout turned the officials of the zoo upside down with his comments.

"San Francisco is a moral disaster area," he said. "There are over 700,000 naked animals running around loose.

"There's a definite correlation between this animal nakedness and the city's high rates of alcoholism and suicide. The sight of so many naked animals also helps to explain why there is so much juvenile delinquency and adult crime."

Zoo officials didn't agree with Prout's views.

"The animals are happy without clothes," said Mrs. Judith Lambert, of the Children's Playground in the zoo, "and people are used to it and think nothing of it."

"We've only just begun our campaign," Prout said. "People are joining us every day.

"Why, we have nearly 10,000 membership applications we haven't even processed.

"The day isn't far off when every four-legged animal over four inches tall and six inches long will be decently clothed."

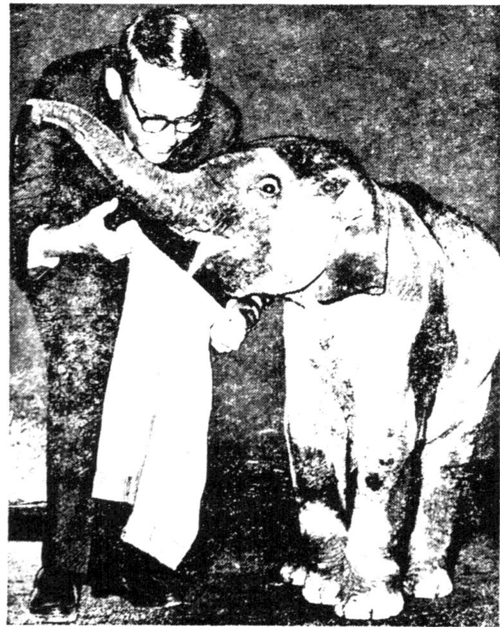

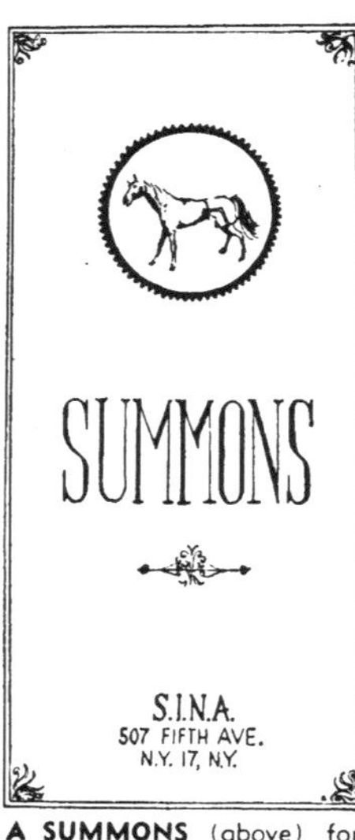

A SUMMONS (above) for contributing to the delinquency of an animal is given by the SINA to owners who don't clothe their animals. Prout displays a pair of trousers (left) to a baby elephant in the San Francisco Zoo.

NATIONAL
ENQUIRER

September 30, 1962 Vol. 37 No. 3
DINO M. GALLO, General Manager
CARL GROTHMANN Editor
TED MUTCH Managing Editor
NAT CHEZAN Asst. Managing Editor
WILLIAM MORIARTY, Circulation Mgr.
VINCENT MANZO, Production Manager
Published weekly by Best Medium Publishing Co., Inc., 655 Madison Ave., New York 21. Phone MUrray Hill 8-1111. Cable address, ENQUIRER NEWYORK. MAIL SUBSCRIPTIONS $5 a year in U.S. and Canada (subscriptions to foreign addresses $8 a year). Second Class Postage paid at New York, N.Y. Member, Audit Bureau of Circulations.

As much as I looked forward to the demand dying down, I couldn't help myself from writing to CBS news anchor Walter Cronkite. "Dear Walter, just a quick note to say hello from San Francisco. This city is crazy about these nuts who want to clothe animals. And they're serious! Might be something here for you." I enclosed the headline stories. A man named Robert Schackne called from CBS in Los Angeles; he wanted to put SINA on the network evening news, but wouldn't accept underlings, only the top man, G. Clifford Prout. I managed to get in touch with Buck just before he was to depart for New York, and he ended up being interviewed by Walter himself for eight minutes on August 21, 1962. Buck concluded the segment by singing the SINA Marching Song, accompanying himself with a ukulele.

Aug. 22, 1962

Dear Buck:

Hope you made it o.k. I called last night after catching Walter Cronkite and found your paramour Paula in your pad. The CBS thing was great and the SINA MARCH came over like crazy! Jeanne and I were rolling on the floor. I had a hunch you would make the scene and tuned in, although normally we don't watch sad-face Cronkite. He smiled afterwards and that was the first time I ever saw him crack!

I got the mail from you on Paul Coates and we are just now breaking it down into good, bad, awful, obscene, and shitty. I am writing for a tape on the Cronkite interview and will also write to see if he will send over all mail as I'm sure he'll get a batch of it! Gad you were on for about 8 minutes! It was stunning, especially with those animals booing and baying in the background....just too much!

I made contact with one of the skywriting outfits you told me about over the phone and they just mailed me their rates, etc. But last night after the Cronkite interview the skywriter called me and said he would like to write SINA in the sky as a sample for you to see.....thinking you were still in L.A. So I told him you were somewhere in Hollywood, etc. and he didn't want to send up the plane unless he was sure that G. Clifford Prout himself would be watching.....a real nut....... so that's when I called your number thinking you just might be still around. Paula answered and I asked her to call the nut, saying she had just talked to you and that you would be "looking up in the sky". So I guess that did the trick because the skywriter called me back and said they would write a sample and hoped "you would be watching!" Too much!

Meantime, I heard that Channel 11 (KTTV) had you on the news yesterday too. I don't know if you did that or if they took something from Paul Coates....anyhow we're starting to get action all over again in L.A. The skywriter said you were spread out in the TIMES and I have written for copies. I'll send these and others from S.F. to you this week so you'll have by time you get in Monday. I'm dying to know how things went with this Bob Shackne from CBS because you know he acted like a real shit when he called up here; I sent him a letter and copy to you....if you got it in Hollywood before leaving.....trying to pacify him and lend further authenticity to SINA.

Will write this week-end as soon as I know the latest score. Keep in tough with the west coast office!

Later,

AA & JA

Too Late To Classify

Clothe Animals? Of All The...

Baring an Issue

Dressing Animals Is Expensive

Don't We Have Enough to Do Without Clothing Horses, Too?

Prout's appearance created another flurry of press, and elicited a call from Don Hewitt, Cronkite's powerful producer. He was furious, having learned that Prout was none other than Buck Henry, a CBS employee. Hewitt found this out from Frank Stanton, the network president. What really enraged him is that I had mailed him a SINA achievement award for CBS's "courage above and beyond the normal boundaries of decency." *The San Francisco Examiner* sent reporter George Murphy to get a story about the Buck/Prout identity crisis, intent on embarrassing its rival, the *Chronicle*, with headlines of its own. I explained that Buck Henry was G. Clifford Prout's double, his spokesman. But, I insisted, that did not preclude the urgent need to clothe naked animals. SINA would carry on.

LET THE PUBLIC SPEAK

Question: How Do You Put Pants on a Bull?

ANIMALS INDECENT?

Kittens in Britches, Etc., Fire Artist's Creativity

Editorially Speaking

Let's Get Those Animals Covered

all shocked by the reptile's nakedness.

UNCLOTHED REPTILE

Kiwanians Not Upset By Sight

Animals With Clothing?

The Brownsville Herald

Your Freedom Newspaper

BROWNSVILLE TEXAS FRIDAY, AUGUST 24, 1962 DIAL LI 2-4331 FINAL EDITION

AMBUSH SCENE—Police stand near one of the vehicles used in ambush of French President De Gaulle. Attempt on his life was third in a year. Story on Page 10, Part I (AP Wirephoto via radio from Paris)

TESTING—Bill Meigs clothes his donkey, Cuddles, who seems dubious over test of a New Yorker's idea. Watching are Bill Meigs Jr, 12, and Bruceann, 5. Times photo

Pet Donkey Resists Clothes-Horse Test

Bill Meigs, an actor-singer, thinks G. Clifford Prout Jr. ought to try dressing a few animals "instead of running around just talking about the idea."

Prout is the New Yorker who is traveling throughout the country trying to get people to put clothes on "the naked animals of America." Prout is president of the Society for Indecency to Naked Animals (SINA).

For the last week Meigs, his wife, Pat, and their children, Bruceann, 5; Monty, 10, and Bill Jr., 12, have been experimenting with their pets, Cuddles, a jenny donkey; Lad, a collie, and Kitty Kover, a cat.

"It isn't easy," Meigs confided Thursday as he held a dress rehearsal at his home, 5831 Shirley Ave., Tarzana.

It was Bruceann who first got the family interested in outfitting the Meigs' backyard menagerie. She dressed Kitty Kover in doll dresses.

"The cat went along with the idea at first," said Mrs. Meigs. "But now every time Bruceann approaches she darts under a bed.

"And Cuddles is getting a little sick of the sugar we pop into her mouth every time we try to slip on her lace panties."

Mrs. Meigs made the panties at the insistence of Bill Jr. and Monty. Lad runs around the yard in a pair of Monty's cut-off Levis and a loud sweatshirt.

"That guy Prout is all wrong on this thing," Meigs declared. "The animals don't like it. They squirm out of their pants as quick as they can.

"We've experimented with the clothes for several days. Being modest in the daytime is for the birds. Since all this nonsense started at our house Cuddles is happiest at night when she lies down and sleeps in the nude."

Who'll Make Kilts for Cats?

Cracker Crumbs

Dogs Won't Wear Pants From Choice

By Frog Smith

BUSINESS is GOOD in SALISBURY . . . There's a reason!

SALISBURY EVENING POST

WEATHER
ROWAN — High yesterday, 88; low last night, 64; 10 a. m., 80; wind, W-8.
N. C. — Fair and Continued warm.

SALISBURY-SPENCER-EAST SPENCER, N. C., SATURDAY, SEPTEMBER 1, 1962

Letters To The Editor

Of Modesty In Animals

Editor Post:

The other evening Walter Cronkite on his 6:45 TV news broadcast interviewed a young man who is much concerned over immorality among our naked animals. He proposed to clothe all of them in shorts modified to suit the animal. It seems to me that he neglected one or two important points. First, should there not be some distinction between male and female shorts? What self-respecting boy animal would like to be mistaken for a girl? For the girls I would suggest a backward pointing ruffle over the hips like an apron. This would also be an advantage for a person walking a pet who would like to know what precautions, if any, needed to be taken about an approaching animal.

THEN NOTHING was said about removing the shorts in case of need. Does the young man plan an attendant for each animal who would render this service? Or perhaps numerous animal comfort stations with 24 hour service. It might do wonders for the unemployment situation if it could be worked. Another suggestion would be to fasten the shorts with a bowknot with short loops and long ends which the animal could reach to untie the knot and drop the shorts. The problem would be to replace them. Even the most intelligent animal would find that difficult. But why could not the general public be alerted to the need? I am sure that if the matter were properly presented over radio, TV and in the newspapers, any right minded citizen would come to the aid of an animal in need.

The young man also neglected to point out the boost to the economy that a new animal short making industry could make on the community. And what about the tremendous laundry problem? Together these might obviate the need for a tax reduction.

It is possible that the Society has literature covering these points. I am sure that an inquiry addressed to Walter Cronkite of the CBS news service would bring the needed information.

Very sincerely,
Cora E. Gray

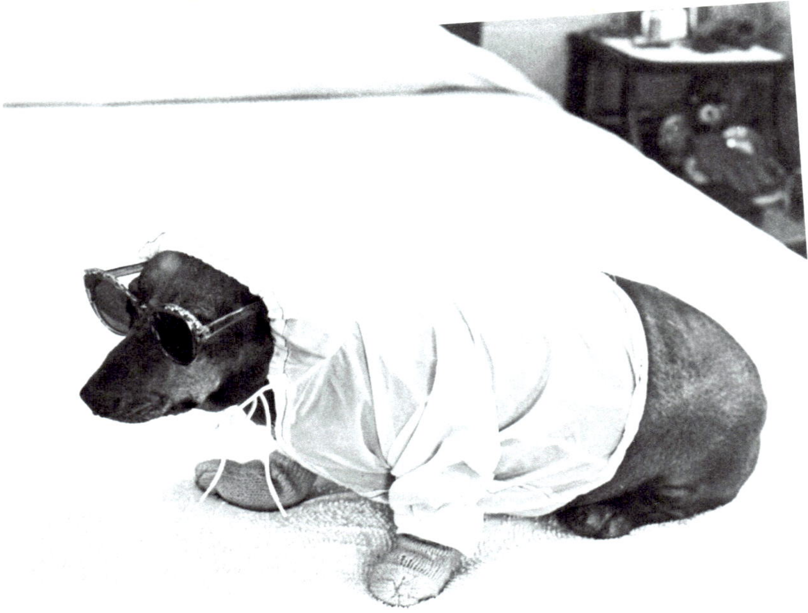

SINA NEWS from

Society for Indecency to Naked Animals

507 Fifth Avenue, NYC

OXford 7-5895

NEWS RELEASE

Walter Cronkite,well known TV personality, obtained an exclusive interview with G. Clifford Prout, President of SINA, that was aired for eight minutes over the entire CBS TELEVISION NETWORK Tuesday August 21st. (6:45 pm P.S.T.)

Mr. Prout was both humble and forthright in his comments as he stressed the need for decency and public sympathy for his world-wide crusade to clothe all animals that stand higher than 4 inches or are longer than 6 inches. Mr. Cronkite seemed both fascinated and amused as the interview was concluded by his singing of the official SINA MARCH "Wings of Decency" a cappella!

Response to the telecast was immediate as thousands of people throughout the United States wrote, wired and called SINA Headquarters to voice their opinions. The SINA switchboard went on 24 hour duty, CLOTHESMOBILES and SINA-CYCLES were ordered to stand by and a form letter was prepared to answer the tidal wave of mail that poured in.

Monday evening August 27th Steve Allen added his weight to the SINA movement by commenting on the gigantic campaign under way in San Francisco, personally directed by G. Clifford Prout.

In the very near future the officers of SINA will debate their issues with a leading psychologist, sociologist and anthropologist during a special half-hour television show that promises to be educational and stimulating.

Further details on the SINA crusade in California can be obtained from Vice-President Alan Abel in the San Francisco field office: WA 1-0482.

* * * * * * * * * * *

August 28, 1962

Dear Buck:

Don't know if you caught Steve's program last night (Mon) but he held up the headline on Nude Animals in S.F. and talked about G. Clifford Prout as though a complete stranger, etc. which made me breath a sigh of relief because I thought he just might launch into a tirade of expose on Buck Henry, etc. just to let his audience he know what was behind most things in the news that were frauds, etc. But he remained true! Will check tonight and rest of week to see if he follows up.

Talked to Bob MacMillan today and he said all the press in L.A. are still hopped up about you and he gets calls daily as to when you will be available for interviews, etc. I told him you might be back in near future, etc. He told me that Santa Barbara News-Press ran a story on you. I acted surprised but actually I planted a press release story with paper to the effect that you and 200 SINA women were going to picket a horse show there Sept. 3rd. I made it sound threatening, i.e. with a band, banners, summons, the works! Will send you this story and the L.A. TIMES which MacMillan promised to send. He and Paul Coates are also interested in another interview with you.

Right now I'm working full speed on the TV format because I want to cash in on the national publicity. I hope Cronkite follows it up. I've also planted a story with HUNTLEY-BRINKLEY show in Washington-N.Y. so they may bite too. What about the TONIGHT show? I don't think Paul Keyes is on it but perhaps you can check to see who is handling the producing or chief writing as I've been planting anonymous notes from "housewives" as to why they don't get the president on SINA on, etc.

Later, AA

September 8, 1962

Dear Buck:

After the frantic calls from Don Hewitt regarding Walter Cronkite, Frank Stanton, etc. and my agreement that SINA would destroy the CBS address plate providing there was no reprisal against Buck Henry, I thought we could settle down to some peace and quiet. No such luck! Following your letter about the EXAMINER a photographer and reporter showed up at our new apartment Thursday afternoon. They piled a lot of questions on Jeanne but she came through beautifully and they learned nothing except that SINA was very real, here to stay, etc. I have no idea how they found our new place because the other apartment was a sub-let from a girl who had specific instructions to tell nothing about anything and I know we can depend upon her.

Lots of love, kisses, embraces and an extra big goose

AA & JA

Sept. 30, 1962

THE GARRY MOORE SHOW
RED WING PRODUCTIONS, INC.

524 WEST 57th STREET · NEW YORK, NEW YORK · JUdson 6-6000

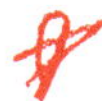

Dear Al:

Among other things - pick up, if you haven't already, this weeks dated Sept. 30 National Enquirer. Page 2 - SINA. Weirdly enough, the byline is actually one of the pennames of that guy Semple, or whatever his name is. I have a friend who works on the Enqiirer. He got hysterical, of course, when he saw it. But the Enquirer itself took the story straight. Thinks I'm r eal.

It is absolutely impossible to get to see that damned Cronkite show. My agency tried and that guy in charge hit the roof all over again. It's really a traumatic thing with him. So I guess I'll never see it.

Listen - will you send me a copy of my letter to Tooney. I haven't got one and I think I'd like to frame them both, along with any other correspondence we might collebt on the Tooney affair.

The stories on Contact, Nevada are great. It's gotta be a publicity stunt but I wish it were for real. Sounds like a town we ought to visit once in a while.

Nothing new. We move pur offices next week to the Henry Hudson Hotel. So what.

Can't seem to get ahold of that damn Insider's Newsletter anywhere.

Later Buck

San Francisco Examiner

Truth, Justice ● Public Service

FRIDAY, SEPTEMBER 14, 1962

DICK NOLAN

THE CITY

●

IT IS OLD STUFF to late TV watchers, who were well aware of the SINA comedy act perhaps a year ago, but Insider's Newsletter has taken note of the gullible (or mendacious) newspapers which gave great space to SINA and the "campaign to clothe naked animals." . . . The man who invented the gag, says the Newsletter, is actor-comedian-writer Buck Henry, who has been giving his dead-pan performance for a long time on stage and on television as a comedy bit. Henry is one of the writers on the Garry Moore Show, if you are curious about how he really earns his bread.

●

SOCIETY FOR INDECENCY TO NAKED ANIMALS

507 Fifth Avenue
New York 17, N.Y.
OXford 7-5895

SPECIAL NEWS RELEASE:

SINA, the Society for Indecency to Naked Animals,announced today that it had instructed its attorneys to file a $6,000,000 libel suit against the "Insiders Newsletter", a Cowles publication.

The decision to sue was reached after an all night meeting in San Francisco by SINA officers called together for this special executive session. G. Clifford Prout, President of SINA, was unable to attend due to a skin allergy, however, Vice-President Alan Abel handled the proceedings and discussed the evidence at hand with top level SINA officers who had flown in from New York for the secret rendezvous.

Mr. Abel presented the facts and received an unanimous vote to proceed legally with all possible speed. He then outlined the bill of particulars that will constitute the law suit so that it would not be necessary to hold press conferences in New York and Los Angeles as has been done in the past.

Some of the information offered at this meeting was: ".....so let us not be shaken by these scandal publications that cling to the sensational side of the news.......especially ones with dubious readership and limited circulation. We have survived past attacks over the four years of SINA history. Our work will continue relentlessly and it remains for the public to see through any attack that would undermine SINA and twist our morality campaign into something facetious................"

Meantime, a special mailing was made to the over 1000 California SINA card holders to intensify their efforts in picketing all zoos and horse shows in the state, particularly the large zoo in San Diego.

Plans are also being made for a SINA WORLD CONGRESS to be held this coming December in New York. Over 2500 SINA Chapter leaders are expected to attend from the United States, Canada, England, France, Switzerland, India and Mexico.

SINA activities for the West Coast are being handled out of the newly established San Francisco field office at 2434 Vallejo St. TELEPHONE: WAlnut 2-0796.

* * * * * * *

SINA

California Disaster Areas

San Francisco and Bay Area
762,000 Naked Animals

Sacramento
23,740 Naked Animals

San Jose
staggering figures-
as yet incomplete

Los Angeles
482,720 Naked Animals

San Diego
(under investigation)

Palm Springs
(clothesmobile enroute)

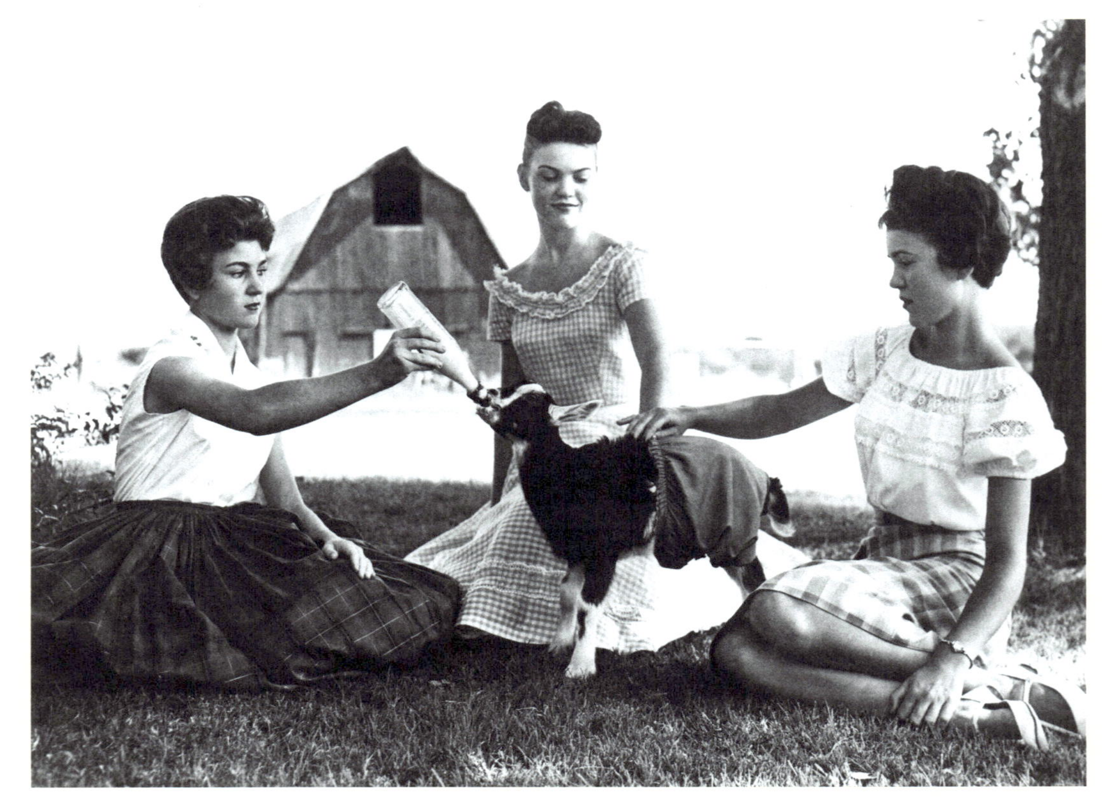

In between writing assignments, Buck appeared in a West German documentary as well as on Jean Shepherd's show *The Dissenters* in Philadelphia, where he sat opposite a female nudist. Receiving an avalanche of mail from students at the University of California at Berkeley, I stepped in for Prout and arranged to give a lecture to an audience of 1500 bright young minds. I told them all about the Prout dynasty, including G. Clifford's grandfather, Otis, who fought in the Civil War against the North and the South. He had his soldiers ride into battle on clothed horses. I described the day when Otis stood on a barrel and raised his sword: "Gentlemen," he declared, "Give me decency, or give me death!" So, they shot him.

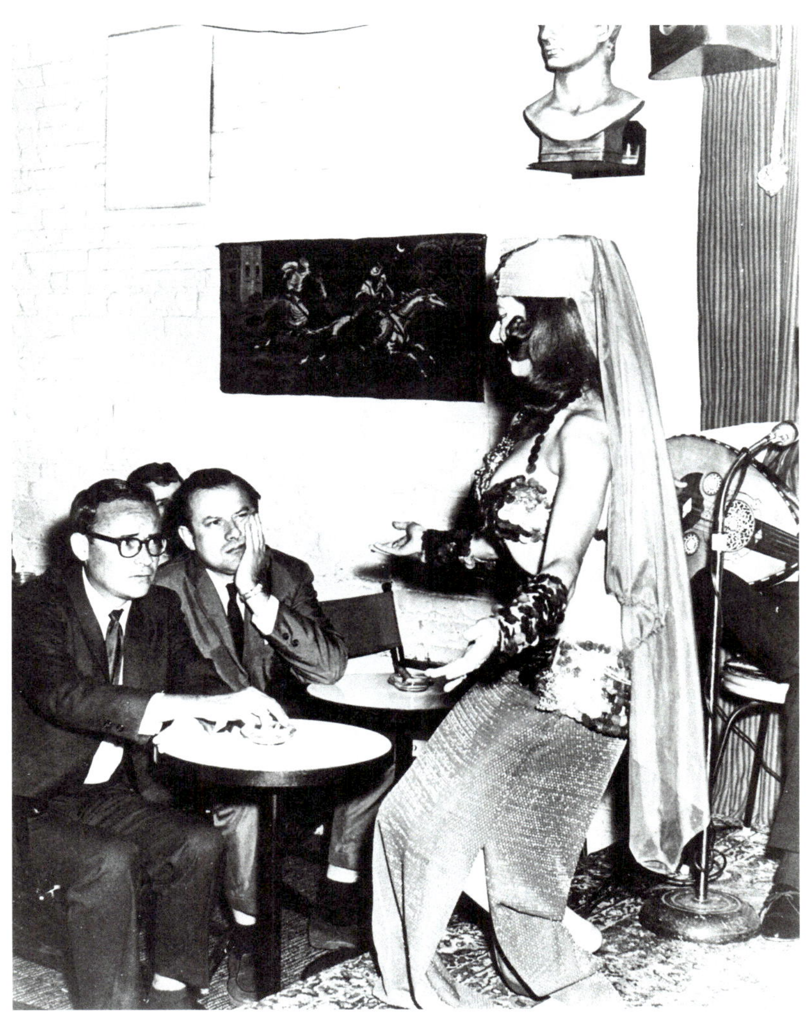

Prout and Abel accept invitation to view dancer who asked to join SINA. Membership was denied due to nature of her work.

? Nov 62

Dear Al :

Christ, what a thrill to hear your mellifluous tones again. I think you'd better get back to NY as quickly as possible. I have taken matters into my own hands and have rented the front of an automobile showroom and the back of Ed Carmelli. So we can start all over again. And this time, we're going to do it right!

I did the Kraut show last Friday. They kept trying to get me to pick a place to do the actual shooting: my sumptuous home, my lovely offices, one of the many prominent SINA meeting halls ---- Jesus, I had to think up a different excuse for each one of them. Finally they gave up and we made the film in a conference room in the Shelton Hotel. Opened with the SINA marching song, naturally, discussed a few salient issues for about ten or fifteen minutes, then closed with a rather thrilling and moving reading of Miss York's "Ode to Decency". I told them I would have to read it because I never had time to memorize it, so they held it a few feet in front of me and told me to try and pretend that I was saying it from memory. Afterwards, they told me that I really would make a wonderful actor - I was so convincing in my reading. Gosh. Gee whiz. Wow. Then I had to sit and try to maintain a straight face while the interviewer asked all the questions over again - in German. It is very difficult to be serious while someone yammers at you in another tongue. They had a couple of high schooly type girls hanging around, gazing at me with a mixture of awe and disgust. I don't know what they were doing there. They will contact you - if they have not already - and ask you for details about our Washington branch - they want to do some local shooting there. Lots of luck.

Obviously their letter was a con-job. I have reason to believe that they are not doing a show about animals and animal protection at all. I think all they're doing is a show on a number of weirdos (unusual people, to be polite). I'd love to know who the others are.

Listen - as soon as you get back, I want to take you up to the Cooper office. I don't know how you feel about agencies or whether you have any connection with any already, but I've talked to them about you and they're looking forward to seeing if you really exist and how many heads you have and all that.

That's all I can think of for the moment. Hang on.

Buck

SOCIETY FOR INDECENCY TO NAKED ANIMALS

507 FIFTH AVENUE • NEW YORK 17, NEW YORK • OXFORD 7-5895

MESSAGE	REPLY
TO	DATE 2434 Vallejo Street San Francisco 23, Calif.

11/30/62

Dear Buck:

I faced a wild hip audience at UC and they tore the house down with laughter as I went through all the jazz on SINA plus a whole new concept involving your Grandfater and the Civil War. Will write it up and send your way as it is sure-fire for laughs and you might find it useful during interviews, etc. None of the info can be proved or disproved so it is a natural for our cause!

I sent you some stuff under separate cover c/o Moore Show at CBS so watch for it if you haven't already received by the time this gets to you. What's new? We're still planning our return to N.Y. end of Dec. keep in touch. More later.

Love & Stuff,

AA & JA

DATE

BY

SIGNED

A DAY IN THE LIFE OF G. CLIFFORD PROUT, JR., PRESIDENT OF SINA

(As recorded in his personal and confidential diary)

7:00 am Alarm went off right on time.

7:05 am Exercised vigorously.

7:10 am Shower, shave, brush teeth, etc.

7:35 am Breakfast of organ music, orange juice, dry toast and coffee. (Must watch my figure!)

8:05 am Long distance call from reporter in London. Gave him exclusive interview on SINA. Promised to air mail autographed photo for his cousin. Wonder how he got my unlisted number?

8:30 am Took cab to office. Left 25 SINA leaflets on seat. Arrived in 14 minutes and 22 seconds. Much better than yesterday.

8:46 am First one in. Switchboard lit up with calls. Three bags of mail unopened. People waiting at reception desk. Nobody to handle anything! Use secret panel in restroom to reach my private office unnoticed.

9:05 am Dorothy arrives five minutes late and I chide her humorously. Instructed her to put through only long distance calls from SINA leaders and the press.

9:15 am Both phones ringing constantly. I whistle the SINA Marching Song to keep my sanity. My two secretaries arrive and begin screening people waiting to see me. One man demands to see me in a loud and threatening voice. He is evicted bodily.

10:45 am Have spoken continuously on the phone and with various civic leaders in person who are anxious to declare their neighborhoods moral disaster areas, want me to speak before their cummunity organizations and others seeking loans whom I direct to nearby banks.

11:00 am Executive Board meeting gets under way with all officers present and cheerful. We pass on 4 SINA Achievement Awards, authorize the formation of 27 new SINA Chapters and elect 68 people to honorary membership in SINA. One member in Chicago is expelled for writing me an abusive letter without sufficient cause.

12:30 pm Departed for luncheon at the Waldorf in my honor and spoke for 40 minutes on the future of SINA. A number of fine young women attended who are seeking affiliation with SINA. They represented their organization called "Women for Decency" and would like to spend all of their free time knitting clothing for needy animals from needy families.

2:30 pm Returned to office and spent three hours on the phone with more long distance calls; dictated 187 letters and telegrams; put through call to White House but was unable to contact the President.

5:30 pm Posed for pictures in my office with SINA delegation from Chicago. Discussed their fine efforts in Cook County and promised to march at the head of their next parade, my schedule permitting.

6:15 pm Took cab home to change clothes for formal dinner at the New York Athletic Club. Made it in 17 minutes and 47 seconds.

6:34 pm Opened the door to my apartment. Took shower and shaved again while listening to the strains of Mozart Symphony which sounded strangely similar to our own SINA Marching Song, "Wings of Decency." Must remember to investigate this further. Also need new needle for phonograph and tablecloth.

7:30 pm Arrived at the New York Athletic Club and took up position outside to serve the SINA Summons to people with naked animals. Served six violators. Last man had huge Great Dane who attacked me at the throat. I skillfully dodged his thrusts and then responded with a hard right uppercut to the mouth that sent him sprawling to the ground quite bruised and embarrassed. Now they both charged me viciously. I jumped into a waiting cab and went to see a movie on 42nd Street.

10:30 pm Came out of theatre after seeing exciting double feature films on plant life in South America and huge ant men of the future. Bought newspapers and hailed cab for home. Left 50 more SINA leaflets on back seat.

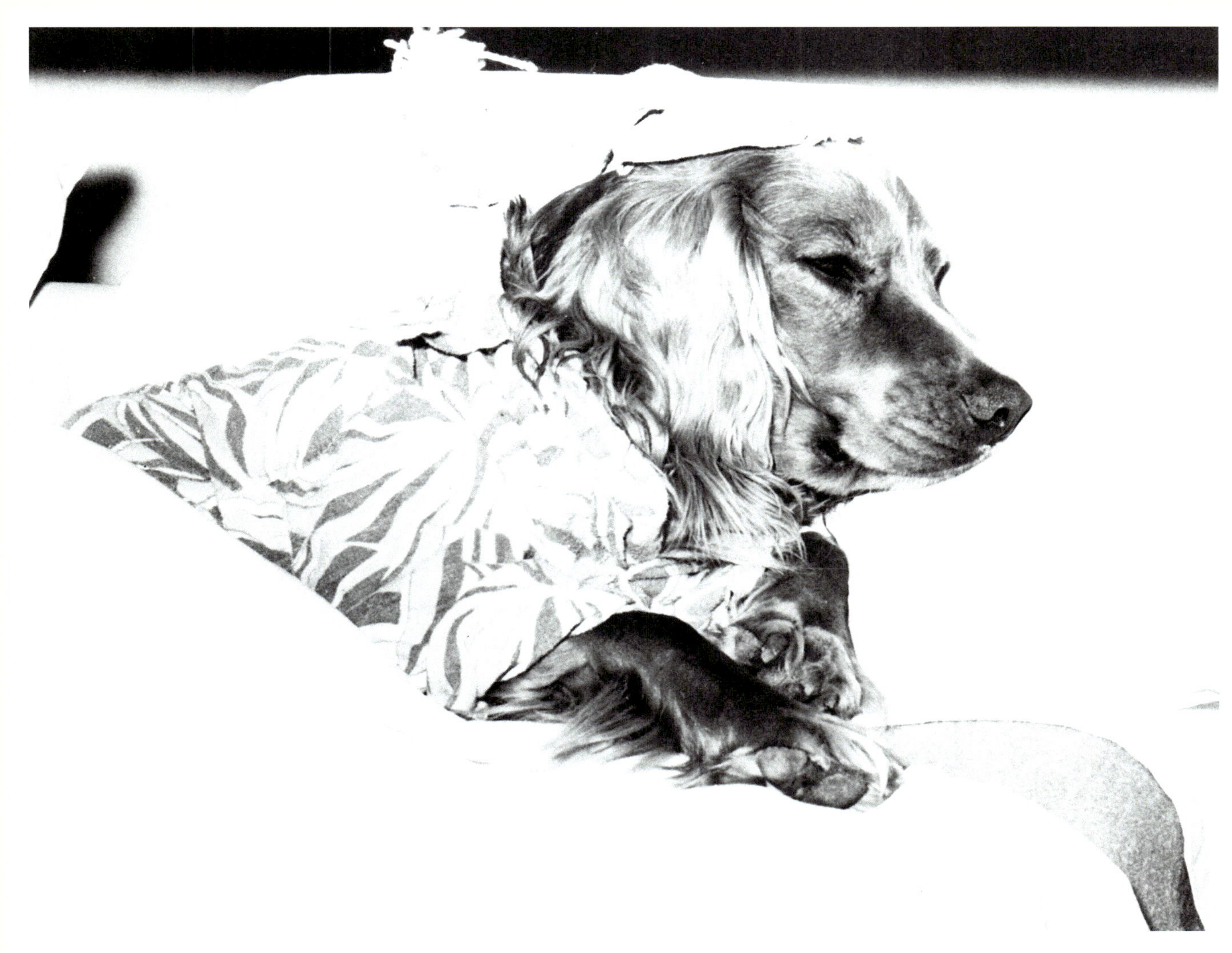

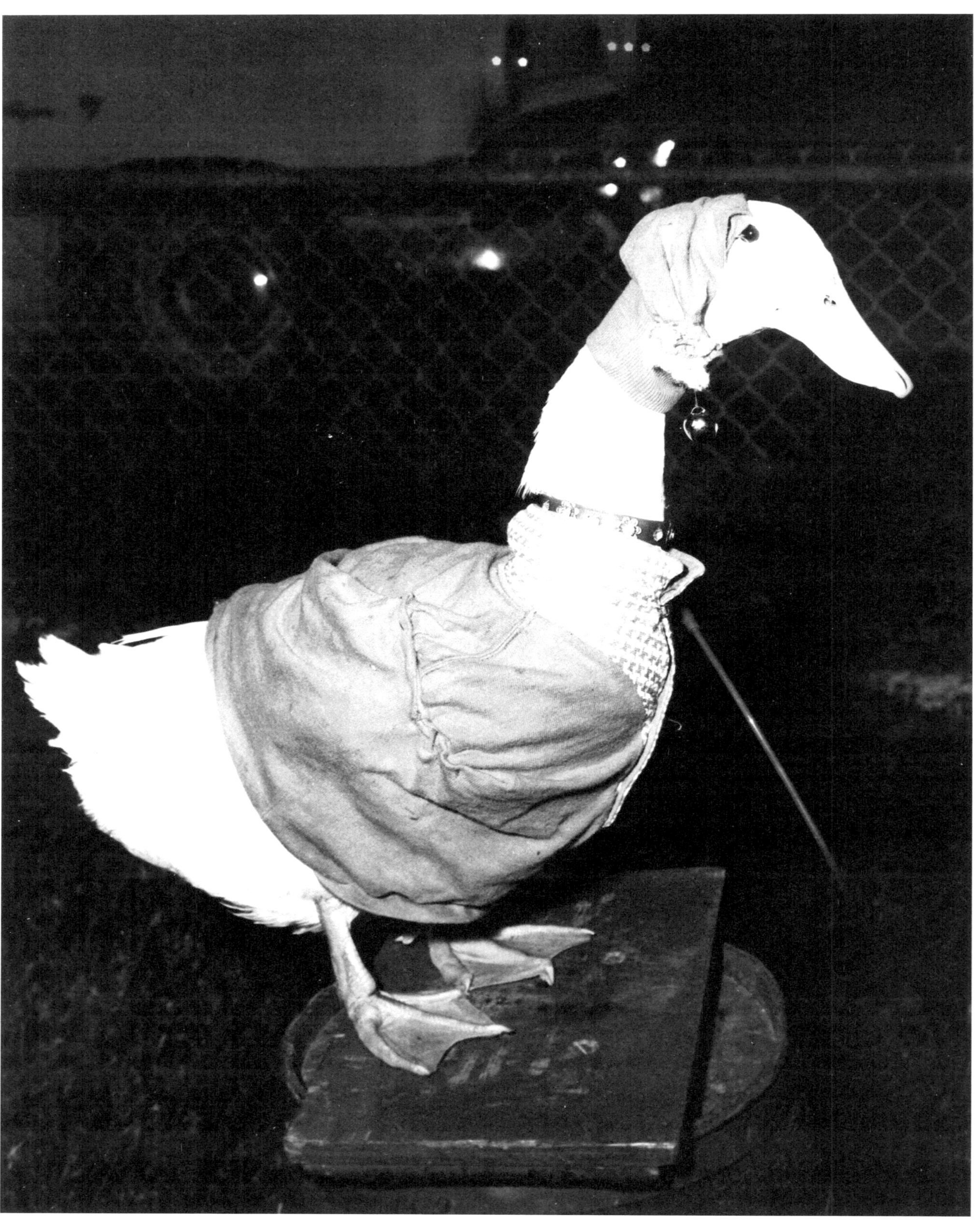

Spencer Productions, Inc.
507 FIFTH AVENUE
NEW YORK 17, N. Y.
OXFORD 7-5895

18 июля, 1963

Премьер Никита Сергеевич Хрущев
Москва,
С.С.С.Р.

Уважаемый Премьер Хрущев,

Представляем вашему вниманию ПЕРВЫЙ СЕКСТЕТ УДАРНЫХ ИНСТРУМЕНТОВ, как один из наиболее знаменитых и захватывающе успешных университетских музыкальных ансамблей Соединенных Штатов Америки.
В состав этой группы входят семьдесят пять единиц различных ударных инструментов, выступающие в театрах и концертных залах с программой длительностью в два часа.
В прошлом году, вскоре после того как вы стуча кулаком по столу выступали перед ассамблеей Организации Об'единенных Наций, до нас стали доходить мнения многих профессиональных барабанщиков с различных концов Америки о том, что ваше стучание по существу было весьма музыкально, искусно и даже с известной техникой ;вплоть до того что эти инструменталисты даже восхищались вашим „фортиссимо состенуто".
Под впечатлением виденного один из членов нашего СЕКСТЕТА написал музыкальное произведение, сюжетом коего являются „Волжские Лодочники" при инсценировке вашего стучания за столом в ООН, как это и передавалось по телевиденью. Эта пьеса озаглавлена „День в ООН" и долженствует собой явить музыкальное оформление попытки об'единить все страны по признакам гармонии.
„День в ООН" оказался самым успешным номером в репертуаре наших позднейших концертов, и поэтому мне пришла мысль в голову предложить вам выступить с СЕКСТЕТОМ в качестве солиста, играющего роль за столом, на особом концерте в Москве, сообразно с обстоятельствами вашего свободного времени.
Несомненно что ваш народ будет рад этому событию, а со своей стороны я уверен что и наш американский народ в этом увидит ваш добровольный жест могущий послужить в целях лучшего обоюдного понимания различия наших олигархий.
Если вы пожелаете принять участие в этом предприятии, то будьте любезны в ответном письме нам указать точную дату предлагаемого концерта. Если это окажется возможным, то нашему СЕКСТЕТУ потребуется ваше содействие в виде оплаты транспорта и содержания ансамбля для реализации нашего концерта. Для репетиции от вас понадобилось бы не больше часа, в вашей роли барабанщика при монтаже „Дня в ООН".
Я уверен что наш Государственный Департамент не окажет препятствий в выдаче нам всем виз на это путешествие.

В ожидании вашего ответа, я остаюсь,

Уважающий вас,

Алан Абель, менаджер
Первого Секстета Ударных Инструментов

Эй Эй: джей эй
приложение

Dear Buck:

I have another idea. I sent a letter to Nikita Khrushchev with all 4 issues of the CHRONICLE. H e will surely piss and moan when he sees that his Ass-tro-nuts were put down and the nude bit across the banner headline. I suggested that the SINA officers do a TV appearance on their central TV hookup so that the people of Russia could form their own chapters to clothe the animals of Russia. I suggested that this came about because we have received so many letters from Russian Citizens asking how they could form such chapters; and I added that this common denominator of "decency" could well cement our respective relationships and perhaps bring about a better understanding of our nations, etc. etc.

I doubt if he will answer; you know his signature alone is worth a fortune but he just might bite on it and it would be worth its weight in gold if he does! Will keep you informed.

Best, etc.

AA

CLASS OF SERVICE

This is a fast message unless its deferred character is indicated by the proper symbol.

WESTERN UNION

TELEGRAM

W. P. MARSHALL, PRESIDENT

1201 (4-60)

SYMBOLS

DL=Day Letter

NL=Night Letter

LT=International Letter Telegram

The filing time shown in the date line on domestic telegrams is LOCAL TIME at point of origin. Time of receipt is LOCAL TIME at point of destination

CONFIRMATION COPY

87 PD INTL

CD NEWYORK NY MAR 26 1963

LT PREMIER NIKITA KHRUSHCHEV

MOSCOW (RUSSIA VIA WU)

REQUEST PERMISSION FOR AUDIENCE WITH YOU IN MOSCOW TO DISCUSS OUR MOVEMENT TO CLOTHE ANIMALS OF THE WORLD FOR THE SAKE OF DECENCY. DECENCY CAN BECOME A COMMON DENOMINATOR OF UNDERSTANDING AMONG ALL NATIONS. OUR PICKETING OF THE WHITE HOUSE BROUGHT MANY LETTERS FROM RUSSIAN CITIZENS TO SINA, THE SOCIETY FOR INDECENCY TO NAKED ANIMALS ASKING FOR CHAPTERS IN YOUR COUNTRY. WHEN CAN WE MEET? AWAITING YOUR REPLY. I REMAIN, YOURS FOR DECENCY

G CLIFFORD PROUT PRESIDENT SINA

507 FIFTH AVE NEWYORKCITY

THE COMPANY WILL APPRECIATE SUGGESTIONS FROM ITS PATRONS CONCERNING ITS SERVICE

SINA NEWS from

Society for Indecency to Naked Animals
507 Fifth Avenue, NYC
OXford 7-5895

G. Clifford Prout, President of SINA, announced that he had advised Nikita Khrushchev in Moscow about the interest from a number of Russian citizens in forming their own SINA chapters for the purpose of clothing all animals that stand higher than 4 inches or are longer than 6 inches.

SINA presently has chapters throughout the world with the exception of the Far East, Russia and other Communist controlled countries, however, Mr. Prout believes that "decency", as advocated by SINA, may well be the common denominator that could cement Russian-American relations and end the Cold War by providing an umbrella of mutual morality and respect.

Mr. Prout emphasized that any SINA information provided Russian people would be solely for the sake of maintaining the SINA Constitution, which stresses the covering of all nude animals, and should in no way be construed as SINA's acceptance of Russian idealogy. Mr. Prout stated: "SINA is just as much opposed to Communism as any other American group; our only interest is in keeping animals and people decent."

President Prout contacted Premier Khrushchev by cable and requested an audience with him at SINA Headquarters in New York City. This historic meeting will undoubtedly be open to the press and all radio-TV networks.

Complete details will be announced as soon as they are received.

* * *

SINA *"DECENCY TODAY MEANS MORALITY TOMORROW"*

I mailed literature to all those who requested it; many of them came from college kids wanting to form chapters. We sent out the SINA Summons, to be handed to people whose pets were naked. By this point we claimed thousands of members. I traveled to speak to whomever would listen and regularly referred to fleets of SINA Clothesmobiles and SINA Cycles, ready to rush to the scene wherever there were errant animals.

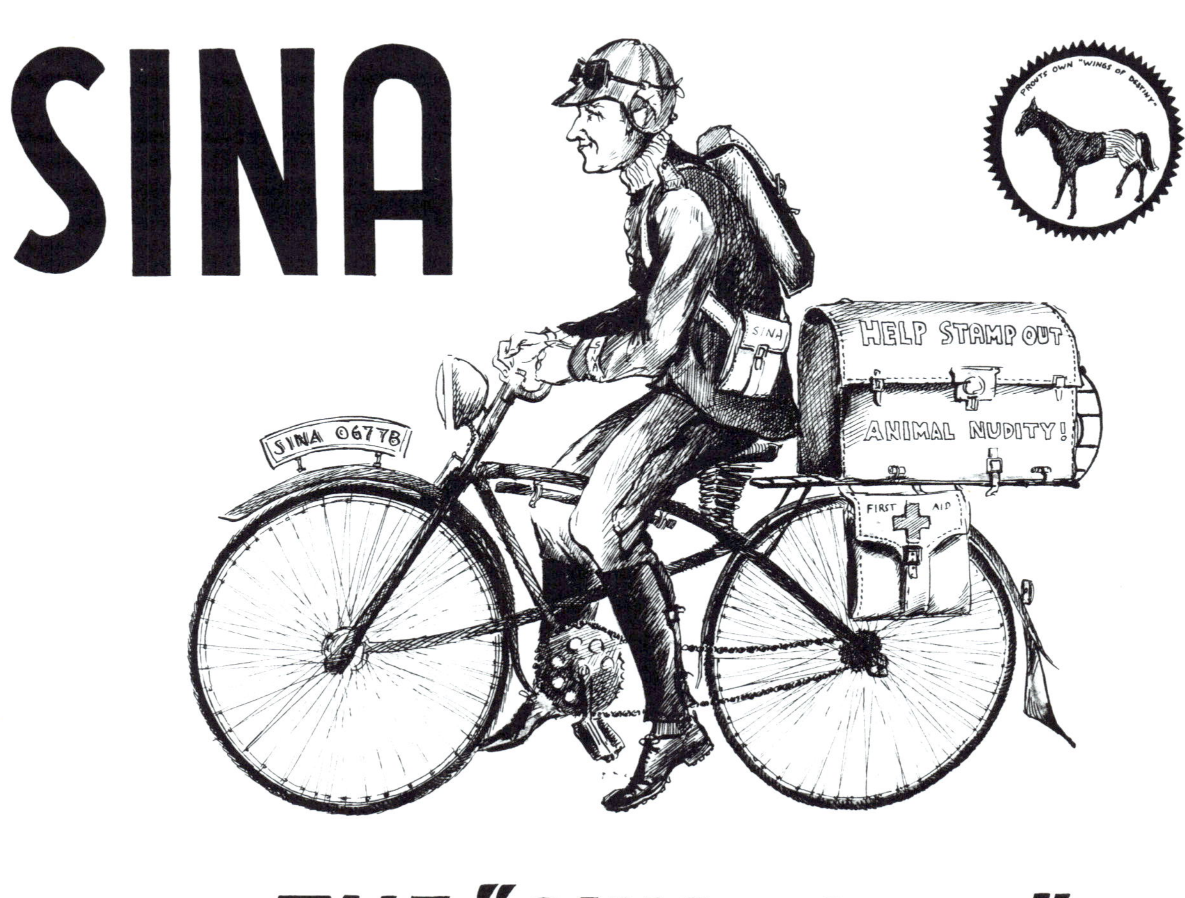

THE "SINA-CYCLE"

©1962

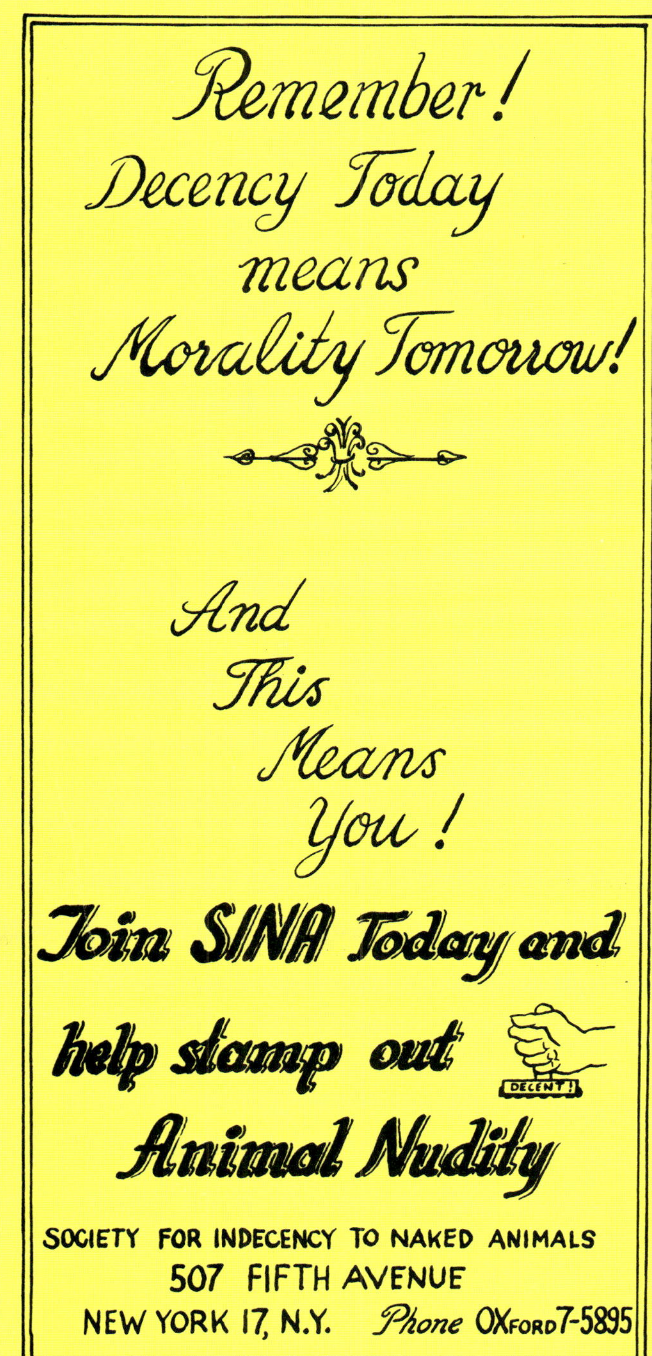

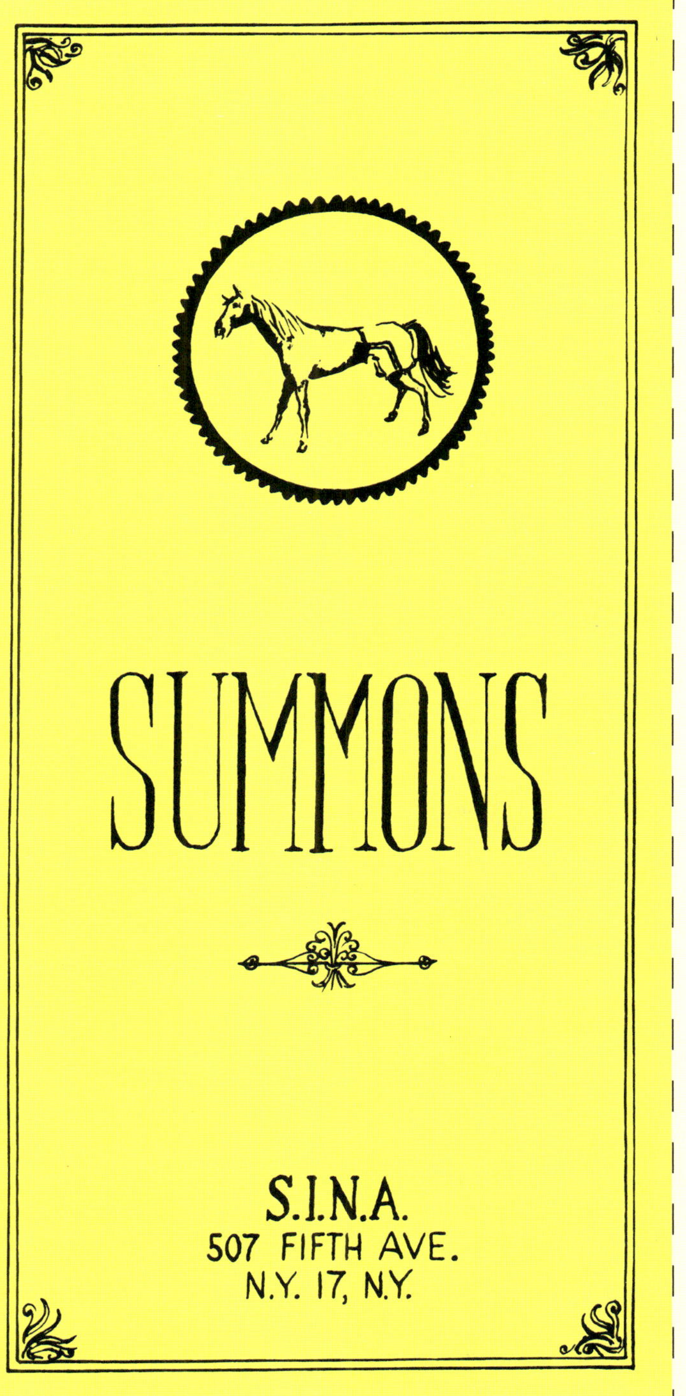

(CUT OUT SUMMONS, FOLD ON DOTTED LINE AND SERVE)

The SINA Summons is issued to all members for the purpose of making a "citizen's arrest" for perpetrating a public act of indecency. For the most part this concerns neighbors, strangers, friends, relatives, etc. who appear in public with a nude dog, cat, horse, cow or any animal that stands higher than 4 inches or is longer than 6 inches.

This summons has been issued by a qualified SINA officer and (or) member in good standing for your violation of ARTICLE II of the SINA CONSTITUTION for appearing in public with a naked dog, cat, horse, cow or any domestic animal that stands higher than 4 inches or is longer than 6 inches.

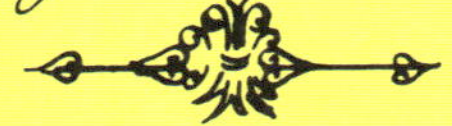

The SINA CONSTITUTION requires that you answer this summons in person or through a sworn statement before the Executive Board of SINA, the Society for Indecency to Naked Animals within ten days after issuance of this document, setting forth a complete explanation of your actions.

If this summons is ignored then in the name of decency you shall be deemed unworthy of ever appearing on the SINA membership rolls and, if you are presently enrolled, you shall be forthwith and also permanently expelled from our organization without delay or prejudice.

In accordance with rules and regulations prescribed by our SINA CONSTITUTION, I, G. Clifford Prout, hereby do affix my seal and my signature

G. Clifford Prout, Pres.
Society for Indecency to Naked Animals.

THE TERRIBLE TURMOIL OF INDECISION

When you begin to feel that you have doubts about what is right and what is wrong, what is good and what is bad, or what is decent and what is indecent, do not despair. All of us have, at one time or another, wrestled with this terrible turmoil of indecision. That's why SINA has been able to lead the way for so many people. Our banners are high and our aims well defined. We stand for decency and decency alone can establish the strongest roots of any civilization. You need to clothe your animals to conform with the moral standards of our civilization; then and only then will you be able to erase the terrible turmoil of indecision.

G. Clifford Prout, Sr.
(1882-1958)

CONFIDENTIAL CONFIDENTIAL

SINA MEMBERSHIP APPLICATION

NAME: NORMAN B.C. HANSEN ADDRESS: 22 COLE STREET - APT#4.

CITY: SAN FRANCISCO, CALIFORNIA ZONE: #17 STATE: CALIFORNIA

TELEPHONE: (HOME) SK 2-7725 OFFICE: SU 1-4114 OTHER: NONE

AGE: 33 FULL DATE OF BIRTH: 9/14/29 SEX: M WEIGHT: 175

HEIGHT: 6'1" EYES: BLUE OCCUPATION (S): INSURANCE INVESTIGATOR

MARITAL STATUS: YES CHILDREN (IF ANY): FOUR

AGES OF CHILDREN: 11,6, 4,3., 1 SUGGESTED BY: NONE

ARE YOU PREPARING THIS APPLICATION ALONE? YES

IF NOT ALONE, WITH WHOM? ________ WHY? ________

WHAT ORGANIZATIONS DO YOU NOW BELONG TO? S.P.C.A.,MICHIGAN ST. U. ALUMNI ASSOCIATION, N.A.A.C.P.

HAVE YOU EVER BEEN ASKED TO RESIGN FROM ANY OF THESE? NO

EXPLAIN: ________ HOBBIES: COIN COLLECTING

WHEN WERE YOU FIRST AWARE OF NAKED ANIMALS? 18 WHAT WAS YOUR REACTION?

(CHECK ONE OR MORE:) Surprised____ Frightened____ Pleased____

Shocked X Curious____ Indifferent____ Embarrassed X

Amused____ Angry X Excited____

WHAT TYPE ANIMAL (S) DID YOU SEE? SHEEP

DID YOU TELL ANYONE? YES IF SO, WHOM? FRIENDS WHAT DID THEY SAY?

THEY LAUGHED

DO YOU HAVE ANY NERVOUS HABITS SUCH AS NAILBITING, TWITCHES, ETC? NO

IS YOUR PERSONALITY: (CHECK ONE) PASSIVE:____ NORMAL X ERRATIC____

WHY DO YOU WANT TO BECOME A MEMBER OF SINA? (Use other side, and answer in your own words.)

DO YOU LIKE ANIMALS? YES DO ANIMALS LIKE YOU? YES FAVORITE ONES: HORSES

ARE YOU A GOOD PUBLIC SPEAKER? YES

ARE YOU AFRAID OF PEOPLE? NO WHY? ________

SELECT THE SINA CLASSIFICATION MEMBERSHIP YOU WOULD LIKE TO APPLY FOR AS OUTLINED IN THE SINA CONSTITUTION. LIFE MEMBERSHIP. IF ACCEPTED IN SINA DO YOU STAND READY AND WILLING TO UPHOLD THIS CONSTITUTION? YES

SIGNED: Norman B.C. Hansen (L.S.)

(This space for office use only):
ACCEPTED ________ REFUSED ________ PROBATION ________

CONFIDENTIAL (Please return within 48 hours to SINA, 507 Fifth Ave. N. Y. 17, N.Y.)

SINA MEMBERSHIP APPLICATION

NAME: Sylvia Chapman ADDRESS: 105 West 31

CITY: Eugene ZONE: ______ STATE: Oregon COUNTRY: U.S.A.

TELEPHONE: (HOME) DI 56026 OFFICE: DI 42187 OTHER: ______

AGE: 24 FULL DATE OF BIRTH: Oct. 22, 1937 BIRTH MARKS: ______

SEX: F WEIGHT: 190 HEIGHT: 5'2" EYES: Green HAT SIZE: 5¼

OCCUPATION (S): Secretary MARITAL STATUS: Single

CHILDREN: None AGES OF CHILDREN: ______ SUGGESTED BY: ______

ARE YOU PREPARING THIS APPLICATION ALONE? Yes

IF NOT ALONE, WITH WHOM? ______ WHY? ______

WHAT ORGANIZATIONS DO YOU NOW BELONG TO? Local dog club

HAVE YOU EVER BEEN ASKED TO RESIGN FROM ANY OF THESE ORGANIZATIONS? NO

EXPLAIN: ______ HOBBIES: Hunting

WHEN WERE YOU FIRST AWARE OF NAKED ANIMALS? when I got my dog WHAT WAS YOUR REACTION?

(CHECK ONE OR MORE) SURPRISED ___ FRIGHTENED ___ PLEASED ___ SHOCKED ___

CURIOUS ___ INDIFFERENT ___ EMBARRASSED X AMUSED ___ ANGRY ___ EXCITED ___

WHAT TYPE ANIMAL (S) DID YOU SEE? Dog

DID YOU TELL ANYONE? NO IF SO, WHOM? ______ WHAT DID THEY SAY? ______

DO YOU HAVE ANY NERVOUS HABITS SUCH AS NAILBITING, TWITCHES, ETC? NO

IS YOUR PERSONALITY: (CHECK ONE) PASSIVE: ___ NORMAL: X ERRATIC: ___

WHY DO YOU WANT TO BECOME A MEMBER OF SINA? (USE OTHER SIDE AND ANSWER IN OWN WORDS)

DO YOU LIKE ANIMALS? Yes DO ANIMALS LIKE YOU? Yes WHAT ARE YOUR FAVORITES: All

ARE YOU A GOOD PUBLIC SPEAKER? mediocre CAN YOU SING THE STAR SPANGLED BANNER A CAPPELLA? ______

DO YOU LIKE TO MARCH? Yes ARE YOU AFRAID OF PEOPLE? Sometimes ARE PEOPLE AFRAID OF YOU? Sometimes

WHY? I'm outspoken CAN YOU CONTROL YOUR TEMPER? Yes

IF ACCEPTED IN SINA DO YOU STAND READY AND WILLING TO UPHOLD THE CONSTITUTION? Yes

DO YOU PLAY ANY MUSICAL INSTRUMENT? piano CAN YOU READ MUSIC? Yes

SIGNED: Sylvia Chapman

WITNESSED BY: P. Chapman (RELATION, IF ANY) Cousin

(THIS SPACE FOR SINA OFFICE USE ONLY)

- -

ACCEPTED: ______ REFUSED: ______ HOLD FOR FURTHER INVESTIGATION: ______

SUBMIT TO NEXT EXECUTIVE SINA BOARD SESSION FOR CONSIDERATION: ______

CONFIDENTIAL HANDLING: ______ RETURN TO SENDER: ______ DESTROY: ______

DATE RECEIVED: ______ DATE ACTED UPON: ______ DATE DESTROYED: ______

C O N F I D E N T I A L   I N F O R M A T I O N

SOCIETY FOR INDECENCY TO NAKED ANIMALS

SINA
507 Fifth Avenue
New York, N. Y.

is hereby extended
life membership in
S.I.N.A.

Clifford Prout, President

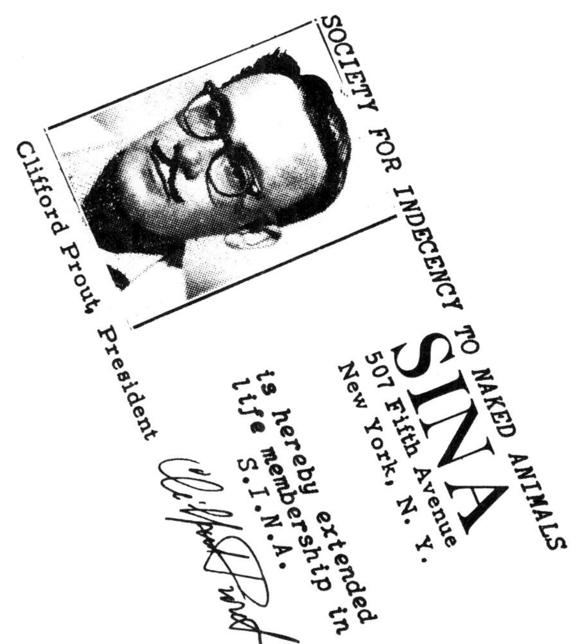
SOCIETY FOR INDECENCY TO NAKED ANIMALS

SINA
507 Fifth Avenue
New York, N. Y.

is hereby extended
life membership in
S.I.N.A.

Clifford Prout, President

SOCIETY FOR INDECENCY TO NAKED ANIMALS

SINA
507 Fifth Avenue
New York, N. Y.

is hereby extended
life membership in
S.I.N.A.

Clifford Prout, President

SOCIETY FOR INDECENCY TO NAKED ANIMALS

SINA
507 Fifth Avenue
New York, N. Y.

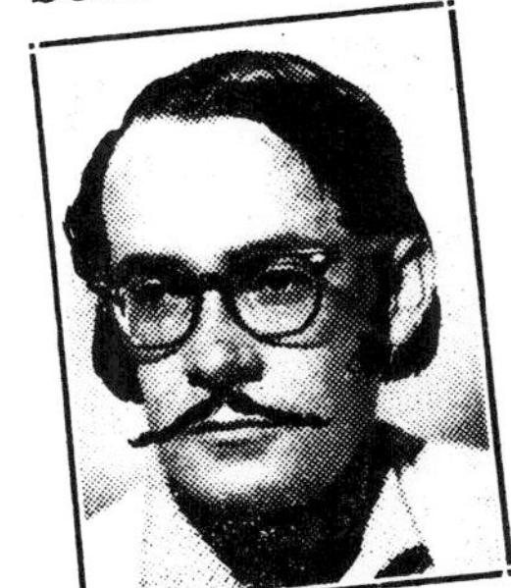

is hereby extended
life membership in
S.I.N.A.

Clifford Prout, President

SOCIETY FOR INDECENCY TO NAKED ANIMALS

SINA
507 Fifth Avenue
New York, N. Y.

is hereby extended
life membership in
S.I.N.A.

Clifford Prout, President

C O N F I D E N T I A L

Constitution, Will and By-Laws of the

Society for Indecency to Naked Animals

(SINA)

Be it known to all people that I, G. Clifford Prout, Sr., by virtue of my resources and hard earned wealth, hereby proclaim the following articles and rules for the foundation and perpetuation of SINA in order to preserve the total decency of our great nation and the world. Therefore, I speak as follows:

ARTICLE I

Section A In accordance with the instructions and details of my last will and testament, dated February 5, 1957, all stocks, bonds, real estate holdings and business interests shall be placed in escrow immediately on the day I, G. Clifford Prout, Sr., take my last breath.

Section B Forthwith, G. Clifford Prout, Jr., devoted son, companion and kind animal lover, as trustee and administrator of his father's estate, shall thereinafter dedicate his life and good deeds towards the formation of a worldwide movement to be known as S.I.N.A. or SINA. (Although the definition of SINA, the Society for Indecency to Naked Animals, seems to be a misnomer, through use of the word "for", let it be known that we are all against animal indecency and the use of said word "for" is merely to retain the image of SINA per se, whereas, the word "against", if incorporated, would introduce the letter "a" (SAINA) and destroy the effect of instant alarm and morality that SINA projects; therefore, in the very broad sense and quite obviously, we are for the removal of the indecency to naked animals.)

Section C All moneys, interest, properties and profits from my estate shall be diligently managed by G. Clifford Prout, Jr. with sufficient funds allocated to SINA at his discretion for the sole purpose of telling the world about SINA.

ARTICLE II

Section A SINA shall be a non-profit and self-sufficient organization with its national headquarters in New York City and field offices around the world located in key moral disaster areas.

Paragraph 1. SINA's basic concept shall be to urge all good people to clothe their animals with proper covering so that vital areas will not be observed by the human naked eye.

Paragraph 2. Insofar as animals are American citizens and people are members of the animal kingdom, then animals shall have the right to be decent and modest such as human beings are, in the light of our present civilization.

Paragraph 3. Be it said here now that all animals shall wear clothing that appear in public; namely, horses, cows, dogs, cats and any animal that stands higher than four (4) inches or is longer than six (6) inches.

Section B All animals that reside in their natural habitat, such as wild game or those animals presently in uncivilized countries, shall not be subjected to SINA indoctrination.

Section C SINA shall not be concerned with any reptile or animals that swim or fly for their chief means of survival.

ARTICLE III

Section A Very large animals, such as those found in a zoo or circus, shall not be the concern of SINA, however, the organizations and promoters behind such barbarian and public displays of indecency shall earn the full wrath of SINA; likewise with the perpetrators of the wild animal shows.

Section B All amphibious animals shall be examined by a duly appointed SINA officer and his findings reported to the SINA Executive Board for classification and consideration under the SINA Code for Decency.

ARTICLE IV

Section A SINA members shall fall into the following classifications:

1. Executive Branch. This will include those paid full time SINA employees in the New York office who are under the direct command of G. Clifford Prout, Jr., hired by the SINA Foundation to organize, lecture and lead the membership.

2. Honorary Membership. This will include anyone interested in obtaining life membership in SINA for the sole purpose of carrying SINA's philosophy into their respective communities. From this group will be selected the leaders and chapter heads who have the time and energy to devote to the formation of local level SINA chapters.

3. Associate Membership. This will include only those people who have no time to actively participate in SINA meetings but wish to stay aware of the movement, carry a SINA membership card, and remain on the mailing list to receive SINA information. (This group will be permitted to sing in the SINA Chorus or play in the SINA Marching Band)

4. Trial Membership. This will include all those who wish to join SINA for a short period of time in order to determine their fitness and moral fibre necessary to remain a Class 2 or Class 3 member.

ARTICLE V

Section A Membership in SINA shall be open to all people for life without regard to their race, color, creed, gender or age.

Section B Each and every applicant for SINA membership must be ready and willing day or night and upon short notice to take the written and oral SINA EMOTIONAL STABILITY TEST. The results of this test, designed by me, will assist in weeding out "oddballs", "crackpots", "undesirables" and other curiosity thrill seekers who might attempt to infiltrate SINA.

ARTICLE VI

Section A SINA will not accept contributions in any shape, manner, or form. There will be no membership dues and any member will be free to join or resign at his or her discretion.

Section B The SINA motto shall always be: "Decency Today Means Morality Tomorrow."

THIS WILL NOTORIZED INTO FORCE JANUARY 15, 1958 AT THE STROKE OF MIDNIGHT AT THE PROUT ESTATE, Webster Groves, Missouri, U.S.A. AND IS OFFICIALLY SIGNED AND SEALED.

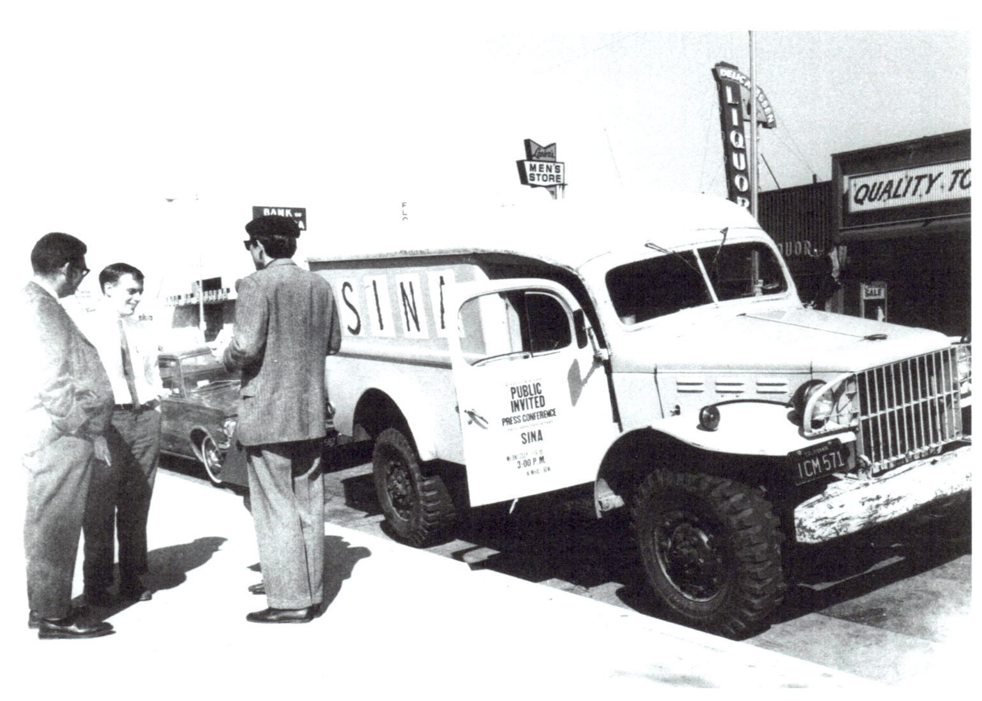

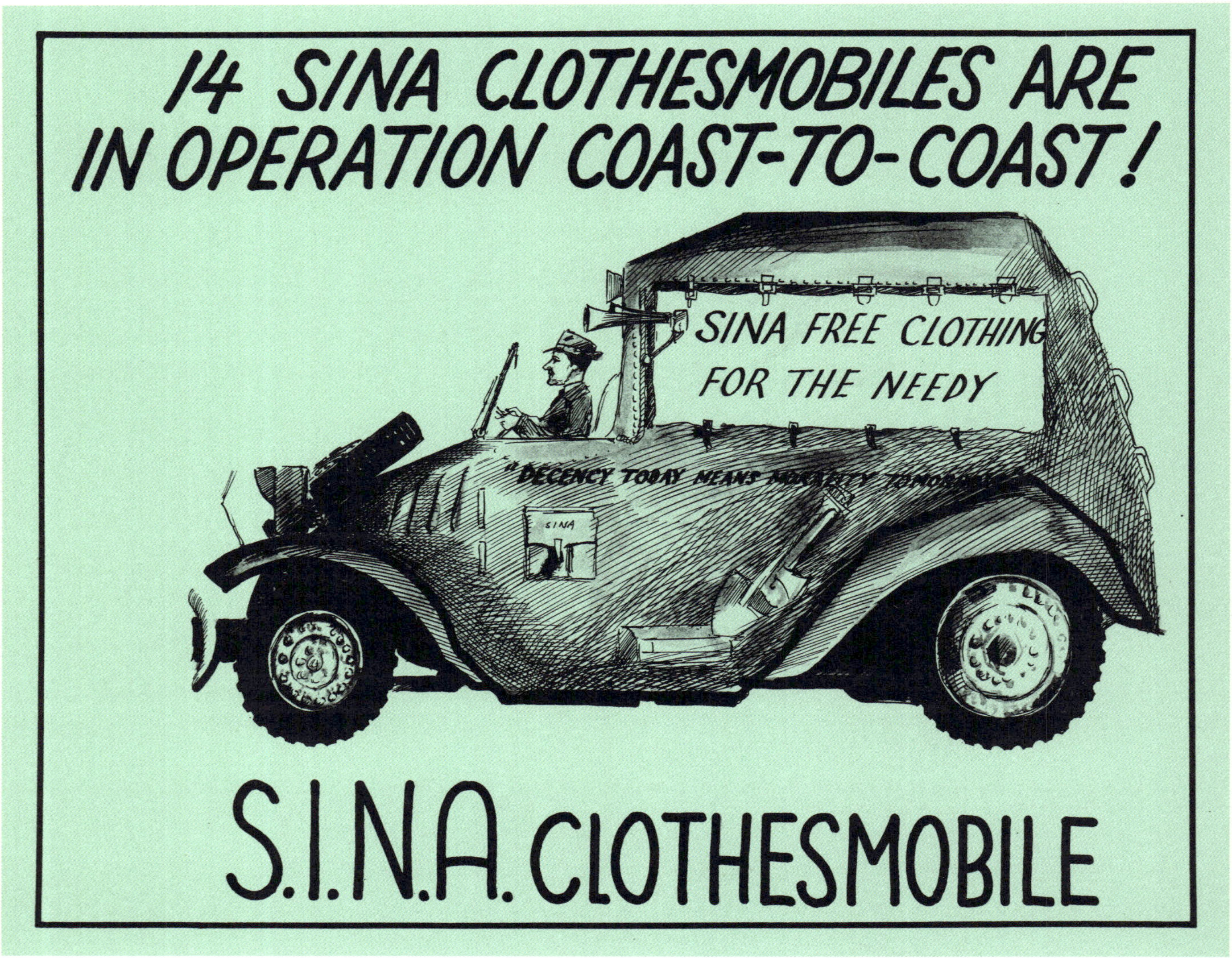

14 SINA CLOTHESMOBILES ARE IN OPERATION COAST-TO-COAST!

SINA FREE CLOTHING FOR THE NEEDY

"DECENCY TODAY MEANS

SINA

S.I.N.A. CLOTHESMOBILE

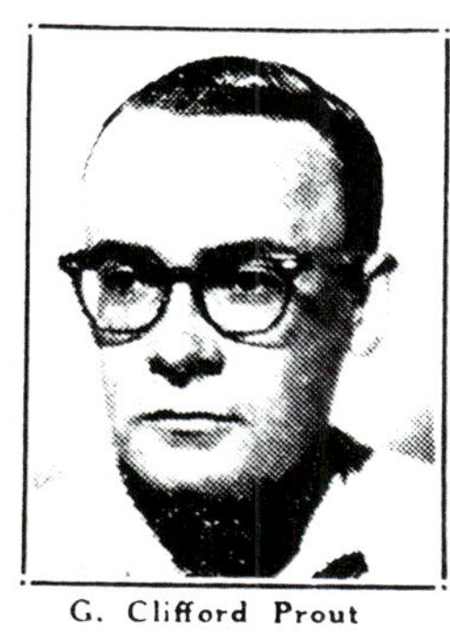
G. Clifford Prout

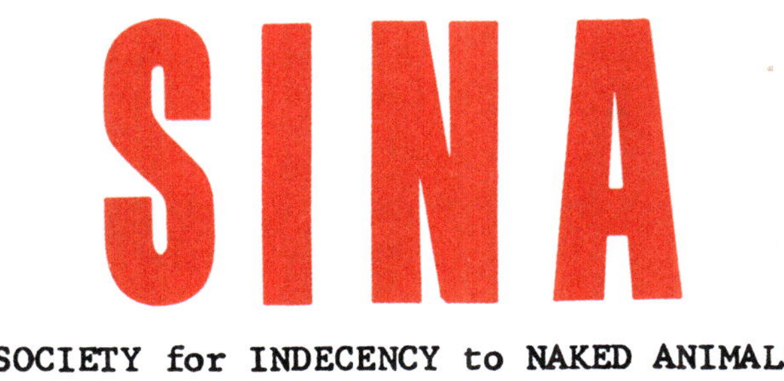

SOCIETY for INDECENCY to NAKED ANIMALS

507 Fifth Avenue
New York, N. Y.

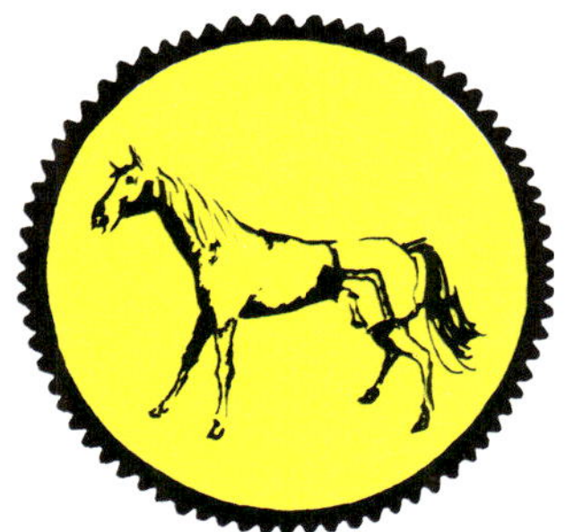

SPECIAL RELEASE TO THE WRETCHED MESS NEWS

SINA, the Society for Indecency to Naked Animals, has declared Routes 20 and 89 between West Yellowstone, Montana and Old Faithful, Wyoming a moral disaster area.

An unusually large number of nude bears and coyotes have been noticed at various crossroads causing unnecessary automobile accidents and shocked expressions on the faces of young skiers and children.

Until the area can be reached by a SINA clothesmobile and these loose animals clothed, motorists are urged to detour by way of route 191 North to Bozeman, Idaho, East on route 10 to Livingston and then South on route 89.

While they last, free car window shades are available from SINA National Headquarters (507 Fifth Ave. N.Y.C.) for added safety and precaution.

* * * * *

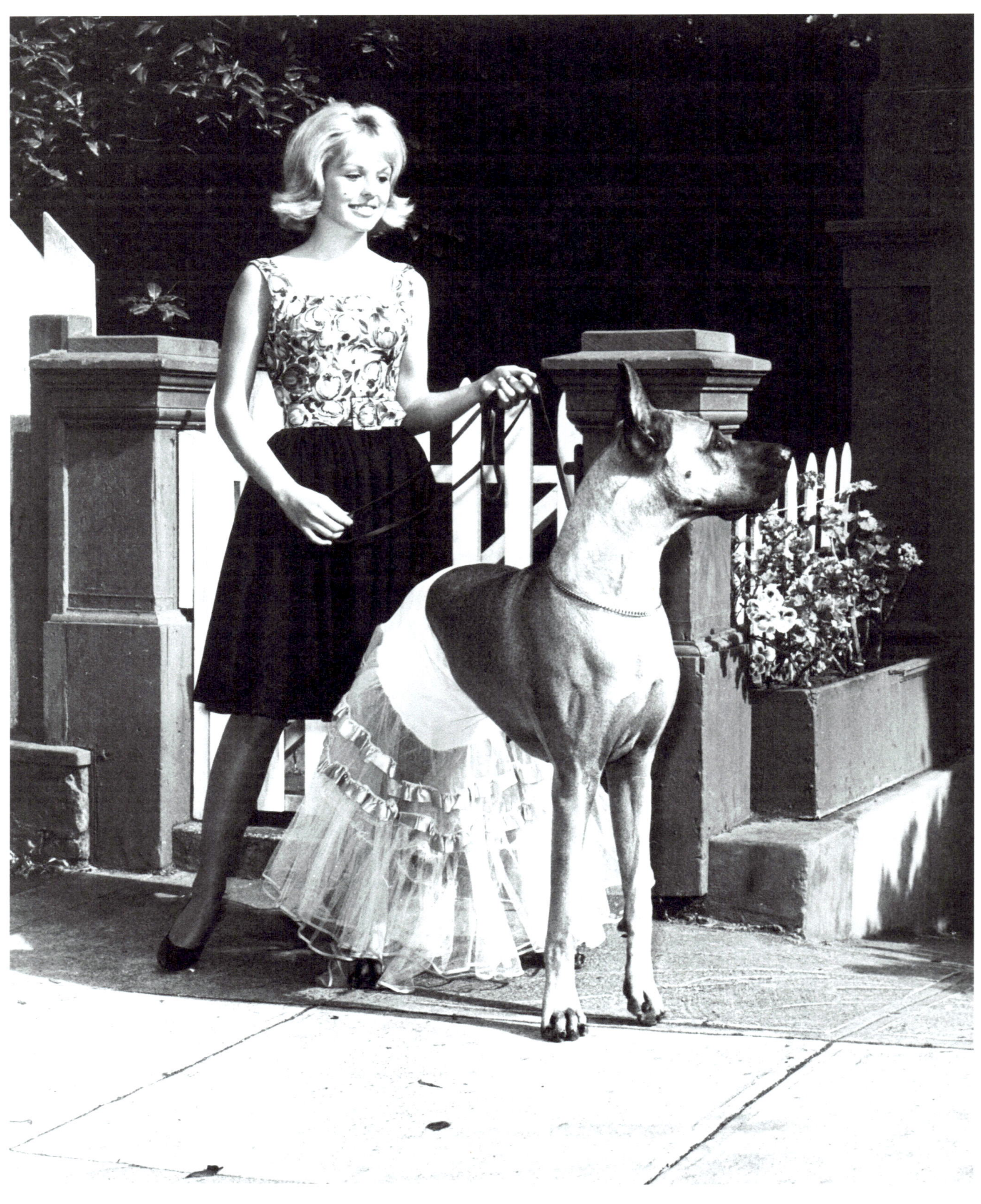

"SINA PEOPLE"

There's a man named G. Clifford Prout
He roams the land and sniffs his nose
Then he looks and listens about
For an animal without clothes

CHORUS

Sina people, where you gonna go
Where you gonna hide and whatcha gonna do
Sina people, you've got woes
Animals don't wanna wear no clothes

Prout says he's against indecency
S.I.N.A. stands for that
Any animal the eye can see
A horse, cow, dog or cat

CHORUS

Sina people, where you gonna go
Where you gonna hide and whatcha gonna do
Sina people, you've got woes
Animals don't wanna wear no clothes

Sina is the name of the movement
Fifty thousand people strong
Meetin and a singin in a great big tent
Prout's own Sina Marching Song

CHORUS

Sina people, where you gonna go
Where you gonna hide and whatcha gonna do
Sina people, you've got woes
Animals don't wanna wear no clothes

They're against four-legged indecency
Animals look so rude in the nude
They cover a pet for morality
And turn him into a decent prude

CHORUS

Sina people, where you gonna go
Where you gonna hide and whatcha gonna do
Sina people, you've got woes
Animals don't wanna wear no clothes

Prout continues to shout his craze
In parks, on streets and over air waves
Animals think he's in a daze
But Sina loves the way he raves

CHORUS

Sina people, where you gonna go
Where you gonna hide and whatcha gonna do
Sina people, you've got woes
Animals don't wanna wear no clothes

FADE OUT

Animals don't wanna wear no clothes
Animals don't wanna wear no clothes
Animals don't wanna wear no clothes
Animals don't wanna wear no clothes

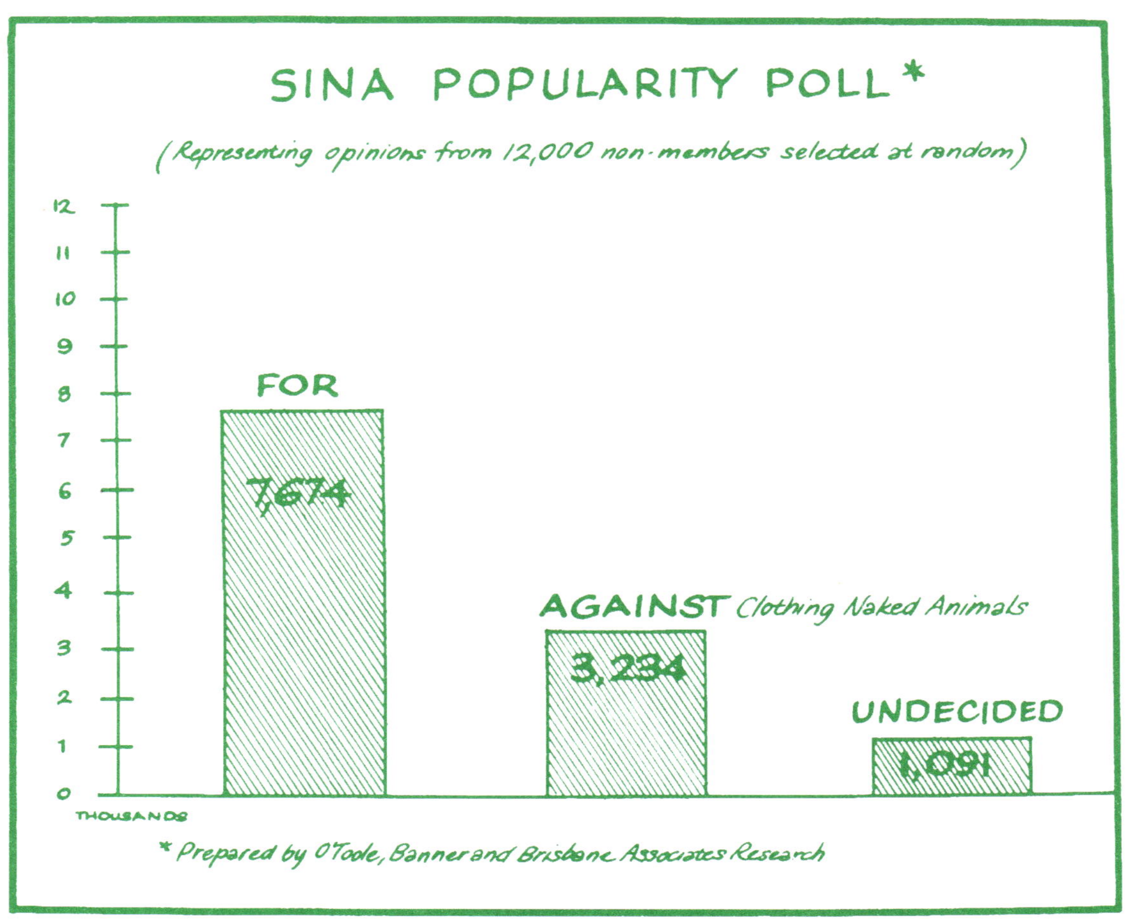
SINA POPULARITY POLL*
(Representing opinions from 12,000 non-members selected at random)
12
11
10
9
8
7
6
5
4
3
2
1
0
THOUSANDS
FOR
7,674
AGAINST Clothing Naked Animals
3,234
UNDECIDED
1,091
* Prepared by O'Toole, Banner and Brisbane Associates Research

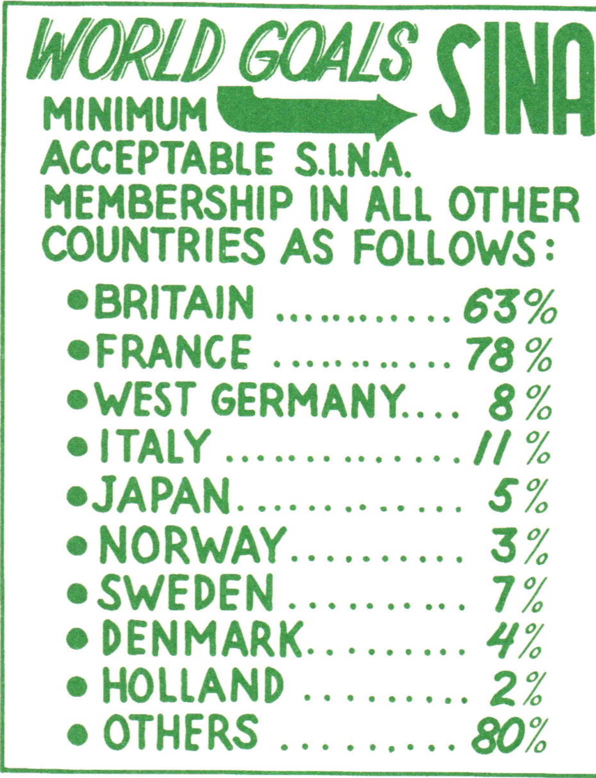
WORLD GOALS SINA
MINIMUM ACCEPTABLE S.I.N.A. MEMBERSHIP IN ALL OTHER COUNTRIES AS FOLLOWS:
• BRITAIN 63%
• FRANCE 78%
• WEST GERMANY.... 8%
• ITALY 11%
• JAPAN.............. 5%
• NORWAY.......... 3%
• SWEDEN 7%
• DENMARK......... 4%
• HOLLAND 2%
• OTHERS 80%

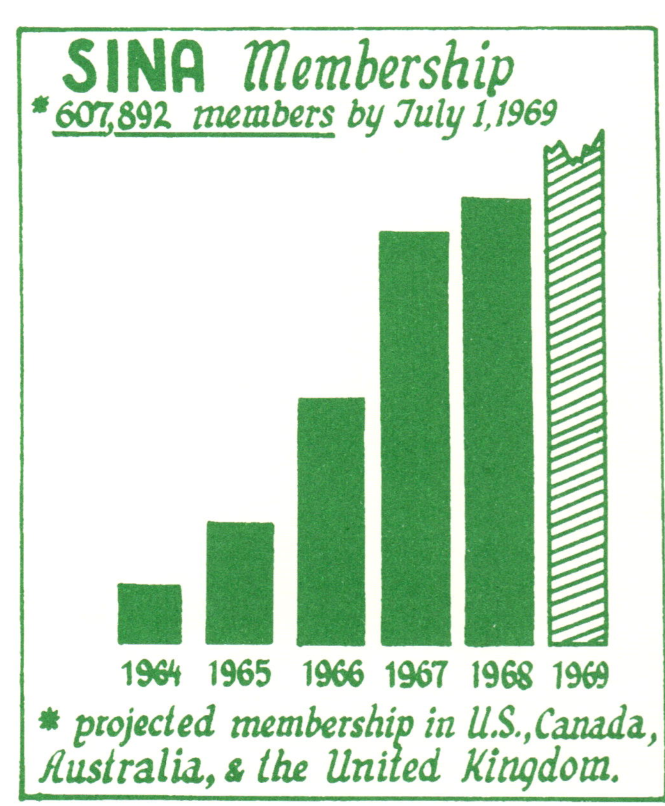
SINA Membership
* 607,892 members by July 1,1969
1964
1965
1966
1967
1968
1969
* projected membership in U.S., Canada, Australia, & the United Kingdom.

THE GREATER EAST ST. LOUIS HUMANE SOCIETY

BR. 4-1354 EAST ST. LOUIS, ILL. "KINDNESS IS OUR BUSINESS" UP. 5-1679

637 North 24th Street
East St. Louis, Illinois

March 6, 1963

Mr. G. Clifford Prout, Jr.
The Society for Indeceny to Naked Animals
New York City, N.Y.

Dear Mr. Prout:

The Society for Indeceny to Naked Animals has attracted national attention through television and press and we know you are pleased that your fathers wishes are being carried out.

The members of our society (all volunteers) constantly receive calls, to do something about the dogs in school yards, especially when females are in season. It is most embrassing to the teachers and children to witness the dogs actions. We want to pick up these little females and keep them away from the public but we do not have a place wherein to keep them. We are stopped in helping in this type situation untill we have a shelter and we are wondering if your organization has any plans for assistance in such projects.

The Greater East St. Louis Humane Society was organized April 20,1960. We do not receive monies from state, city or county, depending entirely upon gifts, annual dues and projects.

We look forward to hearing from you.

Yours very truly,

GREATER EAST ST. LOUIS HUMANE SOCIETY

I. Riedel

Corresponding Secretary
(Mrs. T.W. Riedel)

T. B. QUIGLEY, M. D.
319 LONGWOOD AVENUE
BOSTON 15, MASSACHUSETTS

BEACON 2-3911

26 March 1963

Mr. G. Clifford Prout
Society for Indecency to
Naked Animals
507 Fifth Avenue
New York, New York

Dear Mr. Prout:

I am indeed honored to receive my life membership card in SINA through the good offices of my daughter, Mrs. Jane Alexander of 213 West 14th Street, New York City. I would like to recommend for membership three other doctors who would be equally honored, if accepted:

Dr. Curtis Prout
75 Mt. Auburn Street
Cambridge 38, Mass.

Dr. Hathorn Brown
319 Longwood Avenue
Boston 15, Mass.

Dr. Richard Warren
721 Huntington Avenue
Boston 15, Mass.

Very truly yours,

T. B. Quigley

T. B. Quigley, M.D.

TBQ:sjb

JOHN HATGIS
ATTORNEY AT LAW
115 SUITE 2800
~~20~~ BROAD STREET
NEW YORK, N. Y.

DIGBY 4-5900

August 5, 1963

Mr. G. Clifford Prout, President
SINA
507 Fifth Avenue
New York, N.Y.

Dear Sir:

In reply to your letter of August 2, 1963, I wish to inform you that my name obviously was sent to you without my knowledge or consent.

I wish to inform you at this time that any further use of my name for any purpose, including the mailing of your circulars to me, will leave me no alternative but to seek legal remedy, especially now that you have been put on notice to remove my name from your files.

Please give this matter your prompt attention.

Yours very truly,

John Hatgis

Summary
5/20

age 11 years

320 Riverside Dr
New York 25, NY

against

Mr Prout

please read this whole letter before you angrily dismiss it, for I know what I am about to say will shock you. I have a large brown dog he is completely nude. One fine Sunday in april I took him down to the Riverside park dog pen in new york city. It was a very crowded afternoon in the park. And when I was playing with him I turned him over on his back and his nude rectom was displayed in front of over a hundred persons. Not one of these persons seemed in the least shocked at all. I sadly announce that your cause which is useless too me and many other people is foredoomed to failure.

Never yours
Dan Levitt
R.S.V.P.

P.S. my adress is on the top of this page. I am a violator so send the police here to put me on jail for life

Feb. 18, 1963

Dear Mr. King

I Think that this putting clothes on animls is reticulous. I am only nine years old. But I think that putting clothes on animls is indecent. The man that came to your show Monday is nuts. Now I don't want you to get the wrong idea I was sick on Monday.

Yours truly Kenneth E. Myers

Good Boy

no good

Hillbilly - horse

SINA Membership List
Pasadena Chapter

Pasadena Chapter Headquarters
1395 Wicks Road
Pasadena, California

J. Clifford Prout
507 Fifth Avenue
New York 17, New York

Dear Sir,

I received one of your summonses in the mail the other day and am replying in the necessary ten days. I promise that I will go by the SINA Constitution. I have a dog and the day that I recieved your literature I promply bought him one of the best skirts around.

I was also imformed that if I could get the required number to join SINA you would make me a chapter President. I am enclosing with this letter, a list of people that would like to become members. Could you please send me some more of the literature, like more Summonses or anything else that you might have. I have tried to get things in the local newspaper here and they are coming through with several articles. We are also trying to get SINA on local TV and Radio. Just thought you would like to hear this.

Here is my membership list:

Mr. Harvey Woodard	39 East Howard Street, Pasadena, Calif.
Mr. John A. Bevetta	3125 Montrose Ave. La Canada, Calif.
Mr. Peter Haggerty	1395 Wicks Road, Pasadena, Calif.
Mr. Glenn Mazair	869 East Alemeda Street, Altadena, Calif.
Mr. Richard Kenna	1176 Menlo Drive, Altadena, Calif.
Mr. Harold Willis	2168 Glenrose Ave. , Altadena, Calif.
Mr. John Walsworth	2312 North El Molino Street, Altadena, Calif.
Mr. Wesley Whitmore	1929 Lyons Drive, La Canada, Calif.
Mr. Wendell Whitmore	" " " " " "
Mr. James M. Swedlow	2521 Santa Anita Ave., Altadena, Calif.
Mr. Tom Harris	1530 Washburn Road, Pasadena, Calif.
Mr. & Mrs. D. L. Pratt	1385 Wicks Road, Pasadena, Calif.
Mr. & Mrs. N. C. Sweet	2031 Layton Street, Pasadena, California
Mr. Jerome Tarpin	3295 North Marengo Ave., Pasadena, Calif.
Mr. Mark Morelli	1375 Chamberlin Street , Pasadena, Calif.
Mr. Nick Randall	1370 Chamberlin Street, Pasadena, Calif.
Mr. W. W. Nixon	4328 North Washington Ave., Pasadena, Calif.
Mr. & Mrs. C. F. Haggerty	1395 Wicks Road, Pasadena, Calif.
Mr. Terry Cunning	529 Pembt Street, Pasadena, Calif.
Mr. James Russell	12 East Manor Street, Pasadena, Calif.
Mr. Jeff Speigel	1375 Wicks Road, Pasadena, Calif.
The Night Editor	The Independant- Star News, 525 East Colorado, Pasa.
Mr. Bruce Barnes	980 North Orlando Drive, San Marino, Calif.
Mr. Robert Upshaw	290 West Ventura Ave., Altadena, Calif.
Mr. Fred Yowell	4325 Oak Drive, La Canada, Calif.

I am quite confident that after the newspapers have had a chance to play this up we will be a large chapter. I Hope that you can forward us that material that is needed. Thank you.

Michael Haggerty
Michael Haggerty

SOCIETY FOR INDECENCY TO NAKED ANIMALS

507 FIFTH AVENUE • NEW YORK 17, NEW YORK • OXFORD 7-5895

MESSAGE	REPLY

TO Mr. Mike Bartel
1228 Griffith Street
Wasco, California

DATE March 2, 1963

Dear Mr. Bartel:

One of my secretaries just called my attention to your earlier letter for an application form; this was buried under four or five thousand pieces of mail so you can understand how we get so far behind! Therefore, I am waiving the application form, naturally, since I notice you are already an honorary member of SINA and I am enclosing a charter made out for you and the people of Shafter.

Both you and Kris Carey should be able to do a fine job in getting more memberships and I trust you will be able to sign up a few hundred more people as time goes by.

Please keep me informed of your success.

Yours for decency,

G. Clifford Prout, President
SINA

GCP:ja
enclosures

DATE charter
4 Songs
4 Dogs
4 leaflets
36 membership cards
Contest
Washington
Nudists
Summons
Day
Poem – music
Newsletter
State union

SIGNED

DETACH AND FILE FOR FOLLOW-UP

20. J.W. Gilmer
21. Robert L. Kendall
22. Clifford Harrington
23. John Saindon
24. James Parker
25. George Terry
26. Mark Siemens
27. Annette Smith
28. Janice Hager
29. Pat Borjon
30. Miss Helen Lewis
31. G.A. Parrett

MIKE BARTEL

Society for Indecency to Naked Animals

hereby grants this charter

to

Andrew Lampert

in the city of

Brooklyn

and the state of

New York

for the purpose of forming and perpetuating the S.I.N.A. movement whenever possible and through all members available in this charter area.

Date Granted: 10/10/18

[signature] **Honorary President**

[signature] **Executive Vice-President**

"Decency Today Means Morality Tomorrow"

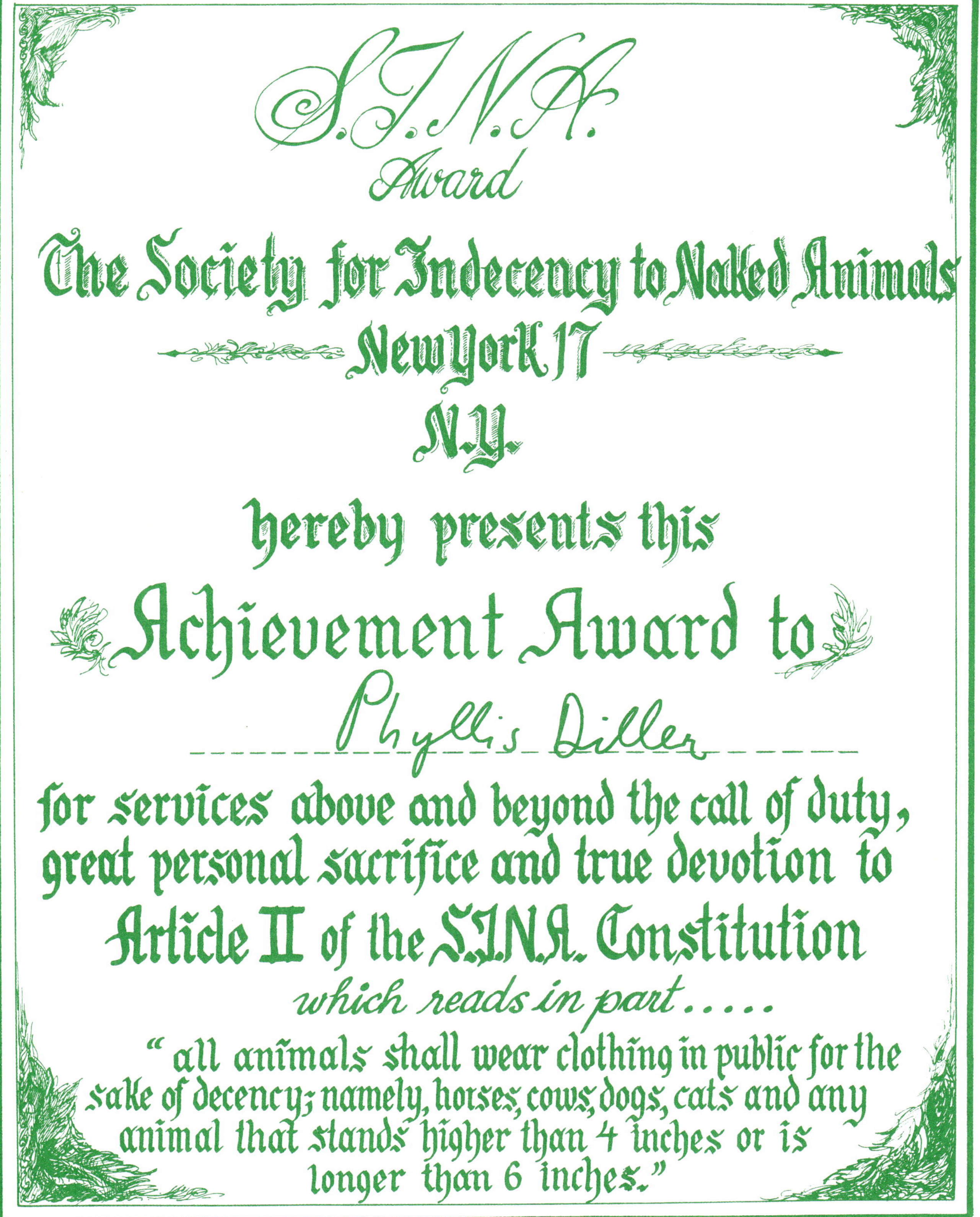
S.I.N.A.
Award
The Society for Indecency to Naked Animals
New York 17
N.Y.
hereby presents this
Achievement Award to
Phyllis Diller
for services above and beyond the call of duty,
great personal sacrifice and true devotion to
Article II of the S.I.N.A. Constitution
which reads in part.....
"all animals shall wear clothing in public for the
sake of decency; namely, horses, cows, dogs, cats and any
animal that stands higher than 4 inches or is
longer than 6 inches."

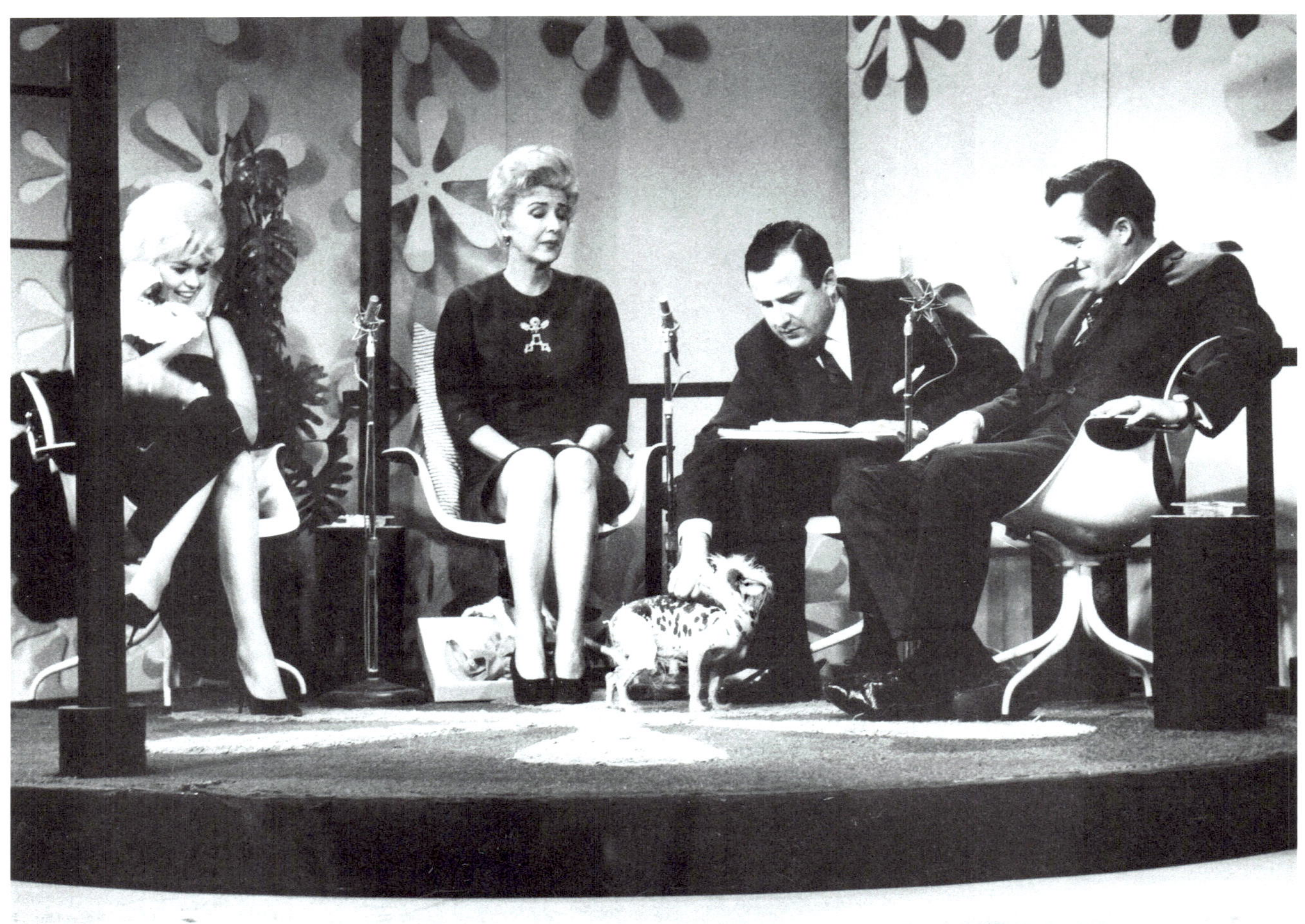

I appeared on many television shows, including *The Mike Douglas Show* where I argued about the importance of animal morality with former striptease artist Gypsy Rose Lee and sex goddess Jayne Mansfield. At the University of British Columbia in Vancouver, a fraternity tossed a chicken on the stage during my lecture and attempted to throw me into a swimming pool.

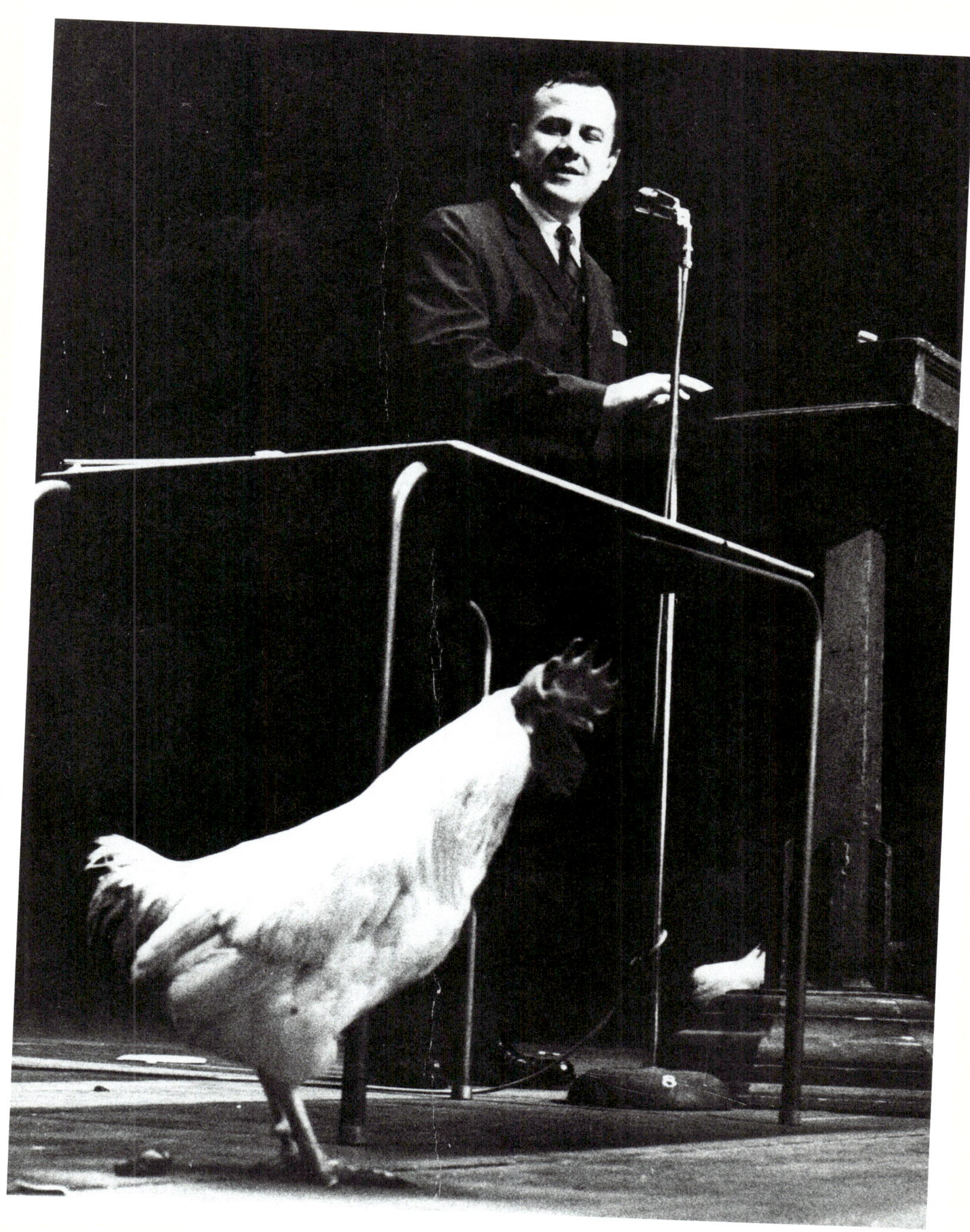

We created a magazine with a horse in Bermuda shorts on the cover. Inside were patterns for animal clothes, a crossword puzzle that couldn't be worked and cartoons that weren't funny along with plenty of philosophy and righteous wisdom:

"A nude horse is a rude horse."

INSIDE SINA

Official Organ of the Society for Indecency to Naked Animals

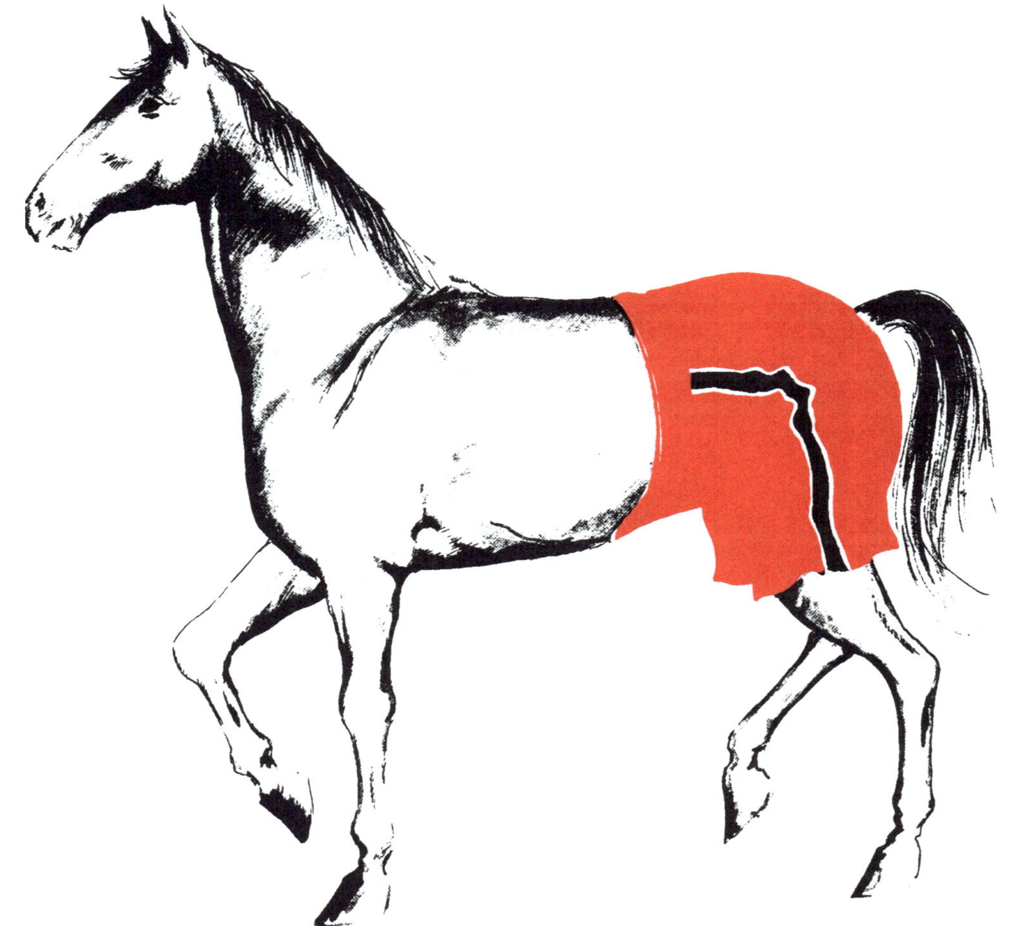

"Decency Today Means Morality Tomorrow"

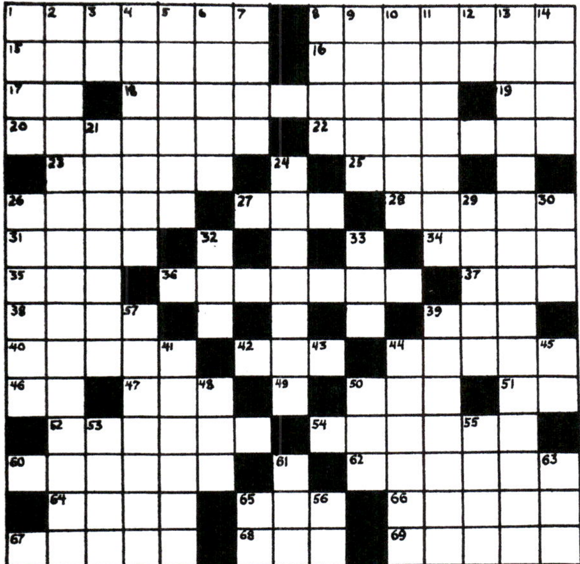

SINA CROSSWORD PUZZLE

ACROSS

1. ———— Today Means Morality Tomorrow
8. Platitudes
15. A sneeze
16. Type of dress worn in Middle East.
17. Preposition
18. Darwin's Theory of ————
19. Knockout
20. ———— France, a writer
22. Living in a glass house
23. Archaic spelling of only
24. Indefinite article
25. Scots for out
26. Rootless plants such as seaweed
27. Years one has lived
28. Period of ten years
31. Upland Dialect, girl
32. First letter of French alphabet
34. Drunkard
35. Ab. of a British branch of Intelligence
36. Anthropologic name for jawless fishes
37. Kind of Indian
38. What a senior citizen does
39. Ab. College of Trysting Experimentalists
40. Tool used to hand cut grain
42. Interjection
44. Sold his soul to devil in dramas by Goethe and Marlowe
46. College name for teaching assistant
47. ————, a mouse!
49. Alpha
50. Obese
51. Chinese unit of measure
52. Melodic
54. Contemporary artist living in France
62. African village
64. Salts
65. Winged mammal
66. Solitary
67. Foe
68. Beasts of burden
69. Term of distance

DOWN

1. Facts and Figures
2. Logical belief in economy
3. Ab. chancery
4. Forever
5. Long novella by female author.
6. Chinese workman
7. Christmas
8. Close fitting
9. Horn of which is used in love portions
10. One-legged creature
11. Prisoners
12. Ab. South
13. Motto meaning to proceed carefully (3 words)
14. Fitted with shoes
21. In a furious manner
24. Class of fish
26. Horrified
27. First word of English dictionaries
29. Opposite of uncouth
30. River in Scotland
32. Cry of anguish
33. Tea, French
36. Article
39. Cross between a buffalo and a cow
41. Belief opposing religious doctrine
43. _ B-C
44. Spot on sun brighter than rest of photosphere
45. 7th note of musical scale
48. Folks
50. Healthy
53. Native of Yha
55. Popular organization for decency
56. Tight situation
57. Barren and unfruitful
60. Primary consonant in zygapophyseal
61. Famous women's store
63. Votes of affirmation
65. Perspiration problem

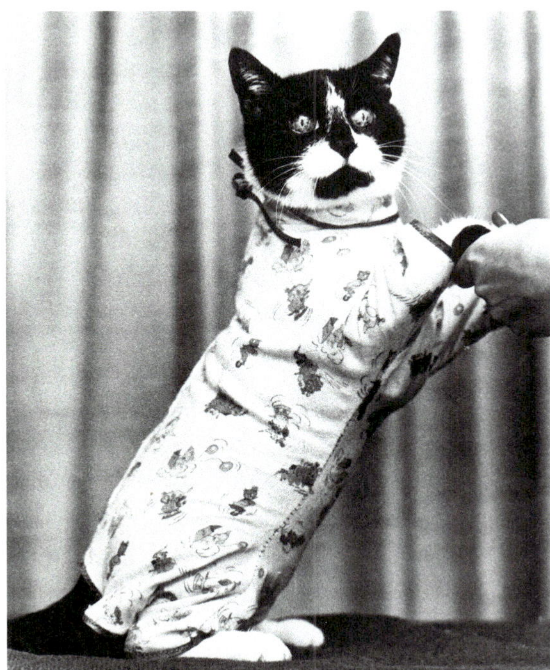

This cat was given the "Award of Decency" by SINA when it appeared in the St. Petersburg Times

Photo by George Trabant

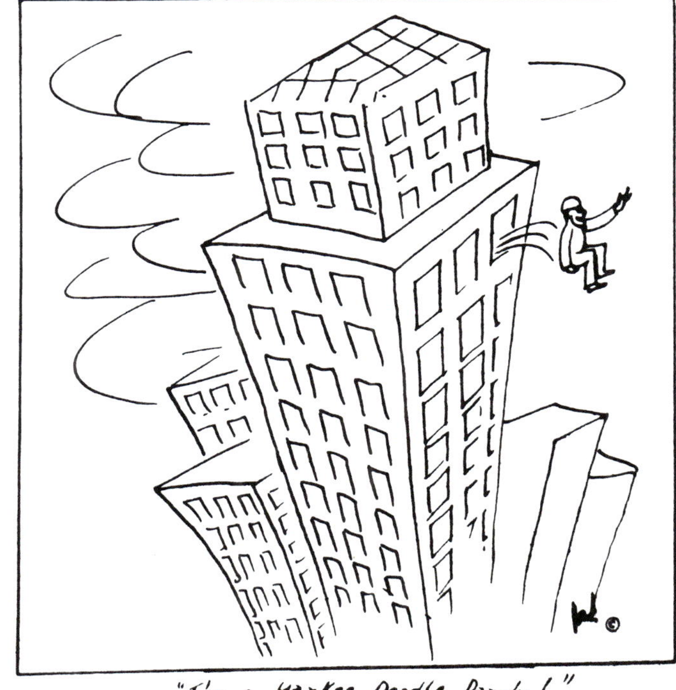

"I'm a Yankee Doodle Dandy!"

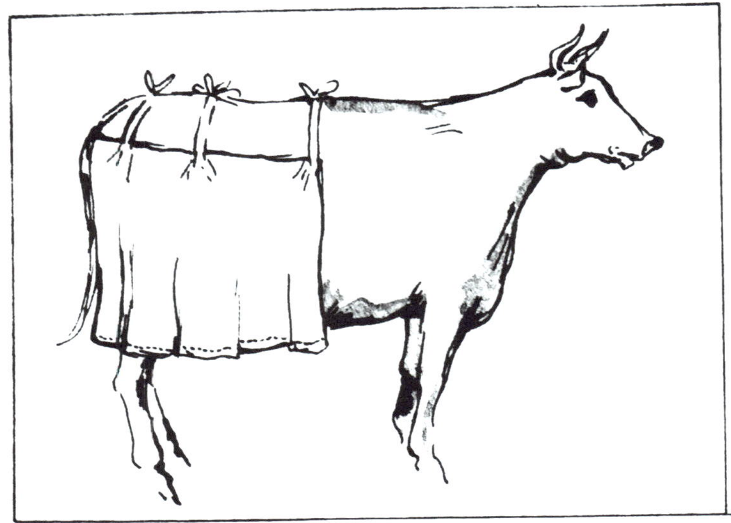

A Cow wearing an apron

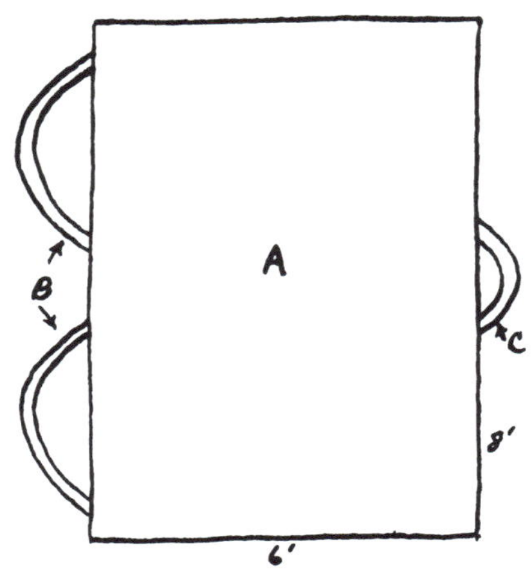

APRON for Cow

A. 6' x 8' coverlet

B. Shoulder straps - Adjust to fit animal

C. Tail loop

SINA SUGGESTED GARMENTS
And Their Patterns

These patterns for basic animal clothing are simple and easy to make. Most people will be able to make garments directly from these sketches. For those less handy, trace the patterns on graph paper. Then sketch same on larger graph paper that corresponds with the size of your animal. If in doubt, use a pantograph.

BLOOMERS for Cat

1. Left leg
2. Right leg

A. Sew "A" sides together
B. Sew "B" sides together
C. Opening for tail
D. Draw-string through waist band to gather and tie
E. Elastic through leg band to gather

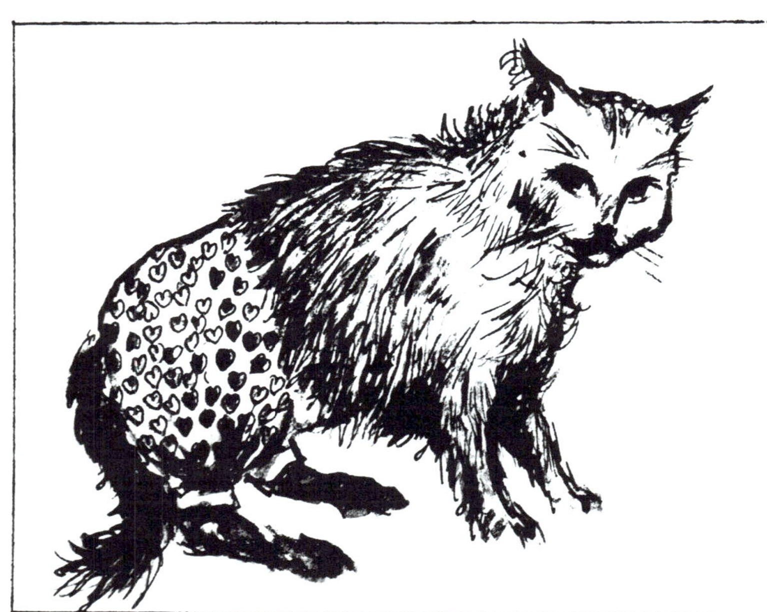

A Cat in bloomers

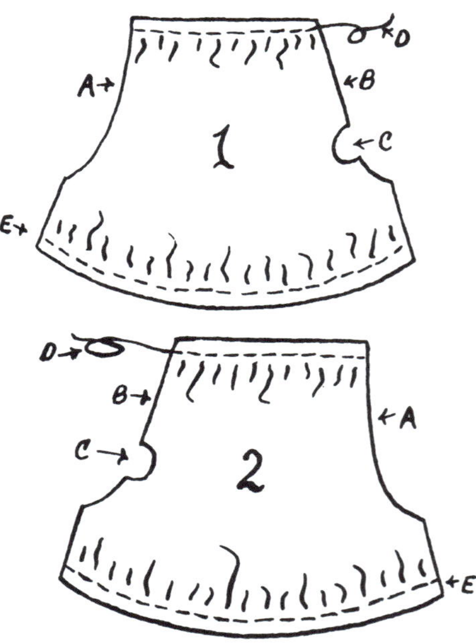

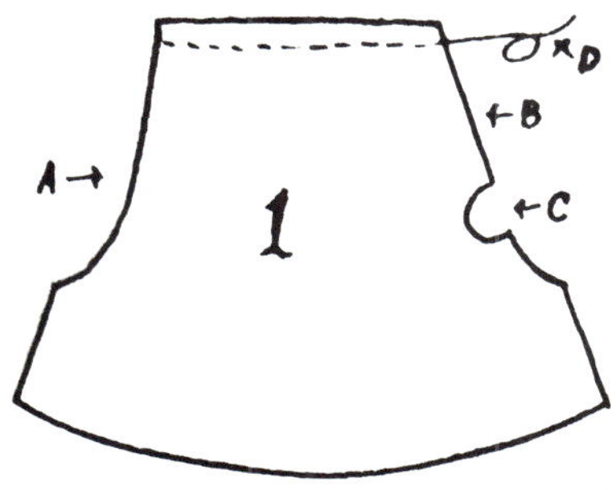

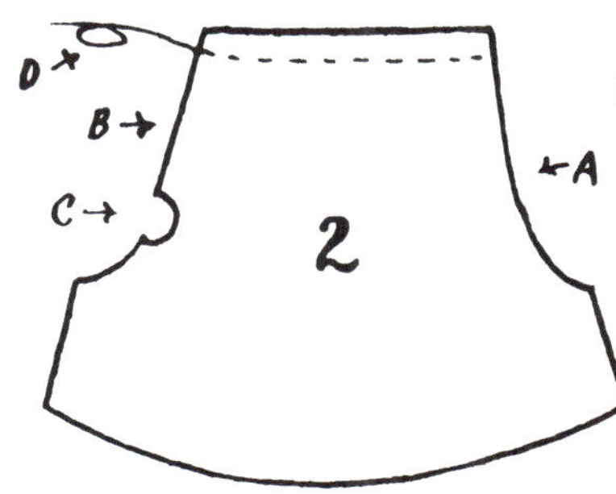

BOXER SHORTS for Dog and Horse

1. Left leg
2. Right leg

A. Sew "A" sides together
B. Sew "B" sides together
C. Opening for tail
D. Draw string through waist band to gather and tie

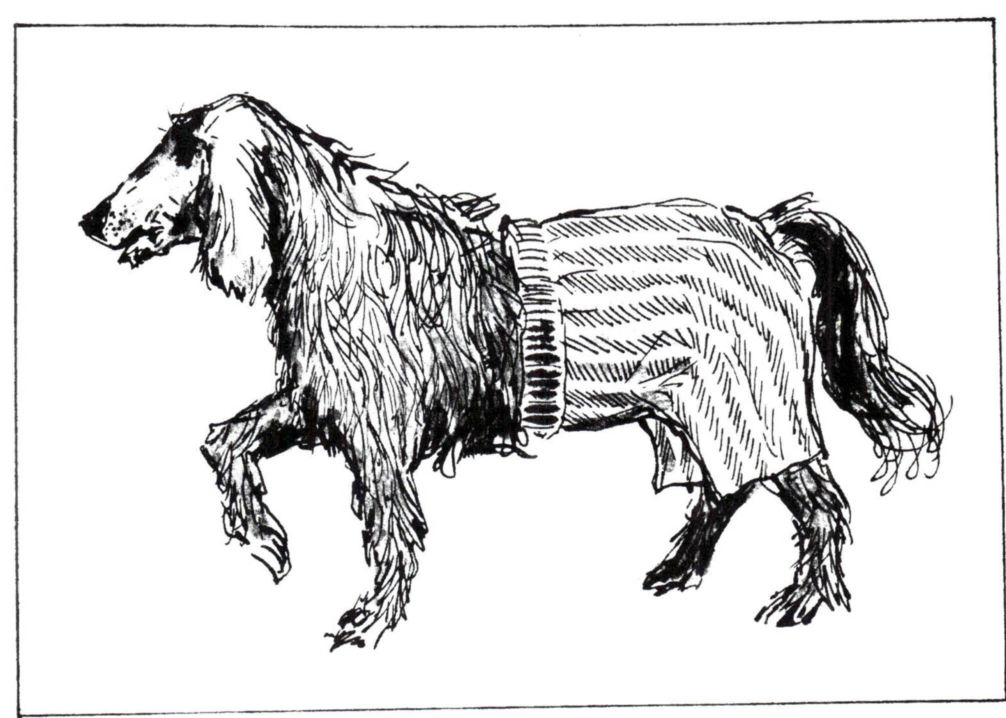

A Dog in boxer shorts

EMERGENCY THROW-OVER

A. Waist band
B. Draw string - Pass through band hem to tie
C. Stationary tie string
D. Gathered ruffle - Make 1½ times band length

The throw-over is designed as an emergency garment. Make and have ready in various sizes for small, medium and large animals.

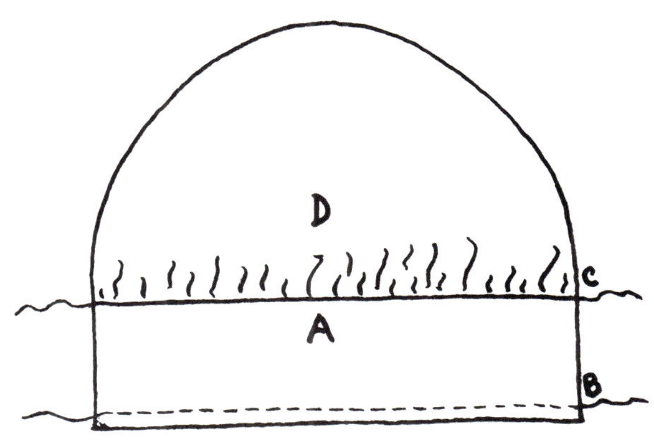

The N.Y. postal service impounded 500 copies, refusing to mail them because they were found to be "objectionable." Jeanne and I picketed the main post office along with our doorman, Bill Moran. We also had dogs wearing picket signs. Our protest worked and the magazine was released.

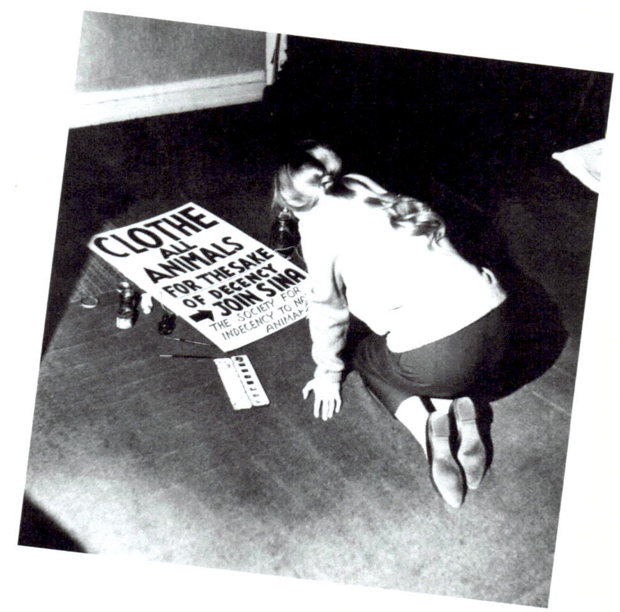

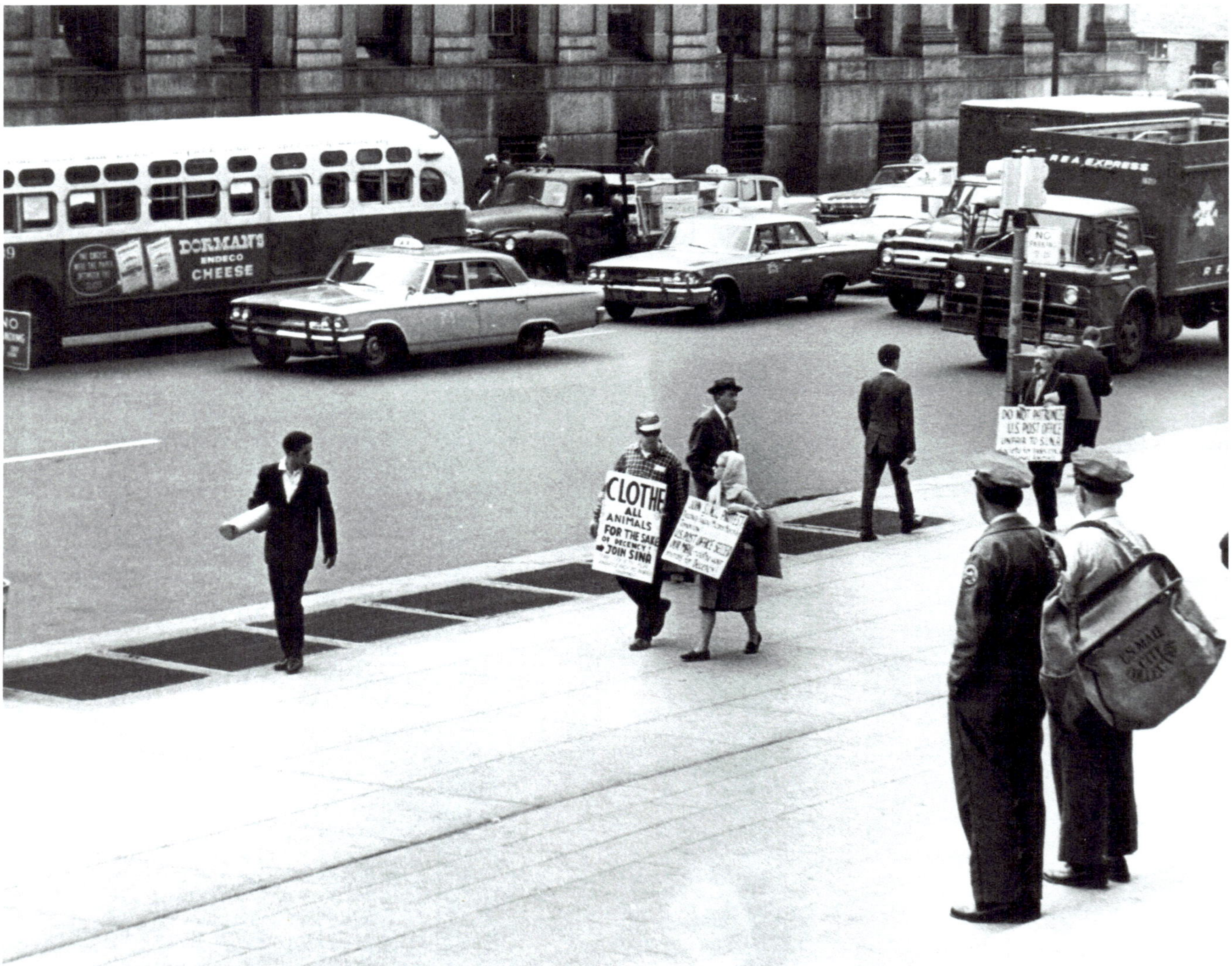

SINA NEWS

from

Society for Indecency to Naked Animals

507 Fifth Avenue, NYC

OXford 7-5895

FOR IMMEDIATE RELEASE

SINA, the Society for Indecency to Naked Animals, voiced a strong protest to Attorney General Robert Kennedy over the United States Post Office's seizure of SINA mail.

According to Vice-President Bruce Spencer, New York Post Office officials confiscated numerous pieces of mail enroute to important destinations and then advised SINA it would be impounded until a ruling was received from Washington.

Mr. Spencer said: "We have asked the Attorney General to double check the backgrounds of people running the post office because if they question our crusade for decency, they could well be concerned with inconsequential matters that have resulted in their present deficit, all at the taxpayers' expense."

Meantime, as a show of strength, SINA chapters in key cities around the country are planning to picket their local post offices, urging the public to use telephone, telegraph, teletype and other forms of communication. All heavy mail users are being asked to unbundle their mail and stuff corner boxes to capacity.

These measures will continue until the post office publicly agrees to recognize the authority expressed in the First Amendment of the Constitution and permits SINA's unrestricted use of the mails to carry on its movement to clothe all animals for the sake of decency.

(SINA, a four-year old organization, is dedicated to the philosophy that since we as humans are biologically animals, and accept the social custom of wearing clothes, then animals too should be permitted to share our propriety. SINA is concerned mainly about dogs, cats, horses, cows, and other domestic animals that stand higher than 4 inches or are longer than 6 inches.)

* * *

SINA ***"DECENCY TODAY MEANS MORALITY TOMORROW"***

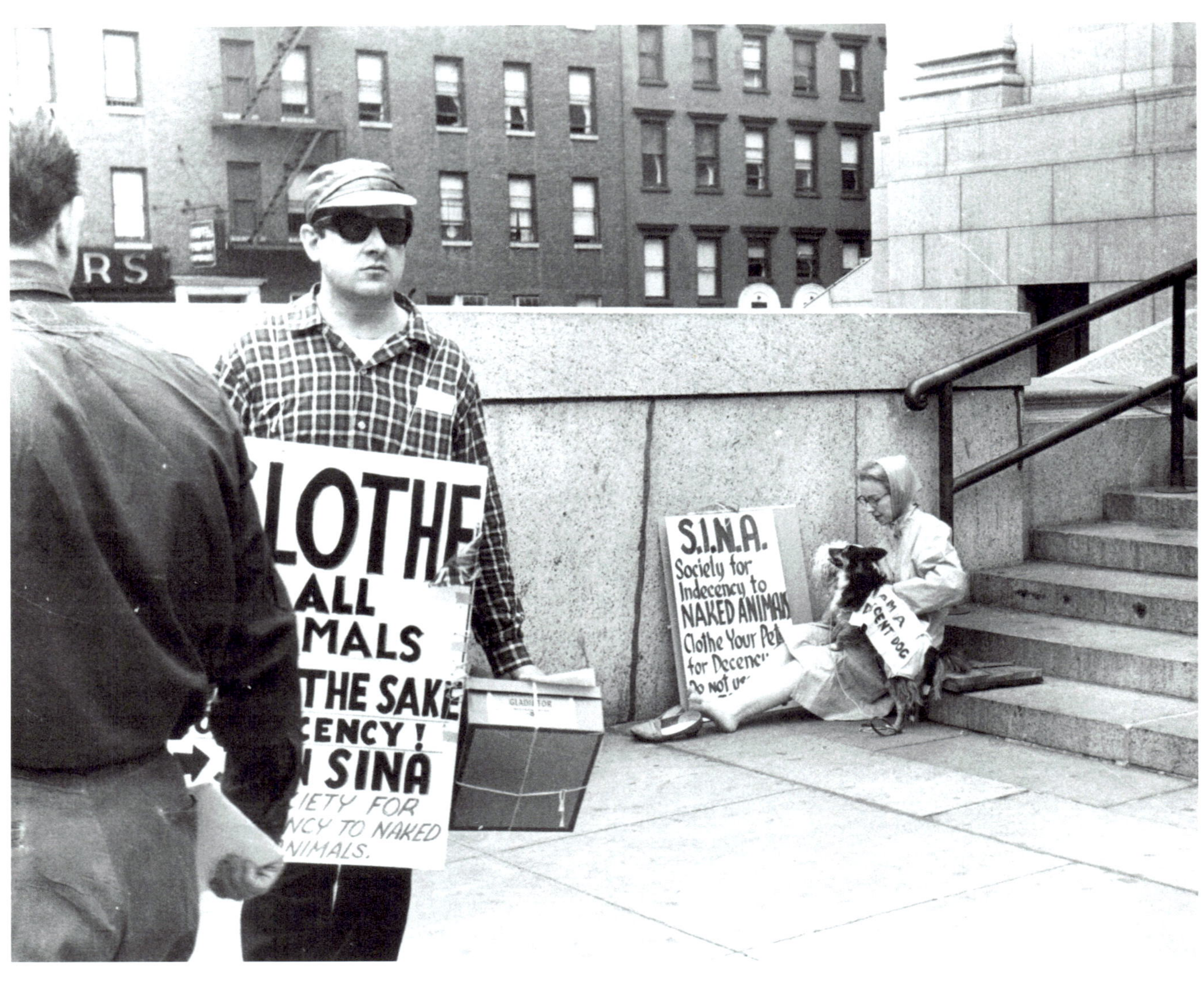

The N.Y. Telephone Company terminated our office phone, Morality 1-1963, claiming we were getting too many calls. People wanted to hear our recorded messages, and this was somehow threatening their equipment. So, we picketed them, too.

A. T. & T. IS
UN - AMERICAN

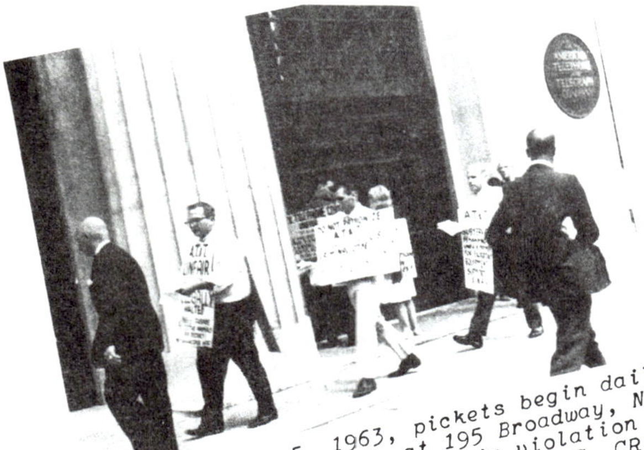

Monday, August 5, 1963, pickets begin daily strike against A.T.&T. at 195 Broadway, New York, in protest against their violation of the United States Constitution. (U.S. CRIMINAL CODE SECTION 241)

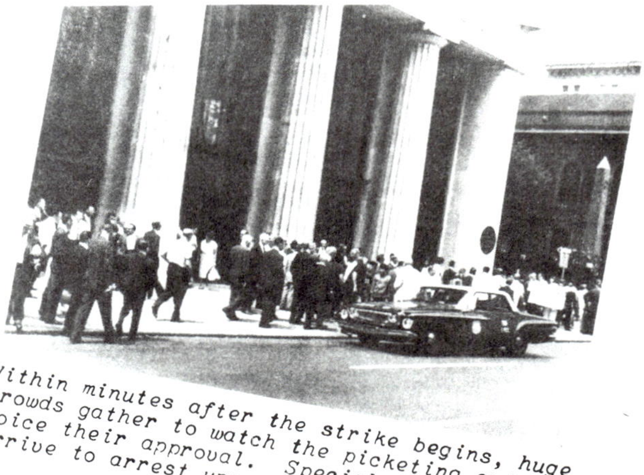

Within minutes after the strike begins, huge crowds gather to watch the picketing and voice their approval. Special police forces arrive to arrest unruly strike breakers.

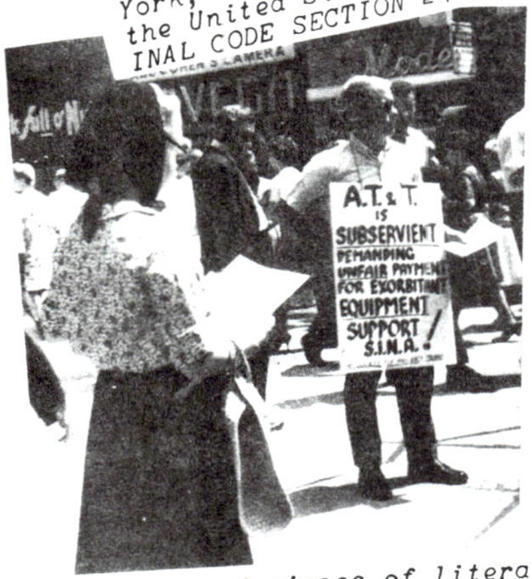

Thousands of pieces of literature are being passed out daily. Here, an employee reads the facts, then decides not to return to work.

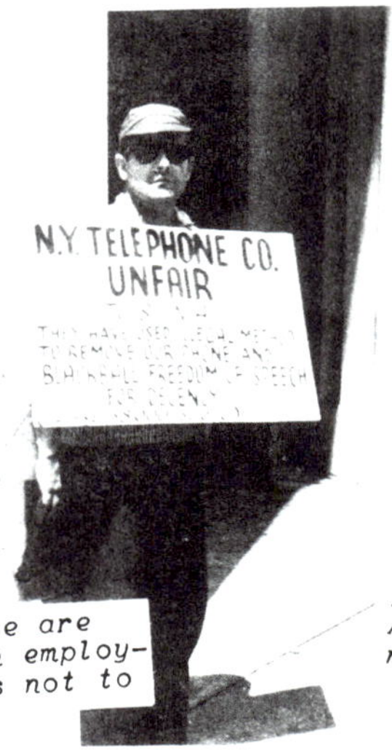

One of the pickets poses with his sign. The strike is continuing indefinitely, spreading to all major cities in the country against the entire Bell System.

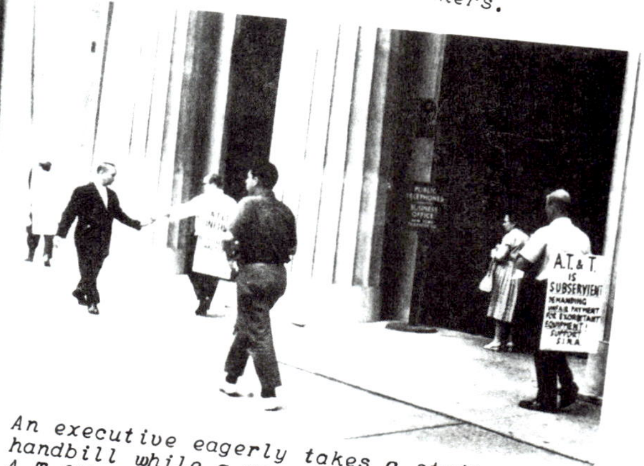

An executive eagerly takes a striker's handbill while a woman ponders entering A.T.&T. to pay her phone bill, then decides not to.

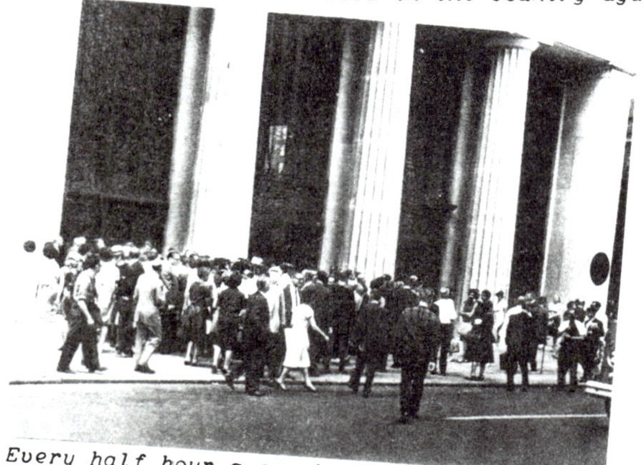

Every half hour a speaker mounts his soapbox in front of A.T.&T. and explains the issues to sympathetic crowds.

HELP

BREAK

THE

TELEPHONE

HABIT

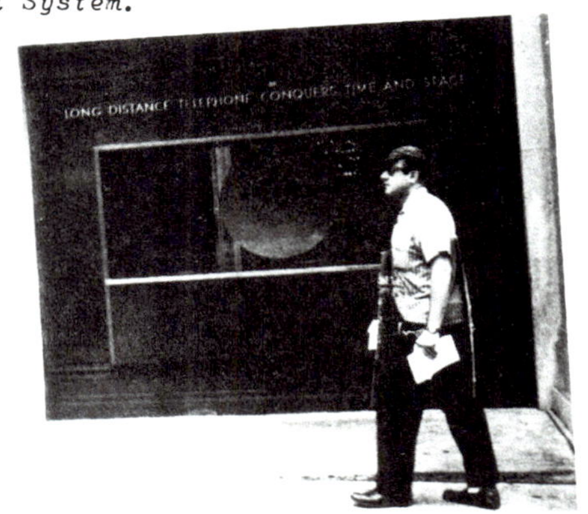

It is high noon and the normally crowded A.T.&T. clock area is deserted as patriotic citizens refuse to cross the picket line.

DO NOT PATRONIZE A.T.&T.

Society for Indecency to Naked Animals
507 Fifth Avenue
New York 17, New York

FOR RELEASE TUESDAY MARCH 5, 1963

G. Clifford Prout, President of SINA, held a confidential meeting with key SINA leaders in the basement of his Greenwich Village apartment Sunday March 3rd to form final plans for the White House picketing, as a protest against the riding of nude horses by Mrs. Kennedy and daughter Caroline.

President Prout had originally planned for 250 members to march from Baltimore en masse, however, the situation had gotten out of hand when several hundred New York SINA members voiced their intention of joining forces in Washington, causing a possible traffic jam on Pennsylvania Avenue.

Therefore, Mr. Prout issued the following orders:

1. Key SINA leaders will march on Washington first, as an advance scouting party to establish a command post and a general picketing area at the White House, arriving on or about 0900 hours Tuesday March 5, 1963.

2. Little by little, in groups of fifty, additional SINA marchers will be sent into the line so as to eventually surround the White House in gradual and dramatic stages.

3. This build-up of SINA forces will continue until Mrs. Kennedy makes some overture of recognition and/or resolution for the clothing of their horses when riding in public.

4. All picketing will be carried out peacefully with the highest moral standards of the SINA Constitution prevailing.

5. Bruce Spencer, Vice-President of SINA, will be in complete charge of the field operation at the White House and will report directly to GCP who will fly between New York, Baltimore, and Washington at random by helicopter.

After our New York City efforts, I read in the newspaper that President Kennedy gave express orders to encourage peaceful demonstrations in front of the White House. How could SINA resist a presidential mandate? On March 5, 1963, Jeanne and I and Bill Moran picketed the White House, begging Jackie to clothe Sardar, her horse, and Macaroni, her daughter Caroline's pony. Again, there were flashbulbs and microphones as reporters and photographers clamored for our story. From the White House, there was "no comment."

Walking back to our hotel after a day of pacing back and forth, stopping only to answer reporters' questions, we were amazed to see ourselves on the front pages of *The Washington News*, *The Evening Star* and *Baltimore Sun* on the newsstands.

THE EVENING STAR
Washington, D. C., Tuesday, March 5, 1963

DECENCY FOR ANIMALS

Put Macaroni in Shorts?

By DAVID BRAATEN
Star Staff Writer

The White House was being picketed in the name of decency today, specifically, decency to dumb animals.

The placard carried by the lead picket, Bruce Spencer of New York, told the story:

"The indecency of naked animals can be corrected," the sign read, "through new Federal laws and SINA—the Society for Indecency to Naked Animals We are now over 50,000 strong."

Why picket the White House? Mr. Spencer was asked.

"We hope that Mrs. Kennedy will set an example, and at least clothe the family's animals in public," he explained. This would mean Bermuda shorts for Sardar, Mrs. Kennedy's favorite mount, and for Caroline's pony, Macaroni.

Any mares or fillies in the White House stable could be made decent in specially designed bikinis, Mr. Spencer said, and Pushinka, the Russian dog, would presumably rate a tasteful maternity dress.

Once the example is set by the Kennedys, Mr. Spencer feels, the movement to clothe animals will sweep the country. It can't come too soon, he added.

"There are overtones of great moral disaster as far as youngsters are concerned, growing up seeing naked animals," he said.

The society is mainly concerned with domestic animals, Mr. Spencer said—dogs, cats, horses and cows. Mice are too small and bird clothing would be impractical, he said.

As for bare bears and nude gnus at the zoo, Mr. Spencer said:

"This could be a big problem. We feel that people should no more take children to a zoo than to a burlesque show. Zoos should be solely for serious nature study."

A passerby asked bluntly: "Who gives a damn about naked animals? What kind of people join this outfit? Are they nuts or something?"

"We have no screwballs in our organization," said Mr. Spencer patiently. "We have an emotional stability test for applicants."

Mr. Spencer did not say what the society's position is on unclothed, inanimate animals, like statues. If they decided to solder shorts onto equestrian statues, they could spend SINA's whole inheritance without even leaving Washington.

It has been suggested, unworthily no doubt, that the Society for Indecency to Naked Animals is a gigantic spoof. Its title, for instance, belies its purpose, which is to fight AGAINST indecency to naked animals.

Mr. Spencer explained this. The man who left the money — about a half million — to found SINA, G. Clifford Prout, "was a bit eccentric."

"His son, G. Clifford Prout, jr., is president of the organization," Mr. Spencer said. "Other relatives tried to break the old man's will, so the son doesn't dare change a word of the society's name."

Mr. Prout, the younger, and his assistants have been spending the half-million for about four years now, traveling back and forth across the country spreading the word. Mr. Spencer didn't know how much was left.

But he did explain how he can take the society's work seriously and shrug off the giggles and taunts of the skeptics. As vice president of SINA, he pulls down $8,000 a year, plus travel expenses for himself and his wife Jeanne.

"Laughter doesn't bother me in the slightest," he said. "It is the first phase of successful indoctrination."

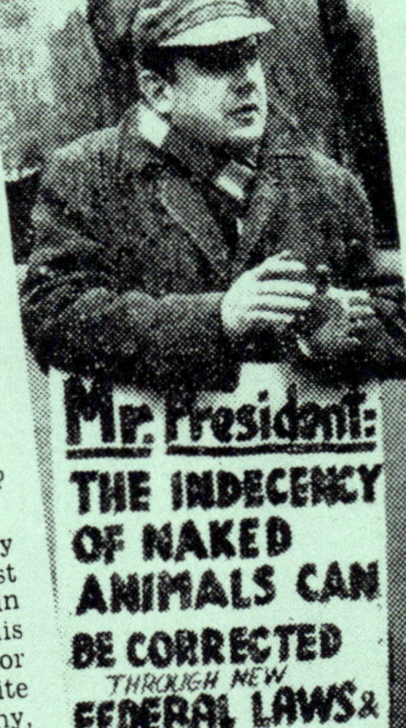

Bruce Spencer at the White House.—Star Staff Photo.

PICKETS AT WHITE HOUSE URGE CLOTHING ANIMALS

Washington, March 5 (AP)

The White House was picketed today by pleaders for an end to "the indecency of naked animals."

The pickets asked that President Kennedy and his family lead the way by clothing their own dogs and horses.

They handed passersby leaflets urging "clothe all animals protect our children from the sight of naked horses, cows, dogs and cats."

The White House maintained an official silence.

TROUSERS FOR MACARONI?

Pickets Implore Jackie To Clothe Her Animals

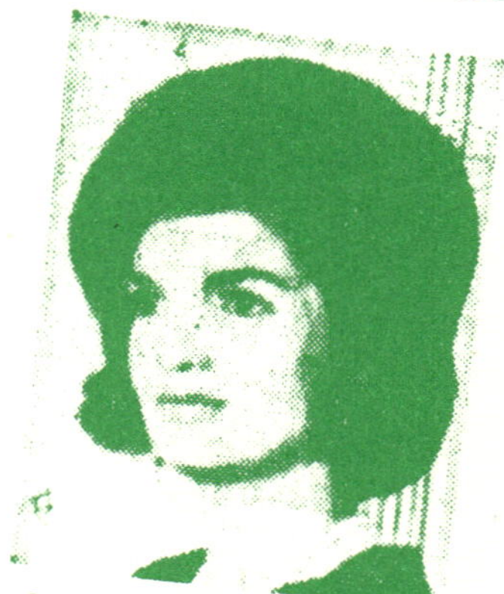

MRS. JOHN F. KENNEDY
. . . animal lovers' target

Just Plain Lack Of Horse Sense

Society Thinks Kennedys Should Clothe Horses

Upon returning to New York, we couldn't get off the phone to eat or go to the bathroom because of calls from reporters. They tried to push their way into our apartment, camping outside on the stoop. *Time*, *Newsweek* and *Life* magazines were preparing stories. So were *The New York Times*, *Chicago Daily News*, *Louisville Times*, *Der Speigel*, *Woman's Wear Daily* and many others. Jeanne dealt with the SINA office while I debated the virtues of SINA on TV shows in Toronto and Boston.

Group Will Ask Mrs. Kennedy To Dress Horse

BALTIMORE (AP)—

Jackie's Horse Needs Pants?

SINA Pickets President

'Nude' Animals Indecent?

Clothing for Animals Sure-Fire Method to Get Economy Moving

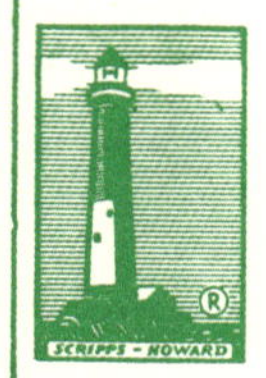

Index

Business ... 14
Classified ... 36-41
Comics ... 44, 46
EDITORIAL 18
Night Clubs ... 30
Radio-TV ... 42, 43
Sports ... 31-35
Theaters ... 26, 27
Travel ... 21-25
Women's ... 28, 29

The WASHINGTON DAILY News

FINAL EDITION — TUESDAY, MARCH 5, 1963

1013 13th St. N.W.—DI. 7-7777 — Second Class Postage Paid at Washington, D. C.
42d Year—No. 101 — Published Daily Except Sunday

Weather

Rain. High in 40s, low in 30s. Rain ending tomorrow.

Today at
9 a. m. ... 46
10 a. m. ... 46
11 a. m. ... 46
12 Noon ... 46
1 p. m. ... 45

See Weather Maps on Page 2

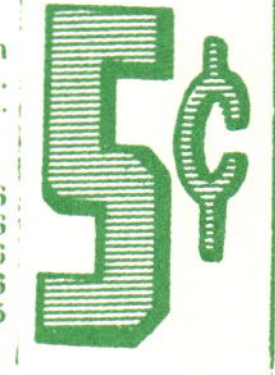

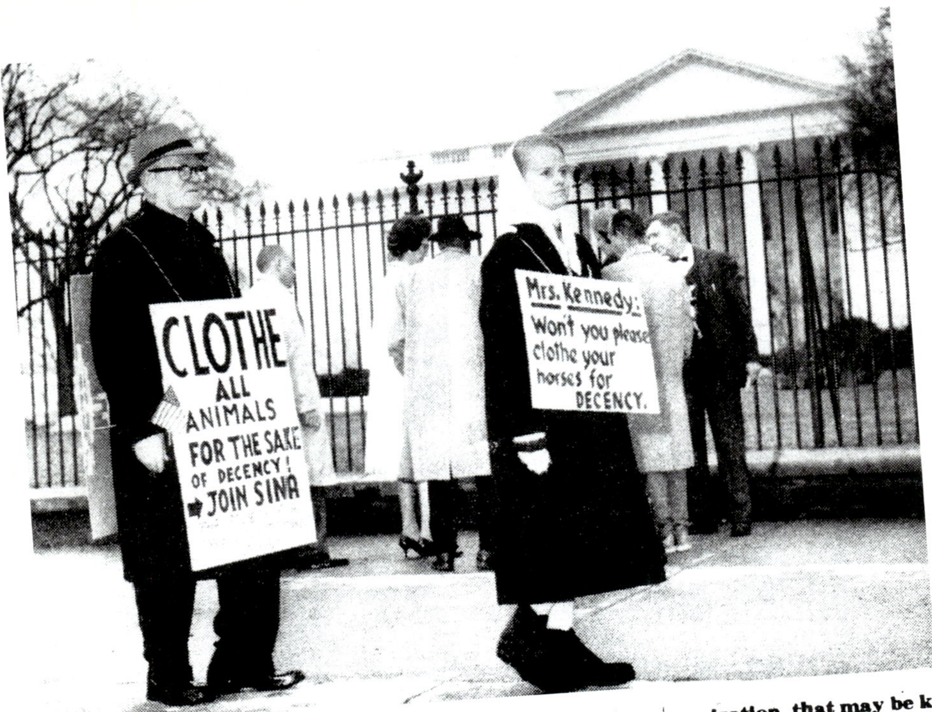

BARE TRAP—The Society for Indency to Naked Animals, n organization that may be keeping its full purpose under wraps, picketed the White House yesterday. SINA, as it likes to be known, is against the nudity of horses, cows, dogs and cats, tho it seems indifferent to fish. Bill Moran, left, said he is a doorman in New York and a volunteer picket. Jeanne Spencer, right, said she is the wife of SINA's paid vice president. Its President, G. Clifford Prout, has remained in New York, as invisible as a kitten in a kimona. (See editorial on Page 26.)

Pickets at White House Beckon First Lady to Clothe Her Horse

Nice Pair Of Shorts For Macaroni?

Let's Clothe Those Pets, Pickets Beg Of Jackie

Pickets Ask Pony Pants

Must dress horses in public, Mrs. Kennedy,

'Clothe Animals,' White House Pickets Urge Kennedys

The New York Times reporter Milton Bracker threatened us with a lawsuit as he sought to ferret out the facts. What was the truth? At this point, it hardly mattered. SINA was a force. When I objected to the Fifth Avenue Association about a naked paper mache horse in a window, they removed it. A manufacturer putting out a line of animal clothes asked for the SINA seal of approval. A pet store owner wanted to create a chain of stores with a SINA tie-in. I had already returned a check for $40,000 from a lady in Santa Barbara. To take money was a line I didn't want to cross.

Nonetheless, our high profile earned me the attention of the Internal Revenue Service. They believed the press story that Prout had inherited $400,000 and wanted their cut of SINA's back taxes. What to do? I gathered up all my records and receipts and went to the IRS office where the agent wasted no time threatening me with stiff penalties and jail time. Motioning him closer so others in the room could not hear, I told him that "SINA is a fairy tale, a hoax, a joke" and forcefully explained that he could lose his job for trying to collect taxes from a non-existent organization.

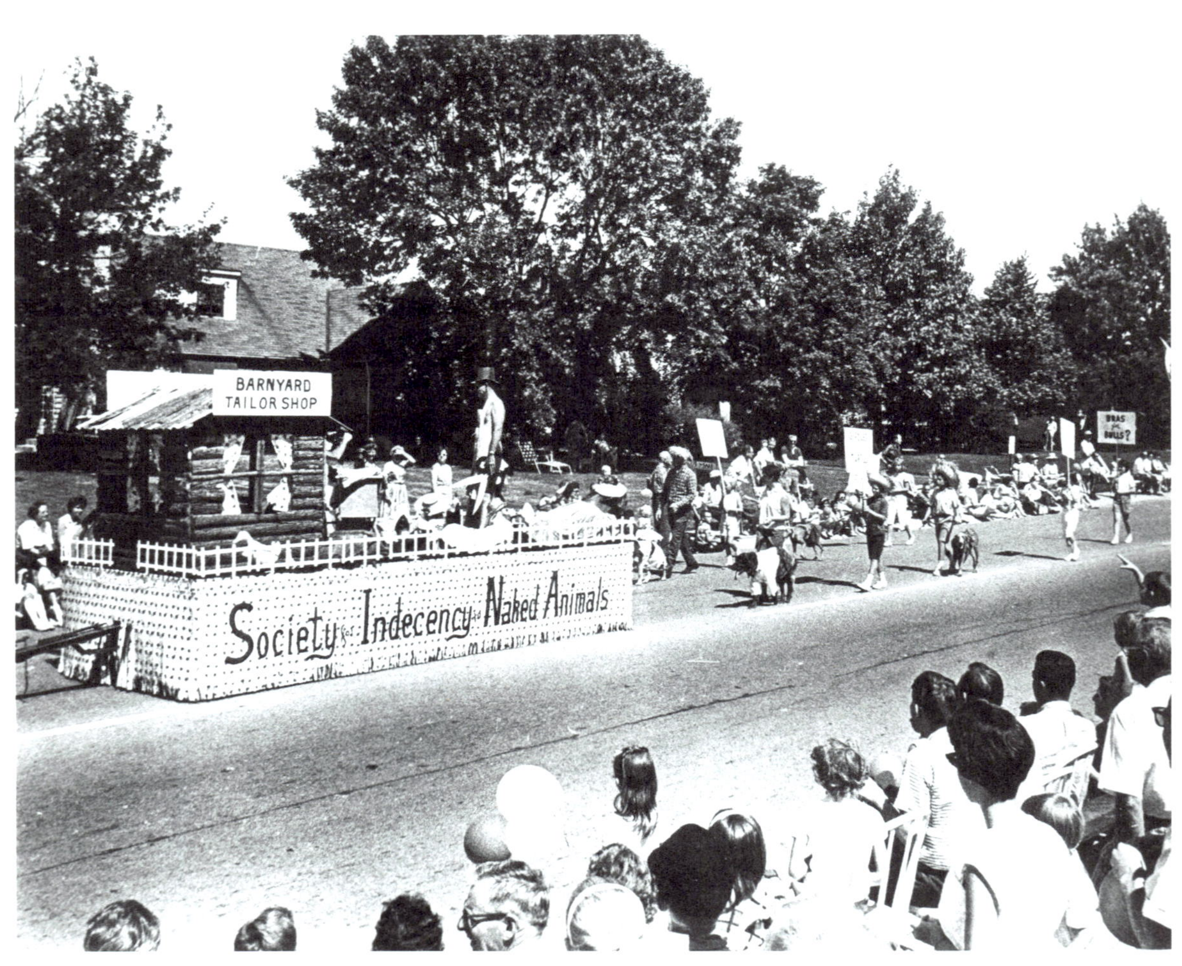

Clothes For Animals? It's All A Hoax

PALM SPRINGS, Calif. (UPI) — A nation-wide "drive" to clothe naked animals was unmasked Thursday as a hoax perpetrated by television gag writer Buck Henry who posed as G. Clifford Prout Jr., but who genuinely is Buck Zuckerman of New York.

All three are one and the same man — Zuckerman.

Resting in the desert sun at a resort hotel where he is registered as Buck Henry, writer for "The Gary Moore Show," he said: "I had no particular reason for dreaming up the Society for Indecency to Naked Animals ("SINA.)"

Henry, who as Prout picketed the White House in an attempt to dress animals decently, says, "Everything fell illogically into place.

"I did it partly to amuse Buck Henry, but Prout takes it all very seriously. I know Prout quite well. He's a great guy. I wouldn't say he's eccentric, but has the qualities of most men his age (32) only more so."

Playing it straight - faced, Henry - Prout - Zuckerman said he believes zealot Prout has as much right to be taken seriously as anyone else.

"He's very sincere about SINA. He no longer is shocked by seeing unclothed animals. He just feels a deep pain when seeing naked animals."

Newspapers, television news shows and periodicals took Prout seriously during his campaign to clothe animals, much to the amusement of Henry-Zuckerman. Asked if he was a split personality, Henry refused to answer.

Gagster Henry - Prout - Zuckerman said he would return to his home on New York's 56th Street within a few days, but has every intention of continuing Prout's campaign for discouraging nudity among animals.

Even though I instigated and promoted it for many years, I'm still mystified as to why The Society for the Indecency to Naked Animals managed to get all the attention that it did. The public got so emotionally involved in the idea of animal nudity; they hated it, they loved it, they jumped to join the movement. Some wanted to hurt me, most laughed and many suspected it was a joke — but they still got involved. Ultimately, I couldn't have kept it going were it not for an eager press looking for a good story. I might have stuck with it for longer, but on March 14, 1963 Buck called from Palm Springs where he was vacationing. "Alan, news people are surrounding me here and they want the truth. What should I tell them?" I said, "Go ahead, Buck. Bring the curtain down."

Zuckerman---the Naked Truth

Palm Springs

The bespectacled president of the Society for Indecency to Naked Animals acknowledged yesterday that his real name is neither G. Clifford Prout Jr., nor Buck Henry but Buck Zuckerman of New York.

Prout or Zuckerman makes his living as Buck Henry, a writer on the Garry Moore TV show.

He heads SINA under the name of Prout and exists under the name of Zuckerman "to preserve Buck Henry's sense of the past."

In his role of Prout last September, Zuckerman said he adopted Buck Henry as his writer's name to "keep from being pestered by crackpots and oddballs."

The controversial Society for Indecency to Naked Animals believes decency will be encouraged only if the "vital areas" of animals are clothed.

Our Correspondent

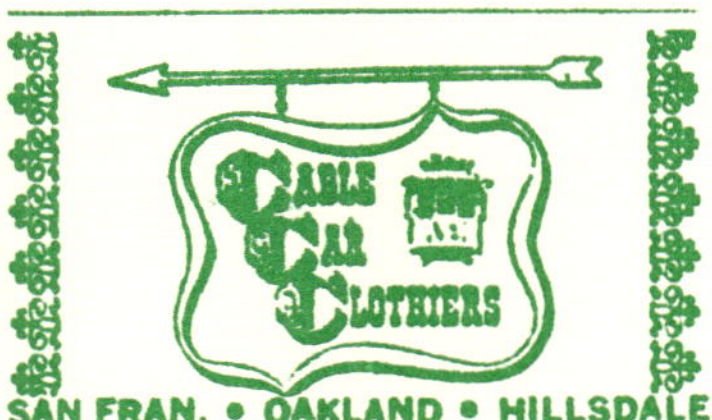

Some months later, In January 1964, I planted the final SINA hoax-reveal story with Art Buchwald. His syndicated column appeared in over two hundred newspapers. I was more than pleased.

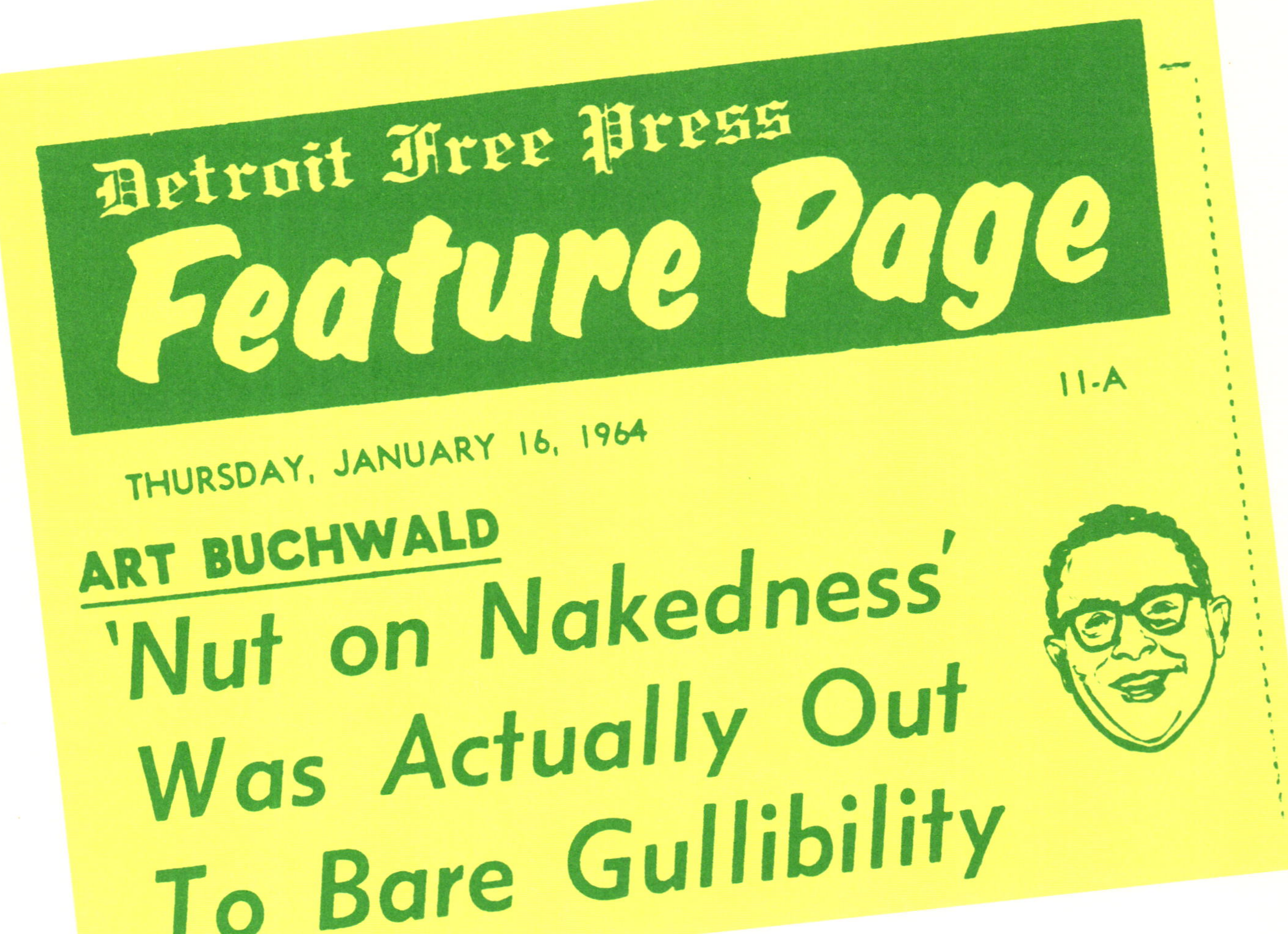

Detroit Free Press

Feature Page

11-A

THURSDAY, JANUARY 16, 1964

ART BUCHWALD

'Nut on Nakedness' Was Actually Out To Bare Gullibility

BY ART BUCHWALD

WASHINGTON—In 1959 a young American writer named Alan Abel formed a society called SINA, the Society for Indecency to Naked Animals, dedicated to clothing all animals in public for decency's sake.

Press, radio, and television gave it wide publicity, and many people offered money and support.

Others suspected a publicity stunt which would soon reveal a commercial link-up, and still others felt that Mr. Abel was some kind of nut.

But despite skepticism, Mr. Abel managed to exert great influence.

• • •

HE HAD an unclothed papier mache horse removed from a Fifth Ave. window in New York when he threatened to picket the store.

Zoo directors became furious when he said that taking your children to the zoo was like taking them to a burlesque show.

Clothing manufacturers offered to tie up with SINA if they would give their endorsement.

A lady in Santa Barbara wanted to give SINA $40,000 for the cause.

And so it went. But through it all everyone kept wondering what Mr. Abel's angle was. Now it can be revealed.

• • •

MR. ABEL TOLD us in Chicago that his organization was formed to show how gullible the American people really are.

"You could call it a great morality play," he said. "I was trying to satirize our customs. People say one thing and do another. We find this in politics, business, sex, and in every part of our life.

"Even the title of my organization was contradictory. It means the opposite of what I was trying to do.

"Although people laughed at us, they never understood us. The naive believed we were for real, the smart alecks were sure we had an angle. Hardly anyone guessed we were pulling their leg."

MR. ABEL SAID the gag didn't cost him much money. "It may have cost about $20 a week, and since neither my wife nor I drinks, that wasn't much. We returned all money sent to us and turned down all commercial tie-ups.

"But even I didn't realize how big this thing could become. I discovered that any crackpot group, so long as it sounded official, could put pressure on any important organization in the United States and scare the hell out of it.

"I discovered that people not only didn't read, they couldn't hear. On Labor Day I got a SINA band together and marched in a Labor Day parade in New York City. I had a cello in the band, a bugle, two trumpets, and a snare drum, and we played 'The Stars and Stripes Forever,' each in a different key.

"But because we were carrying the American flag, everyone along the way applauded."

• • •

WHEN MR. ABEL wanted pickets, he hired them at $1.25 an hour. His "president," Buck Henry, was an actor who played the role on TV shows, interviews, and press conferences.

"What have you proved?" we asked.

"I think I've proved that one person can turn the country upside down. I've also proved that Americas give in to nuts very easily and are afraid of them.

"The question is how do you awaken people when they can be taken in so easily? I don't think, even though the secret is out, that people will change their attitude toward SINA. Once you plant the idea in people's minds that animals should be clothed, it's hard to turn back."

Satire On Our Customs

The Coverup Was A Hoax

Naked Animal Campaign A Joke

Animal Nudity Hoax Unveiled By 'Official'

VANCOUVER (CP) — The Society for Indecency to Naked Animals (Sina) is a hoax.

The organization, devoted to putting clothes on animals, is a giant banana skin on which the whole world slipped, its chief trouble-shooter and vice-president said Wednesday.

"There is no Sina," Bruce Spencer of New York told 700 laughing University of British Columbia students. "It's been a big hoax through the last five years."

Spencer told the students this was the first time he has revealed publicly that the organization is a joke. On the stage with him were six unclothed roosters and a sweatered pig.

Spencer said the hoax was perpetrated by him, his wife, New York actor Buck Henry and the doorman at the apartment where Spencer lives.

"SINA was supposed to be a social satire on narrow-minded people. It should have been recognized as such but it wasn't — instead the press picked it up and thousands of people took it seriously."

"Then we continued it as a spoof on people taking things seriously."

"To keep our image alive I rented a door to a locked broom closet in a prestige office building and put up a sign saying 'SINA National Headquarters.' "

Just For Laughs

Alan Abel Was Just Pulling Nation's Leg

tuesday, march 26, 1963 *temple university NEWS*

Nature of anti-naked animals society exposed

Clothed Animals? The Naked Truth

Animal Society Fooled Many Americans

SINA: The Great American Hoax

SINA Founder Proved He Had Naked Animal by Tail

Anyone Can Turn U.S. Upside Down

How Gullible Can We Get?

Editorial . . .

A Lesson

Although we feel certain that America is the GREATEST we must admit that we Americans are also probably the most gullible of people — at least of civilized peoples.

We recently were reading a column by Art Buckwald which reviewed, and went into greater detail, a subject an Enterprise-UPI story had told about some time ago. It was the story about the Society for Indecency of Naked Animals. . Now that — of course — sounds zaney enough to be immediately branded as a hoax. But that would be only if people were not so gullible. Instead — one Alan Abel, who had "organized" SINA as a prank, was amazed to find the money start flowing in in the form of donations.

Some publicity was all that was needed — (like in the case of the Beatles). Of course there were many who decided that Mr. Abel was "some kind of a nut" but there were many others who were sold completely and who believed the idea was a good one.

A threat of picketing resulted in prompt removal of a paper mache horse (nude, of course) from a Fifth avenue store. Zoo keepers were outraged because Abel gave a sobering announcement that zoos were as bad as burlesque shows. Some clothing manufacturers offered to tie up with SINA if SINA would give their garments their endorsement. (Sounds like the Beatles again, eh.)

The money kept coming in, along with all kinds of commercial tie-up offers. A Santa Barbara matron wanted to give SINA $40,000. That was turned down and all contributions sent in without prior warning were returned.

Abel explained that "the whole thing had gotten out of hand." He had planned it all as a prank and as it mushroomed he just couldn't resist riding along with it. He commented, "It (the gag) may have cost us about $2C a week (postage, etc.) and since neither my wife nor I drink that wasn't much."

And Abel added, "People can't understand why I did it. When I tell them that all I was doing was satirizing the gullibility of the American people, they won't believe me."

There should be a lesson in that for all of us.

Congressman's Report

'Gag' Organization Spoofs Odd-Ball, Crackpot Ideas

By GEORGE F. SENNER, JR.
Third District Arizona

Postscript:

Naked Animals Put-on Is Off but Not Over

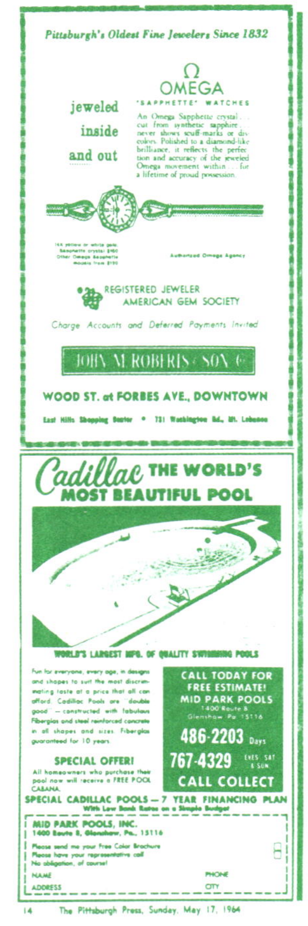

Pittsburgh's Oldest Fine Jewelers Since 1832

Ω OMEGA

jeweled inside and out

"SAPPHETTE" WATCHES

An Omega Sapphette crystal . . . cut from synthetic sapphire . . . never shows scuff-marks or discolors. Polished to a diamond-like brilliance, it reflects the perfection and accuracy of the jeweled Omega movement within . . . for a lifetime of proud possession.

Authorized Omega Agency

REGISTERED JEWELER AMERICAN GEM SOCIETY

Charge Accounts and Deferred Payments Invited

JOHN M. ROBERTS & SON CO.

WOOD ST. at FORBES AVE., DOWNTOWN

Cadillac THE WORLD'S MOST BEAUTIFUL POOL

Fun for everyone, every age, in designs and shapes to suit the most discriminating taste at a price that all can afford. Cadillac Pools are "double good" — constructed with fabulous Fiberglas and steel reinforced concrete in all shapes and sizes. Fiberglas guaranteed for 10 years.

SPECIAL OFFER!

All homeowners who purchase their pool now will receive a FREE POOL CABANA.

CALL TODAY FOR FREE ESTIMATE!
MID PARK POOLS
1400 Route 8
Glenshaw Pa 15116
486-2203 Days
767-4329 EVES SAT & SUN
CALL COLLECT

SPECIAL CADILLAC POOLS — 7 YEAR FINANCING PLAN

MID PARK POOLS, INC.
1400 Route 8, Glenshaw, Pa., 15116

Please send me your Free Color Brochure
Please have your representative call
No obligation, of course!

NAME PHONE
ADDRESS CITY

14 The Pittsburgh Press, Sunday, May 17, 1964

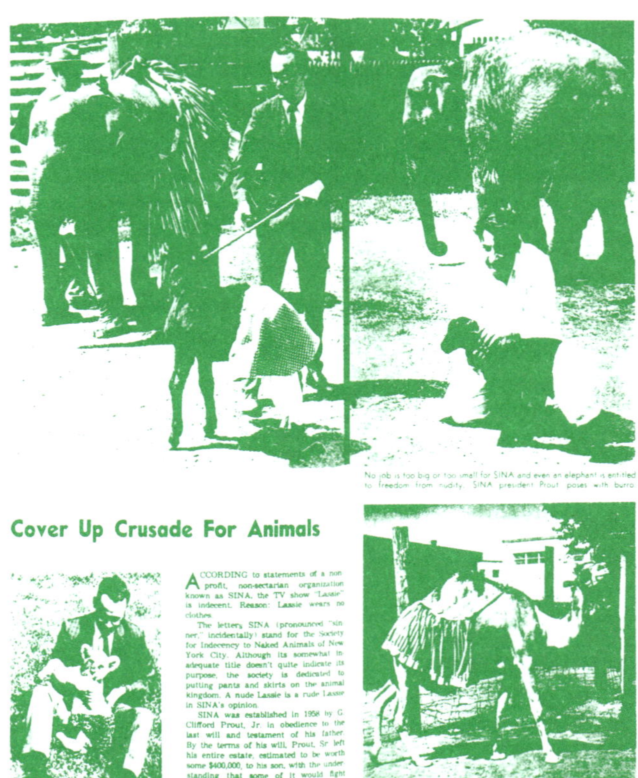

No job is too big or too small for SINA and even an elephant is entitled to freedom from nudity. SINA president Prout poses with burro.

Cover Up Crusade For Animals

ACCORDING to statements of a non-profit, non-sectarian organization known as SINA, the TV show "Lassie" is indecent. Reason: Lassie wears no clothes.

The letters SINA (pronounced "sinner," incidentally) stand for the Society for Indecency to Naked Animals of New York City. Although its somewhat inadequate title doesn't quite indicate its purpose, the society is dedicated to putting pants and skirts on the animal kingdom. A nude Lassie is a rude Lassie in SINA's opinion.

SINA was established in 1958 by G. Clifford Prout, Jr. in obedience to the last will and testament of his father. By the terms of his will, Prout, Sr left his entire estate, estimated to be worth some $400,000, to his son, with the understanding that some of it would fight against nudniks in the animal world.

SINA president shows how a leopard's spots would look on trousers for a lion.

"If the boys back home could only see me now" seems proud boast of this camel strutting in an apron at outdoor menagerie in New Jersey.

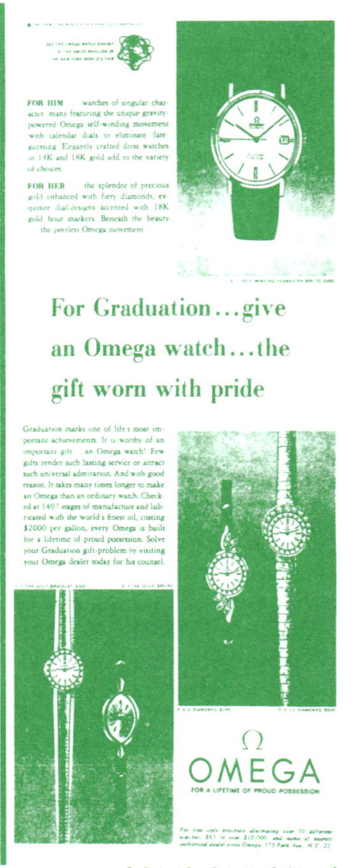

FOR HIM . . . watches of singular character, many featuring the unique gravity-powered Omega self-winding movement with calendar dials to eliminate date-guessing. Elegantly crafted dress watches in 14K and 18K gold add to the variety of choices.

FOR HER . . . the splendor of precious gold enhanced with fiery diamonds, exquisite dial-designs accented with 18K gold hour markers. Beneath the beauty . . . the peerless Omega movement.

For Graduation . . . give an Omega watch . . . the gift worn with pride

Graduation marks one of life's most important achievements. It is worthy of an important gift . . . an Omega watch! Few gifts render such lasting service or attract such universal admiration. And with good reason. It takes many times longer to make an Omega than an ordinary watch. Checked at 1497 stages of manufacture and lubricated with the world's finest oil, costing $2000 per gallon, every Omega is built for a lifetime of proud possession. Solve your Graduation gift-problem by visiting your Omega dealer today for his counsel.

Ω OMEGA

FOR A LIFETIME OF PROUD POSSESSION

The Pittsburgh Press, Sunday, May 17, 1964 15

In spite of SINA having been exposed as a hoax multiple times, the May 17th, 1964, issue of *The Pittsburgh Press* devoted two full pages of its magazine section to a straight story on "the $400,000 left to G. Clifford Prout for the purpose of clothing all animals." Our answering service was still receiving dozens of calls a day and over a hundred letters a week, all asking for SINA literature.

A little while later, a New Jersey newspaper published a serious editorial reply to a SINA press release it had received. The irony is that I never sent it; someone else did. Was it in jest? Were they serious? It was difficult to tell anymore. More SINA articles that I did not plant began to sporadically appear, including a number of stories in a small California newspaper that rivaled mine for ridiculousness. How did this happen?

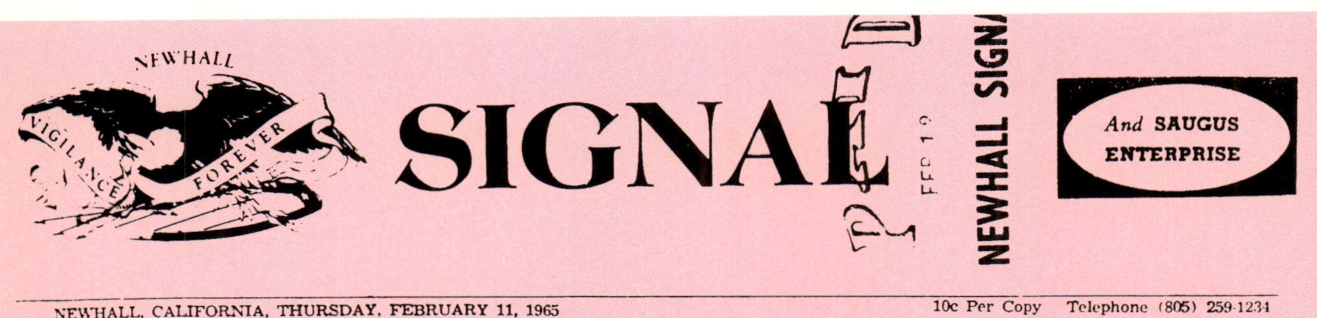

NEWHALL SIGNAL

VIGILANCE FOREVER

And SAUGUS ENTERPRISE

NEWHALL, CALIFORNIA, THURSDAY, FEBRUARY 11, 1965 — 10c Per Copy — Telephone (805) 259-1234

SINA Makes Air Drop Over Moral Disaster Area

Africa USA, Newhall

Ranch Feed Lot Inspected

Residents of Valencia Valley were treated to an astonishing spectacle yesterday when a veteran aircraft, with "SINA" emblazoned on the side in giant letters, circled the area and dropped what was reported to be "emergency animal clothing" to a waiting vehicle.

On the ground, two individuals who identified themselves as Ben and Rain Jacopetti, SINA field agents, gathered up the supplies and loaded them into the back of the clearly marked SINA transport ambulance.

At the scene of the air drop several people ran out onto the field and grabbed up the clothing as it came down to the ground.

"I think the clothes were grabbed up by anti-SINA forces in an attempt to deter our progress," Rain Jacopetti stated.

The air drop culminated weeks of effort by the Society for the Indecency of Naked Animals to alleviate the problems of animal nudity throughout this area.

The SINA program was called to the attention of our readers a week ago when the editors of this newspaper received a telegram from the society's main office in New York. President, G. Clifford Prout Jr., had reported that Newhall-Saugus had been declared a "moral disaster area" due to the abundance of animals displaying themselves in an unclothed condition throughout the valley.

To oversee the project, the two SINA field agents slipped into the area early yesterday morning driving their emergency vehicle. The pair conducted on-site inspection tours of surrounding residential areas, making note of the homes in which naked pets were allowed to wander unclothed in public.

Shortly before noon, the Jacopetti's called on local merchants in efforts to find clothing stores which might carry animal fashions.

"Disgraceful," said Ben Jacopetti, when he was unable to locate the latest styles in animal wear needed to cover the "vital areas" of pets.

After the air drop, the representatives made unan-

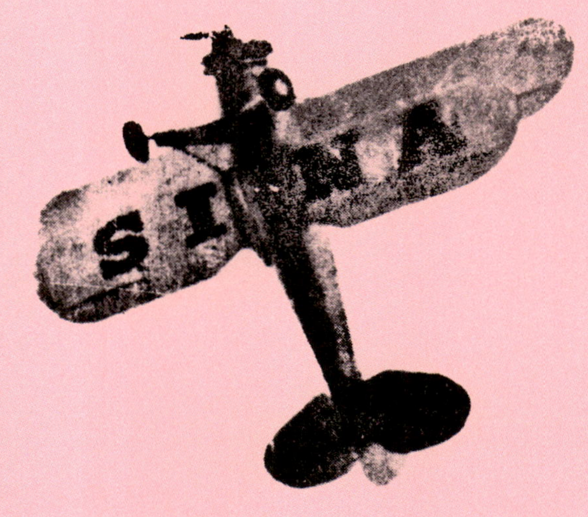

Reporters including Gay Talese from *The New York Times*, Hy Gardner of the *New York Herald Tribune* and CBS Radio's Jack Sterling still requested interviews "with anyone from SINA who can explain its philosophy." I begged off at first (I was busy on an assignment for *Playboy*) but quickly reversed course. How could I resist?

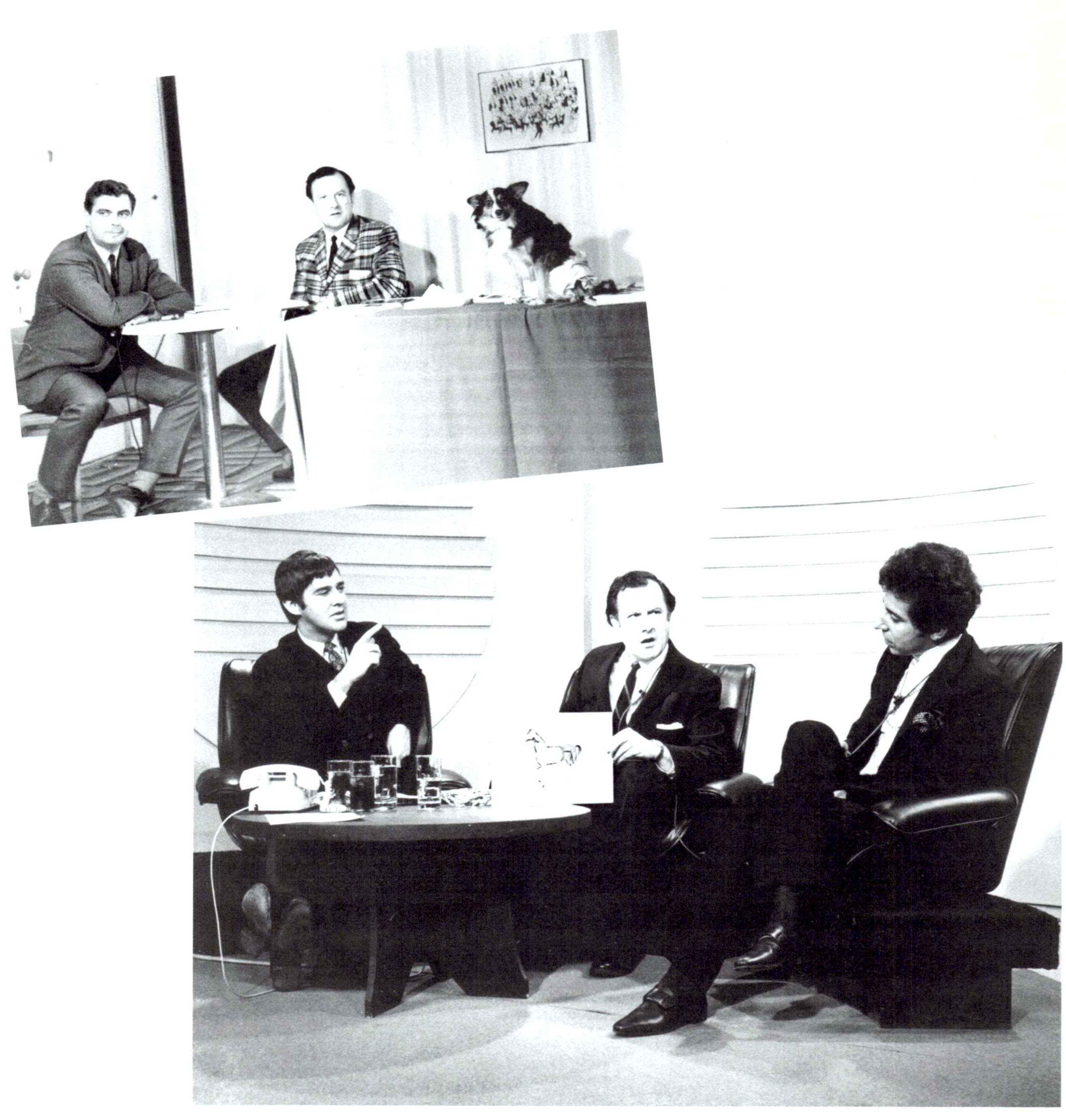

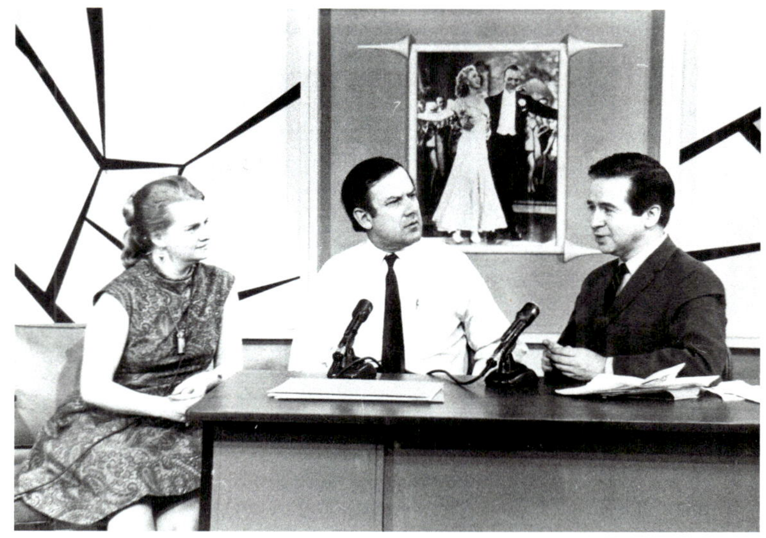

Meanwhile, I accepted speaking engagements from groups that wanted to hear about my personal experiences in sustaining a nonexistent morality movement. These included everything from the congregation of a Unitarian Church to a meeting of pediatric surgeons at the Harvard Club. There were dozens of radio and television requests; I appeared as Bruce Spencer and as myself. The audience responses were gratifying.

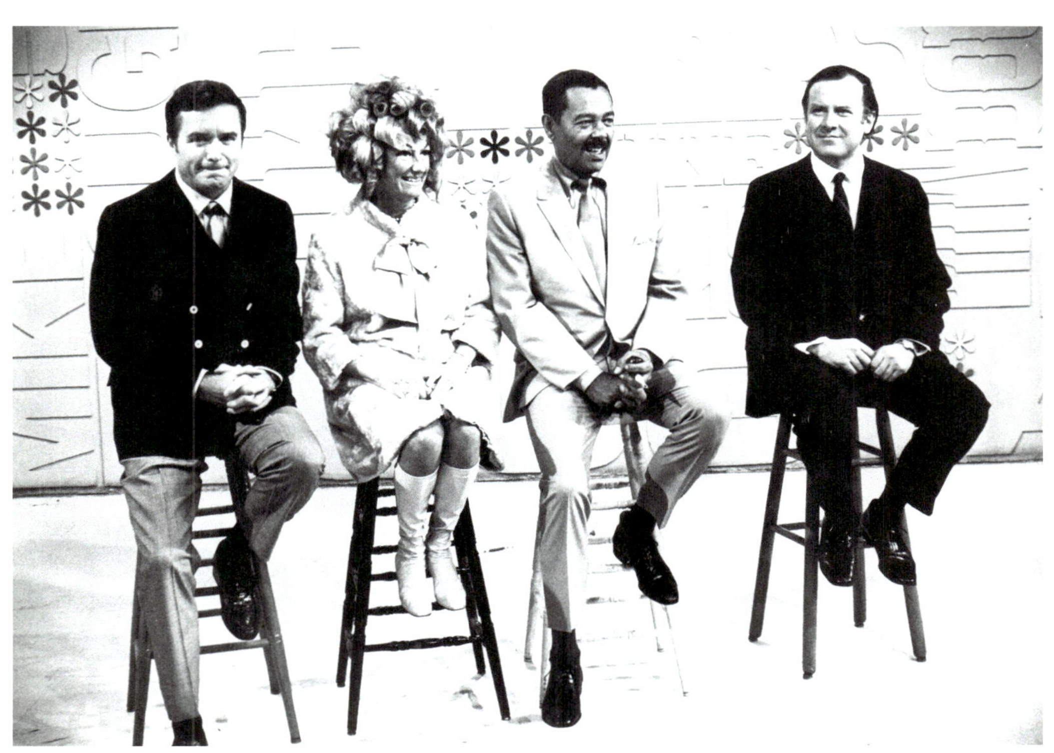

Sidney Fields from the *New York Daily News* pestered me for an interview throughout April 1965, and finally I played the moral crusader's role for old time's sake, just to see if he was putting me on for a change. He wasn't. His factual account on SINA ran on May 27, 1965, reaching nearly five million readers.

ONLY HUMAN

By Sidney Fields

Never the Altogether

Alan Abel gets terribly upset whenever he sees an animal without clothes on. He's the only known spokesman for SINA, the Society for Indecency to Naked Animals. But his distress is considerably diminished by his $8,000-a-year salary, plus traveling expenses.

"At first flush people tell me I must be kidding," said Alan in his 8-by-8 foot midtown office crammed with boxes full of his literature. "But I'm not. We are concerned with dressing animals higher than 4 inches and longer than 6."

It must be quite a wrestling match to get a skirt on a snake, a bikini on a bird, Bermuda shorts on an elephant, a girdle on a gnu, or a bra on a cow.

"There's no reason why farmers can't put a fence around their pastures," said Alan severely.

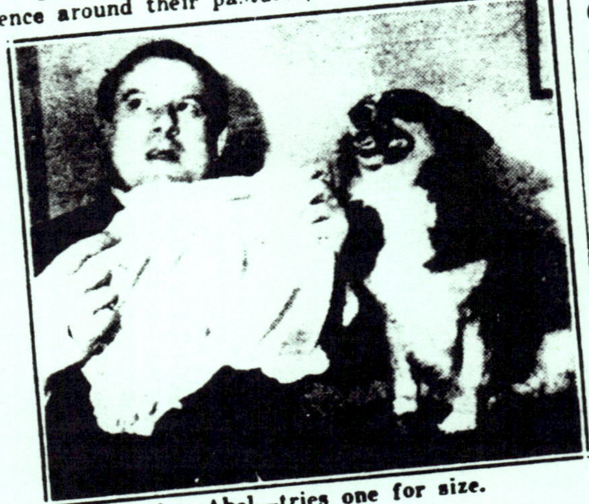

Alan Abel—tries one for size.

"As for zoos, we urge parents not to take their children. No, we haven't been very successful with zoos."

Alan swears that this great moral crusade of our time was started by a man hiding behind the name of G. Clifford Prout Sr., who left $500,000 to his son, G. C. P. Jr., to be spent at the rate of $50,000 a year beginning in 1959. It's the Society FOR Indecency to Naked Animals. Shouldn't it be the Society Against etc.?

Can't Break the Will

"The will says 'For,'" Alan explained. "It has to stay because people have tried to break the will."

The society has been accused of everything from being "warped" to promoting animal clothes and lecture fees. To which Alan snarls: "These are dastardly charges. We do not solicit money or dues and do not charge for our literature."

He had to close his San Francisco office because of "local harassment." People kept phoning and asking how to dress their naked piranhas and crocodiles. When he tried to leave his pamphlets in an animal hospital, Alan was thrown out. No, he's never been hit—yet.

"That's probably because most of the people I've argued with were smaller than me," he said. He's 6 feet, weighs 200 pounds.

Joined Crusade in 1959

Alan is 38; places his native town as Columbus, Ohio; his education from Ohio State; his previous profession as a band drummer, and adds that he met Prout Jr., at a party and was asked to join the great crusade for animal decency in 1959.

"Our very first victory was to get a Fifth Ave. store to remove a naked papier mache horse from its window," Alan said.

Prout Jr., is credited with composing the official marching song. Its directions read, "Start with muted trumpet far away" and "sing with spirit." The society's "Ode to Decency," directed at the animals themselves, holds this immortal stanza:

"Yet, here you are in nature's state,
Unmindful of our modern ways.
Cover at last your nudiness
And do as SINA says."

"We inevitably attract a lot of strange people," Alan said. "Odd ladies and men with beards, knapsacks and guitars."

Little Dog Wasn't There

Women barge in and want him to fit their pets with clothes at once. The pets include hamsters and turtles. One lady demanded that he see to it that a barking dog on a TV commercial be dressed. The dog isn't shown. A man asked for his pamphlets for use in a debating society. The society was in a Massachusetts prison.

"And we get a steady stream of letters from people who want money," said Alan.

One man wanted him to select the ten best-dressed animals in America. Another was stunned to find that no provisions had been made to clothe statues in public places.

A real crisis came when the society announced it was about to turn its full wrath against nudist colonies. There was a deluge of 50 nasty letters from the sun worshippers. One, named Zelda Supplee, invited Alan to come to her camp with his animals.

"But she insisted," he said, wincing, "that we all come out in the nude."

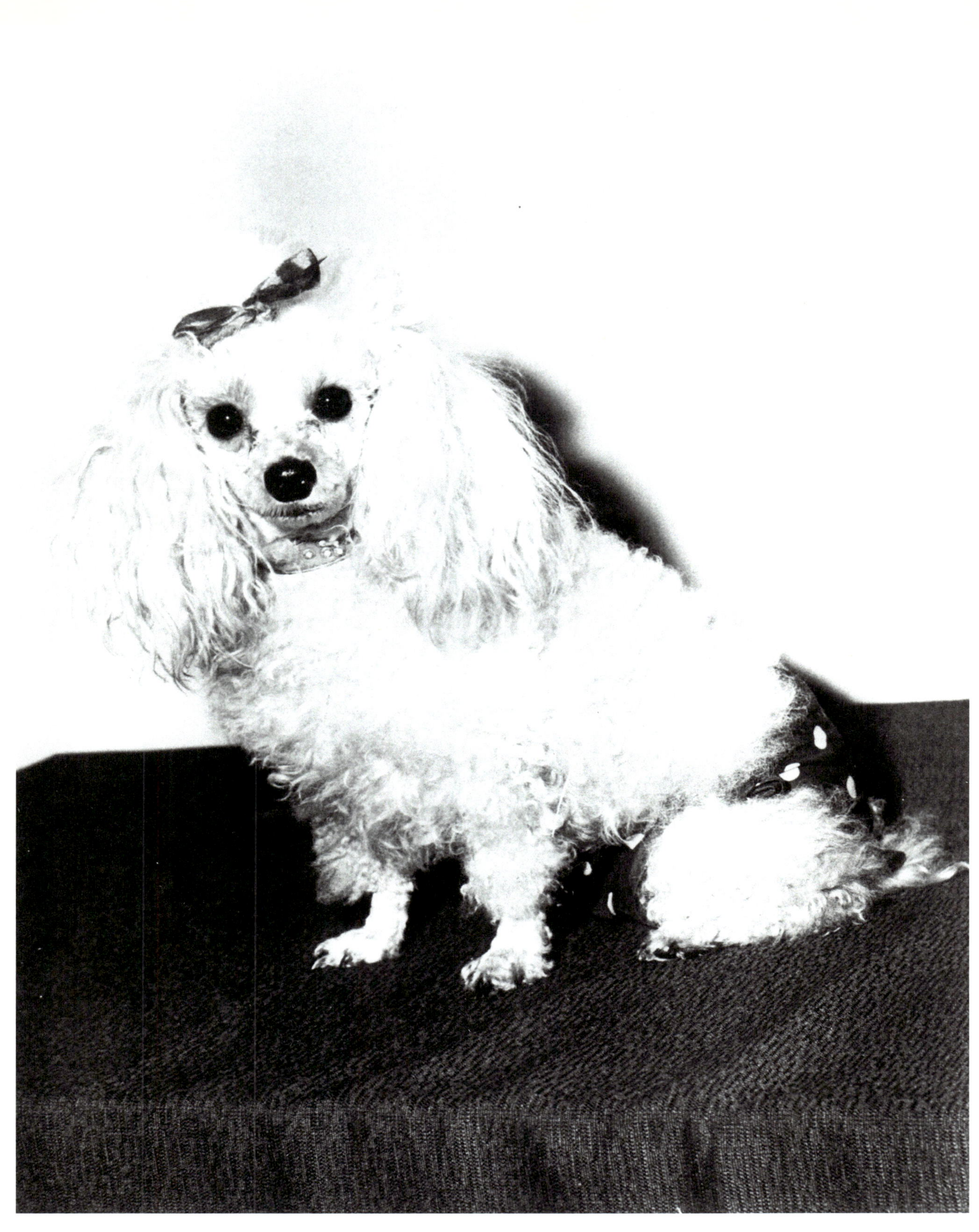

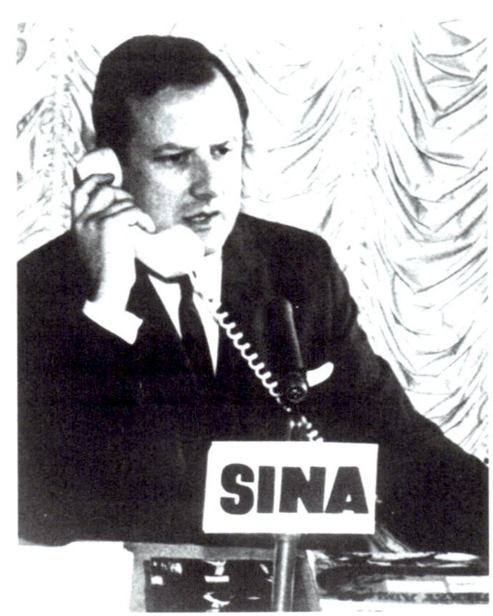

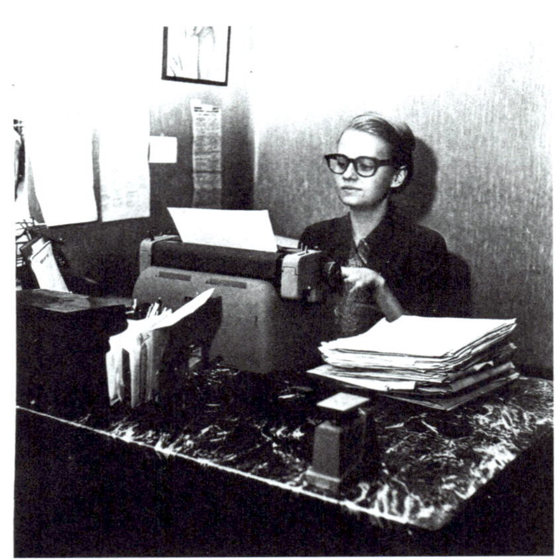

SINA's implausible six-year heyday was followed by a much more improbable afterlife. Buck went on to write *The Graduate* and many other hit films, some of which he even starred in. Jeanne and I moved on to perpetrate dozens of other major media hoaxes. Over time, a lot of people have been taken in by SINA. Some of them have refused to forgive me, and others never found anything funny about the spoof. Then there are those who were unable to dismiss SINA as a prank. The indelible print of news stories and the sound of my determined, deadpan voice on radio and television has managed to linger on and on.

The thing is that SINA was never especially believable, but it didn't need to be. Once a false idea is broadcast or put into print, it develops immunity to fact. How long can an obviously absurd idea survive if treated seriously? The answer, it turns out, is longer than the three of us would have ever believed. From an unpublished short story to a gag, a "social experiment" and, finally, a truly fun game to see how long it could last, SINA seems to have achieved an enigmatic state of immortality.

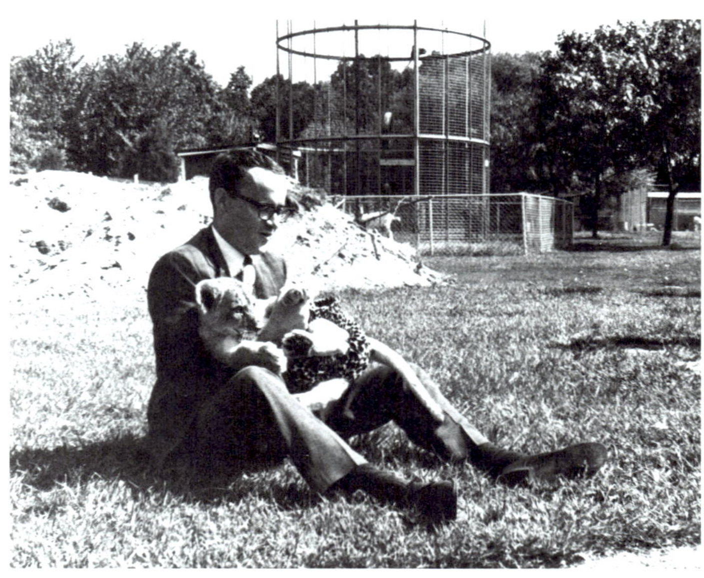

SOCIETY FOR INDECENCY TO NAKED ANIMALS
507 Fifth Avenue
New York 17, N.Y.
OXford 7-5895

Dear Sir or Madam:

Due to the many thousands of letters, telegrams and phone calls we receive every week, it is necessary for us to respond by form letter. This should not be taken as ingratitude on our part; we want to hear from you whether it be good, bad or indifferent because to us every response represents a vote of confidence for SINA.

Accordingly, and with the aforementioned in mind, I, G. Clifford Prout, say to you:

_____Thank you for your kind letter and I appreciate your total acceptance of the SINA Constitution: "that all domestic animals standing higher than 4 inches or who are longer than 6 inches shall be decently clothed, namely, dogs, cats, horses and cows." Won't you join a local SINA chapter today?

_____Thank you for your letter and I'm sorry to know that you feel the way you do about SINA. I suppose you should receive some credit for being so outspoken, but not from me!

_____Thank you and the same to you. Your letter is being turned over to the postal authorities for proper handling.

_____Thank you for your nasty letter. You might be interested in knowing that less than 1% of our mail is from "odd balls" and "crackpots", so you can understand why we tend to ignore you public defenders of immorality.

_____A CLOTHESMOBILE is enroute to your area. ____A SINA-CYCLE has been dispatched.

_____The information you asked for has already been published by the SAN FRANCISCO CHRONICLE during the week of August 13-18. Please refer to those editions.

_____Your membership application for SINA is enclosed. Please return within 48 hours.

_____Congratulations! You have passed the rigid requirements for SINA with flying colors and we welcome you with open arms. Your membership card, a copy of the SINA CONSTITUTION, the SINA MARCHING SHIELD & SONG, the SINA POEM and 2000 SINA SUMMONS are being mailed to you under separate cover in a plain package. Watch for it.

_____We have received your notorized affidavit explaining your reasons for appearing in public with a nude animal and you shall be advised of any diciplinary action by our executive board at its next meeting. Meantime, you are hereby suspended from SINA. Consider your membership card null and void.

_____I have auburn hair, brown eyes, stand 5" 8', weigh 165 pounds, thirty-one years old, single, enjoy swimming, bowling, dancing, volley ball, reading and fencing.

_____Yes. _____No. _____Under consideration. ____We never accept donations.

Faithfully and decently yours,

G. Clifford Prout

GCP:ja

G. Clifford Prout, President
SINA

THE SUNDAY HOME NEWS

NEW BRUNSWICK, N. J., SUNDAY, JULY 24, 1966.

If a clever writer-publicist could perpetrate such a successful hoax on a budget of $20 weekly, fooling not only the American public but also many of the nation's leading newsmen, what might not an organization with subversive or other dangerous motives and unlimited finances accomplish?

DORIS E. BROWN

(See page 89)

D	E	C	E	N	C	Y	■	T	R	U	I	S	M	S
A	C	H	T	O	O	U	■	I	H	N	N	O	A	H
T	O	■	E	V	O	L	U	T	I	O	N	■	K	O
A	N	A	R	O	L	E	■	E	N	P	A	N	E	D
■	O	N	N	L	I	■	A	■	O	O	T	■	H	■
A	L	G	A	E	■	A	G	E	■	D	E	C	A	D
G	O	R	L	■	A	■	N	■	T	■	S	O	S	E
H	G	I	■	A	G	N	A	T	H	A	■	U	T	E
A	I	L	S	■	H	■	T	■	E	■	C	T	E	■
S	C	Y	T	H	■	A	H	A	■	F	A	H	S	T
T	A	■	E	E	K	■	A	■	F	A	T	■	L	I
■	L	Y	R	R	I	C	■	P	I	C	A	S	O	■
Z	I	H	I	E	N	■	S	■	T	U	L	I	W	A
■	S	A	L	S	■	B	A	T	■	L	O	N	L	Y
E	M	N	E	Y	■	O	X	S	■	A	W	A	Y	S

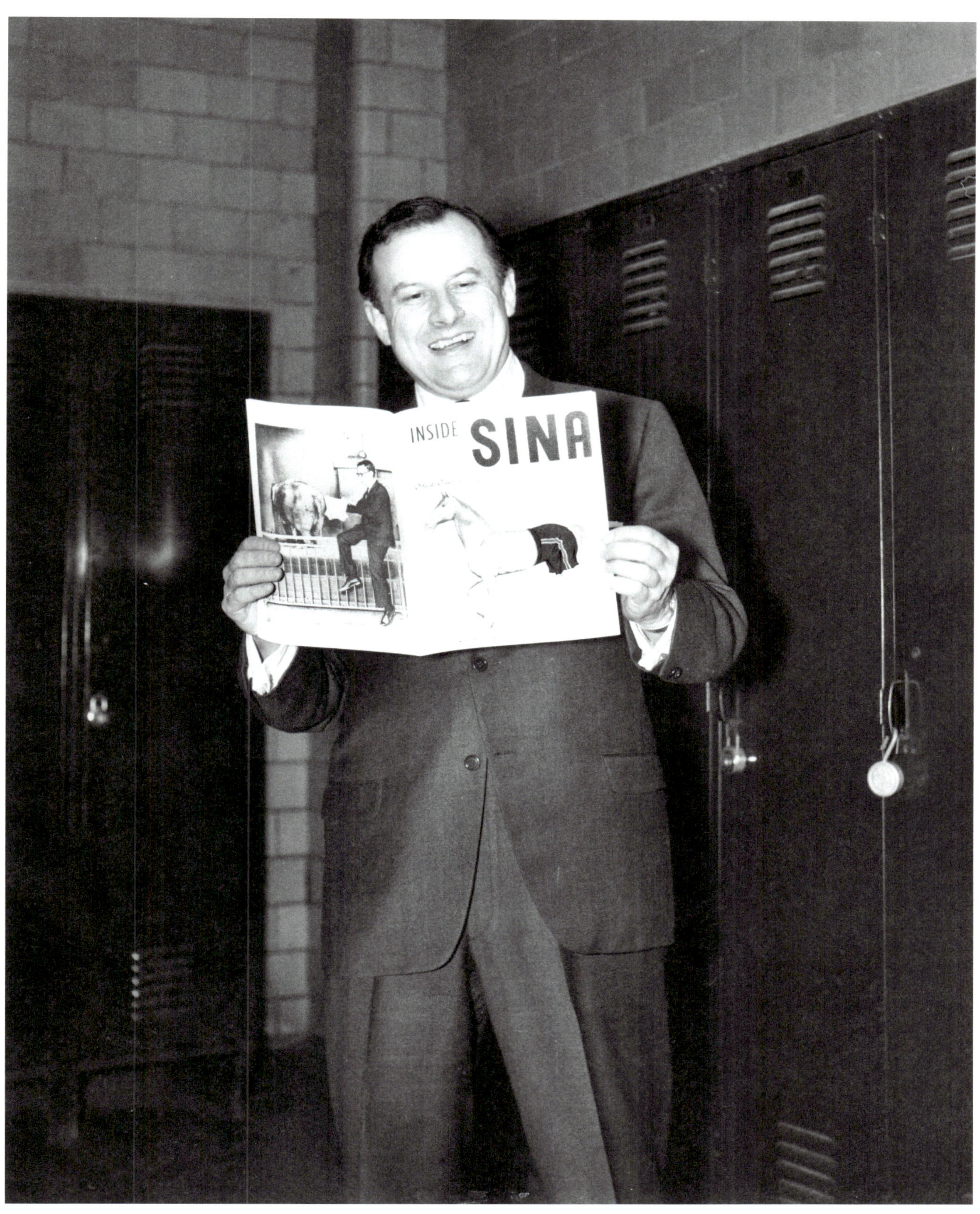
INSIDE SINA

2/7/65

WHAT UTTER

CRAP

Recd. 2/21/65

Arthur Glowka
700 Scarsdale Avenue
Scarsdale, New York